D1738992

THROUGH ALL THE PLAIN

THROUGH ALL THE PLAIN

BENJAMIN JOHN PETERS

CASCADE *Books* • Eugene, Oregon

THROUGH ALL THE PLAIN

Cascade Books
An Imprint of Wipf and Stock Publishers
199 W. 8th Ave., Suite 3
Eugene, OR 97401

www.wipfandstock.com

ISBN 13: 978-1-62032-332-8

Cataloguing-in-Publication Data

Peters, Benjamin John

Through all the plain

xiv + 192 p. ; 23 cm.

ISBN 13: 978-1-62032-332-8

1. Literature 2. Memoir 3. Iraq War 4. Chrisian non-violence I. Title

PS130 P64 2014

Manufactured in the U.S.A.

To Andrea

So violence
Proceeded, and oppression, and sword-law
Through all the plain, and refuge none was found.
Adam was all in tears, and to his guide
Lamenting turned full sad: 'O what are these,
Death's ministers, not men, who thus deal death
Inhumanly to men, and multiply
Ten-thousandfold the sin of him who slew
His brother; for of whom such massacre
Make they but of their brethren, men of men?'

—John Milton, *Paradise Lost*

Contents

Acknowledgments

ONE MAN IS RARELY responsible for a text. I am indebted to those countless teachers, friends, and loved ones who have partnered with me in the shaping of this book. I am but one where they are both many and formative. To all who have participated in the life of Benjamin John Peters, to all who have—if ever so slightly—entered into my journey, I thank you. I am who I am because of you.

To the Marines who died in Iraq, I wake with the burden of honoring your death.

To my professors at seminary who both eagerly and readily taught me the truer meanings of faith and practice.

To my colleagues in Cambodia who extended infinite amounts of grace in an environment riddled with complexity.

To my parents for investing their resources, time, and lifeblood into a quiet, introverted, and, at times, scared boy.

To my wife and children for their bottomless pit of both understanding and support.

To Mike van Mantgem—editor, teacher, and writing confidant—this book *is* because of you.

To Christian Amondson, a friend who saw and believed, thank you for both your insight and critique. Without you, *Through All the Plain* would be a lesser book.

To Caitlin Mackenzie for her skillful, subtle, and clarifying edits.

To Cascade Books for taking the time to read a book proposal from an unknown, agent-less author. I am in your debt.

Acknowledgments

Introduction

THREE BIRTHS. THREE LIVES. Three trajectories. This is a story of reconciliation, of that longing within us all to create one from three.

I was born of my mother in the craggy hills of northern California. Shortly thereafter, she and my father divorced. Life through the eyes of a child is foggy. I have only glimpses and partial memories of my father. I was fourteen when, once again, I entered his household. This was precipitated by the abusive actions of a stepfather. I was weary with both his anger and my mother's acquiescence to it.

In many ways, my life has been a series of choices seeking to reconcile those lost years when my father was but a shadow. Through his absence, I lost identity. I wanted both self and belonging. And so, when approached with the story of a first-century prophet, I ached with hope and was later baptized into a new family. I was taught and mentored in the ways of Jesus. I had no understanding of conservative or liberal. I knew only Christ. I wrestled with old habits and new truths. I would be better than my mother. I would outpace my father. I would find myself in the Church. I would become a son of God.

A final birth issued from death: after September 11, 2001, I enlisted. Six months later I stood on the parade grounds of Recruit Depot, San Diego, and was awarded the Eagle, Globe, and Anchor of the United States Marine Corps. It was pinned on my breast by the man who, more than any other, fashioned me. I was proud, I was honorable—I had found myself, again. I was a warrior defending God and country. I did not question. I obeyed orders. I was born to embody death.

Three births. Three lives. Three trajectories.

This is my story, cemented in history. It is a true story, though not always accurate. As one writer claims, "Memory is creatively reproductive rather than accurately recollective."[1] I will tell it as I remember it, though another's tale would doubtlessly diverge from mine.

1. John Dominic Crossan, *The Birth of Christianity: Discovering What Happened in the Years Immediately After the Execution of Jesus* (HarperOne: San Francisco, 1999).

‡ ‡ ‡

I reached for the doorknob. It was thin and silver, a sliver on which my hope rested. Images raced through my mind, pictures of the desert: heat, bombs, the cries of the fallen. I could never move past this juncture. I was broken. The war had done this. I hated it and myself. This was a chance, however, an opportunity for salvation. I had to open it. I had to stop hesitating. Life must continue. Even if I revered the past, allowed it to shape me, I still had to leave. I had to move on and into the future, so I could embrace the present.

I opened the door.

Sitting opposite me was an elderly man, gray with age and experience. He told me he, once, had returned from war. "Korea," he said. He knew. He understood. He told me wounds could heal. "What do you want?"

What did I want? The silence, thick and tense, hung between us. There would be no return from the ledge upon which I now stood. "I want," I started, "to feel whole."

"And," my counselor followed, "what is that—wholeness?"

"Aren't you supposed to tell me?" I asked. It was my first session. I had never done anything like this before, never chosen to open.

"That's not the way this works." He paused. "Let me try again. Why are you here?"

"They said I had to come."

"Who?"

"The seminary. They said I didn't have a choice. I think they would have asked me to leave if I didn't start coming."

"Really?"

"I don't know." I shifted in my seat.

"Okay, Benjamin. That's fine. Let's start small. Let's get to know one another. Does that work?"

I nodded.

"Great," he smiled, both eager and friendly. "Where are you from?"

"The Northwest."

"Seattle?"

"No. Portland."

"It's rainy there."

"Yes," I said.

"And your family?"

"They live there too."

He scribbled in his notebook before continuing. "Are you close?"

"I live in Denver."

He laughed. "I meant—"

"I know," I interrupted. "It's just . . . they're good people. I don't think my issues are related to them."

"Are your parents still married?"

"No."

"How many siblings?"

"There're seven of us. No. Nine. If you count everyone."

"And where do you fit?"

"I'm somewhere in the middle. And, no, I don't really talk to my brothers and sisters."

"Why not?"

"Look, I'm here because of the war. What does my family have to do with it?"

"Nothing. Everything. They may not be the inciting incident, but they're integral to how you will choose or not choose to handle your trauma."

"Ok. Well. Then it was like anyone else's family. There was a lot of hurt, a lot of . . . stuff. Some of us ran towards each other, and others of us ran away. I ran away."

"And joined the Marine Corps?"

"Something like that."

"And now you're in seminary?"

"Yeah."

"If you don't mind me saying, that seems a contradiction."

"When I was in high school, I wasn't . . . focused. I struggled with both class work and peer pressure. I enjoyed sports, though. They were a release from the tension of having to fit in or get good grades or whatever. I could just go outside and play.

"One day at work—I bagged groceries at Safeway—this guy, no idea who he was, said, 'You played well on Friday.' I was a football player and had recently been written up in a small, local newspaper. I thanked him, thinking that he had recognized me from my picture in *The Chronicle*.

"He invited me to go to church the following Sunday. *Why not?* I thought. It turned out he was the pastor. He came down after the sermon and shook my hand. He thanked me for attending. I don't know. I guess you could say I had a conversion experience."

"Can you tell me about that?"

"Sure. It was . . . I was . . . you know, excited. I took the bait. I threw away my satanic CDs, told my girlfriend we had to . . . you know . . . stop doing stuff, bought a Bible."

"So you would say that you were or are religious?"

"At one point, sure. Now? I don't think of myself that way. My experiences didn't always align with my pastor's sermons. I never really thought of myself as inquisitive, but . . . I wanted answers. I mean, if I was going to stake my life on something as mystical as a two-thousand-year-old story about a guy who returns to life, then I really wanted to know."

"Know what?"

"If it was real or not. If it was worth my time, my effort, my life. I wanted to know if it was really *the* religion, *the* philosophy for life."

"And?"

"And then the war."

"Which changed you."

"Which changed me."

"Can you say how?"

I shifted and started gnawing the side of my cheek. "Violence."

"I see," he said. "Well, we'll get there, only maybe not today, okay?"

"Okay."

"Would you say you were conservative? I only ask, because it helps me to understand your trajectory."

"Yeah. On fire for the Lord and all of that. But then the war happened and I had too many questions. Being 'on fire' was . . . well, it was bullshit."

"When compared to war?"

"Yeah."

"But there was a season in your life when you really embraced your beliefs?"

"I don't know why you keep pushing that, but yes."

"I guess I'm just curious. Is that why you joined the Marine Corps?"

"I don't know. I was an evangelical Christian, alright? I joined the Marine Corp. I went to Iraq. I came home with a lot of questions. Am I still an evangelical? Yes. No. I don't know. I'm not really much of anything, I guess."

"Our time is almost up," he said, looking at his watch. "At some point, we're going to have to talk about Iraq, about what you remember."

"Remember?"

"Yes."

"So much of it's a blur. I remember some things, but other things are a convoluted mess. Like . . . like I made the whole thing up."

"The war or your experiences?"

"Both," I shrugged. "Like I made up the enemy so I could deal with what we were doing. And my experiences, too."

"Why those?"

"Because they belong in a history book somewhere, not in my past."

"Next week," he leaned in, "I want you start telling me your story—all of it. I want to hear every detail, not as it happened, but as you remember it. That's what we need to work through."

"Alright," I nodded. "I can do that."

"You said you wanted to feel whole again, right?"

"Yes."

"That can happen, Benjamin. I promise. But it'll hurt."

"I know."

Part One

1. Beelzebub

I'm not a natural killer; I'm a trained killer. I sat on a school bus at the San Diego airport. The seats were synthetic leather and crackled with shifting movement. The bus, filled with thirty young men dressed as civilians, was weighted in silence. We were Asians, blacks, whites, and Latinos. We were different, but united—we were not elite. We were workers, simpletons, recovering addicts, lawbreakers, and patriots. We were college dropouts. We were ordinary.

Light from a street lamp spilled through the windows. A recorded woman's voice ran on a loop through a speaker, "Please do not leave your luggage unattended." It was both firm and motherly. It made me anxious. I would have closed my eyes, but they'd told us to stay awake and sit up straight, head forward. I was too nervous to let my mind wander. I was twenty-one, a college dropout, and on my way to Marine Corps Recruit Training. Jet airliners had crashed into New York, and it was my duty to respond. Well, that, and I wanted to pay off credit card debt. *What the hell,* I thought, *I'll join the reserves and make some money. It's only eight years of my life. I won't see combat. I probably won't even be deployed.*

I felt a nudge from the guy sitting next to me. "Hey, what's your name?" he whispered.

"I'm Benjamin."

"Right," he stared at me like a lost cause. "My recruiter told me to address the other recruits by their last names. So best get started. What's your name?"

"Uh, Peters."

"Yep, I'm here to kill *sandniggers*. How 'bout you?"

I fumbled for a response.

"C'mon on now, how 'bout it? Why you here?"

"I don't know, not really sure. I guess it's 'cause I want to defend my country."

"Yeah, all that shit, too." He turned his head forward, bored with me.

It wasn't long before we saw a campaign hat, also known as a Smokey the Bear hat, bobbing towards us. An angry man with a shiny shave and a closely cropped haircut boarded the bus. There was no turning back.

"All right, *shitbirds*, whose got my files?"

At the San Diego USO, both our personal and medical data had been collected and assigned to an unwitting recruit. He was from Canada—not that any of us knew. But, later, it was strange to learn that a non-American had enlisted in the United States Marine Corps.

"Me, sir," the Canadian said.

"What the hell! Do I look like your father? No, goddammit," he screamed, answering his own question. "I'm enlisted. From now on, you will refer to me as such. You will," he pitched his voice to include us, "refer to me as, *Drill Instructor*. Do you understand?"

"Yes, sir . . . I mean, Drill Instructor."

"Give me that shit." He held out his hand.

I was aware this had gone too far and wanted off the bus. The Canadian, stiff and glistening, handed over the goods.

After taking one look, the Drill Instructor—DI for short—threw the stack of folders down the length of the bus. "Pick 'em up recruit and they'd better be organized by the time we get to the depot." The DI stalked to the front of the bus and sat. "Move out."

The bus driver turned the ignition.

Wait, can't we talk this through?

The bus pulled away from the curb and towards our training.

It was a dark ride through San Diego before we arrived at the Recruit Depot.

‡ ‡ ‡

On September 11, 2001, I was living in Denver and working as a mattress salesman. I had left the ivy-laden bricks of higher education for the high-pressured world of commission sales. There was a problem, however. I was a terrible salesman. "Hi, welcome to The Mattress Company," I would recite. "Nice weather outside. Would you like to get in bed with me?"

My boss would call me into her office every Monday to discuss my goals, numbers, and ambitions. I didn't have any, nor did I want any. I was a twenty-year-old dropout. To me, it was simple: I needed the money.

Part One

One fall morning, instead of calling me into her fluorescent-whitewashed office, my boss, Elaine, was nervously pacing. She was distraught. "I say kill 'em, that's what I think. I can't believe it. When I was in the Navy—" she stopped.

I nodded my head and smiled. She regularly told tales of her time in the Navy, and I often feigned awareness. I was daydreaming about snowboarding.

"Are you listening to me?"

"What? Yeah! The Navy, right?"

"Go in back and turn on the television," she commanded.

Cool. "Okay," I said.

I turned on the television.

Smoke.

People running.

New York.

I was confused.

Was it an attack, an accident? Why would anybody do this? *Well, a strong response is necessary. They started it.*

When my roommate came home that night I told him I had a plan. We would join the United States Marine Corps—they were the best—and would defend our country. It was our duty, our responsibility. We would enlist together.

He said that he thought it was a great idea.

The next morning we drove to the recruiter's office, signed our papers, and joined the Marine Corps' "Buddy Program," which promised us a place in the same platoon throughout Recruit Training. We would live together, train together, and become Marines together.

Two months later I found myself on a bus with thirty-odd new recruits and one terrifying drill instructor, winding through the gray and empty streets of San Diego.

‡ ‡ ‡

Both patriotism and a heroic ideal had driven me to enlist: young men and women have a responsibility to defend their country in its greatest time of need. This was true. But it was also true that, a year before enlisting, I'd been "born again." I was a new Christian, crisp but crude, struggling with a novel paradigm. The beliefs and practices of the church, in many ways, were as foreign to me as those of the United States Marine Corps. As our bus pulled into San Diego's Recruit Depot, I had one last civilian thought: *Jesus said to love your enemies. Why the hell hadn't I thought of that before?*

"Get off my fucking bus, Recruits," a burly DI resembling Ambule yelled. He was covered with tattoos: lots and lots of tattoos. As I shuffled past him to my appointed place on the yellow footprints—perfectly aligned ranks-and-files used in teaching Close Order Drill—I noticed one rather exquisite tattoo: a dancing mermaid sexing an M-16.

This is unbelievable.

"All right, Recruits, get on my footprints."

We scrambled to do what Ambule said. I was lucky. I arrived first. The Canadian, juggling our files, was several steps behind.

"What the hell, Recruit? Are you trying to piss me off?"

"No, sir . . . Drill Instructor."

Ambule stalked over to the Canadian, punched him in the stomach, and left him to consider his various misdeeds.

Oh shit.

He turned to us.

"You are now property of the United States Government. You will not eat, drink, or shit without the government's approval. That means me, Recruits. I will tell you when and how to breathe." At this, one of the recruits standing next to me chuckled. It was a poor decision.

"What the hell! Who the fuck laughed?"

Unbeknownst to us, another DI had crept up while we were standing in formation. "Shit, Drill Instructor Ambule, can't keep your recruits in check?" The new DI made his way around to the front of the formation. He was wiry and sported a shaved head. He was evil incarnate. His name was Drill Instructor Beelzebub.

"Some recruit laughed. Can you believe that Sergeant Beelzebub?"

"I'm on it."

"All yours." Ambule was smiling.

Beelzebub sauntered over. "It sounded like it came from over here." He contemplated me. "Was it you, Recruit?"

Silence.

"It's okay, Recruit, you can tell me. Was it you?" His teeth were tobacco-stained.

"No, Drill Instructor."

"Hell, it was somebody. Can't you tell me who, Recruit?"

In Recruit Training it's commonplace to betray fellow recruits. I should have sold out the recruit who laughed. But I didn't. "I have no idea, Drill Instructor."

"Oh, you have no idea do you? Well fuck, I say it was you . . . unless you want to tell me different?"

Groaning, the Canadian stirred in front of the formation.

That was the last thing I remember clearly about my first week as a recruit. The next few days were a blur. They shaved my hair, issued my recruit gear, and taught us how to make a military bed. This phase lasted seven days. It was an introduction. They called it "Intake." The day we dreaded was fast approaching, however. Our DIs referred to it as "Black Sunday," the day that we'd be introduced to our platoon Drill Instructors and begin our training in earnest.

It couldn't be worse than what we've already survived. I was naïve, an idiot. Black Sunday was hell.

2. *Bravo Company*

Our platoon leader was named Staff Sergeant Nygo. I still don't know how you pronounce it. Beelzebub was there as well. He was one of Nygo's cronies, always prowling about, pointing his finger at us and yelling. He's what you would call an Enforcer. When one of us screwed up, Beelzebub was the man who disciplined us. It was a "good DI, bad DI" routine. We would screw up, Beelzebub would "slay" us, and SSG. Nygo would "comfort" us. "Slaying" or "quarter-decking" are the terms DIs employ in lieu of hazing. It amounts to the same thing, however. "Mountain climbers," Beelzebub would say. We would start pumping our feet. This would continue for five or six minutes. "Push ups!" We would switch exercises. Five minutes later Beelzebub would scream the next exercise. And on it went—he could be creative.

Throughout the quarter-decking process, Beelzebub would thrust his nose against a recruit and shout obscenities: "You're dog shit on Sunday, Recruit," or "Your father hates you and your mother's a whore," or "Dumbass! I bet you were adopted. Nobody loves you, Peters." Or, if he was feeling particularly malicious, he would creep up to my ear and whisper, "Why did you join the Marine Corps, Recruit Peters? You don't have what it takes. You'll never graduate. I hate you and your fellow recruits hate you. It'd be easier if you died."

He did this to me. He did this to everyone. And what could we do? As for me, I would pump my legs, listen to Beelzebub spew his motivations, and try to forget myself.

There were other DIs. There were always other DIs. All told, there were usually four or so Drill Instructors running about minding the seventy-five recruits in my platoon. With as many of us as there were, you would think we would have tried to break the rules. To the contrary, our Drill Instructors were magicians. They saw all. At night, we might be sitting in front of our racks cleaning our M-16s. It would be quiet except for the sound of clinking rifle bolts. Across from me, a recruit might lean over and whisper to another recruit: "Hey, what do you think we're doing tomorrow?" Before his bunkmate could answer, Beelzebub would materialize. "You wanna talk, Recruits? You still have energy, is that it?" The recruits would shake their heads. "Bullshit," Beelzebub would say, "quarter deck, now!" It was a science. Beelzebub and his ilk knew exactly what they were doing. They knew when to back off and when to come down hard. They were training us for warfare and, like war, they were unforgiving.

A great secret of the Marine Corps is it's nothing like the commercials. On television, all of the Marines are chiseled men wielding flaming swords.

In real life, Marines are people like you and me. They wheeze when they run, smoke cigarettes, cuss like a drunken aunt at Easter, and generally aren't very trustworthy. Most of them, at least during Recruit Training, would as soon as steal your stuff as watch your back. We had all kinds. The Canadians—I use the plural because, as it turned out, not only were there two but they were twins—were skinny, tall, and looked like rats when they smiled. They made me a bit uneasy. But my platoon also counted blacks, Asians, Latinos, and whites among its rank. Some of the new recruits could not, and I mean this literally, could not speak a word of English. We had skinny recruits, fat recruits, stupid recruits, and well . . . more stupid recruits. Let's be honest: the enlisted Marine Corps isn't drawn from the intellectually endowed segments of our society.

When we were finally situated with Senior Drill Instructor SSG Nygo, our DIs assessed each recruit, chose the best from among us, and divvied up the choice jobs: Guide, Squad Leader, and Scribe. The Scribe is a platoon's bookkeeper. He keeps tabs on gear (how much we had and who was using it), on Physical Training scores (each recruit's time in the three-mile run), and mail (he receives it and hands it out). The Squad Leader was responsible for all of the members who comprised his squad. He answered to the Guide, and the Guide answered to the DIs. The Guide is the leader of the platoon. He is supposed to be the fittest, smartest, and best-looking Marine in the bunch. The Guide marches in front of his platoon, carries his platoon's guidon, and, eventually, competes with the other Guides in a Depot-wide Guide competition. The Guide, as our leader, was required to sleep in the middle of the barracks and answer for the platoon, both good and bad. When something went wrong, it was his fault. When we did something well, however, it was due to his leadership. For his trouble, the Guide would graduate Recruit Training as a Lance Corporal. The rest of us would graduate as lowly Private First Classes.

Early on, for no reason that I am aware, they selected me as the Guide.

"Recruit Peters," Beelzebub shouted, "get your ass over here."

"Yes, Drill Instructor." I ran.

"Grab your shit and move it to the Guide's bed, you just got promoted."

"Yes, Drill Instructor."

I had no intention of moving my stuff. I made a show of obeying Beelzebub's instructions, but didn't follow through. The Guide was quarter-decked more than anyone else. He was to be an example. When things went wrong, the Guide was singled out and mercilessly slayed. I wasn't that ambitious. To be the Guide, a recruit had to want it. The Guide was someone who would sell his soul for the Marine Corps. The Guide couldn't fake it. I intended to slide through Recruit Training without becoming totally brainwashed. But if I became the Guide I would be fully assimilated. The Guide had to become a mini-Beelzebub. In many ways, the Guide was our platoon's Faustian craving of what Beelzebub had to offer: mortal sacrifice in exchange for earthly power. *Let some other poor recruit get his ass kicked.*

Dawn came. The Guide's bed was empty.

"What the hell? Where the fuck is my Guide? Peters!" yelled SSG Nygo. "Did Beelzebub not tell you to take the Guide's position?"

Shit. "Yes, Senior Drill Instructor."

"Why the hell are you not moved then, Recruit?"

Play dumb. That might work. "Was I supposed to move in right away, Drill Instructor? I thought—"

"What the . . . you *thought,* who the hell told you to do that?"

"Well—"

"Shut-up Recruit, you're not my Guide, you're a flower. Beelzebub," he called, "take this recruit to the quarter-deck and kill 'em."

What Beelzebub did to me was bad. It was really bad. But I only experienced it one time. The recruit who eventually became our Guide was killed every day.

Our Scribe, on the other hand, was of the Recruit Intelligentsia. He was a University of Chicago dropout who wore military-issued black-rimmed glasses. His name was Recruit Hernandez. He was the administrative nuts-and-bolts of our platoon and, because of his unique position—he did most of the work our DIs should've been doing—he wasn't quarter-decked that often. I envied the role of Scribe, but I preferred my role as a Platoon Wallflower. *Blend in and they won't notice you. If they don't notice you, then they can't kill you.*

At Recruit Training, each platoon is broken down into four squads of about fifteen to twenty people. A Squad Leader is in charge of the recruits who comprise his squad. The Squad Leader gets slayed for the mistakes made by his platoon. Like the Guide, the job of Squad Leader is for ambitious Marines, and so went to those aspiring young recruits who were vying for the Guide's position. The buddy I enlisted with—my former roommate, Recruit McDougal—was a Squad Leader, and I didn't envy him. He embraced that role; he sought the challenge. Whereas the Marine Corps was a shock to my system, for Recruit McDougal it was a blessed break from the monotony of college. We were still friends, familiar faces in a barrack full of cogs, but our relationship had changed. He was a leader; I was his follower.

I had no desire to be the Guide, the Scribe, or a Squad Leader. Both the Guide and the Squad Leaders were singled out too much for my taste, and the Scribe had too many extra responsibilities. Recruit Training was hard enough as it was. My experiences during Recruit Training revealed aspects of my personality I'd never before acknowledged. I discovered I didn't want responsibility for another's success. More to the point, I didn't want to be accountable for another's mistakes or weaknesses. I was scared of too much attention. I was scared of what it would do to me, of who it might make me, which was strange, because at twenty, I didn't know who I was. I only knew that, in a sense, the Marine Corps was stealing my opportunity for self-realization, injecting fragments into a plastic casting. But I didn't want somebody else's mold. I wanted to find my own path to wholeness, not a prescribed identity found in the Corps' green book of recruit knowledge.

I was the middle child in a large family riddled by divorce. If there was one thing I craved, it was self-discovery. I think that's why, after my senior year of high school, I dove into Christianity and, later, the Marine Corps with an on-fire fervor, hoping they would provide me with both a place of belonging and an identity I could call my own. I knew nothing of theology or biblical studies or the dissonance between Christianity and warfare. I knew nothing of paradigms or structures or making decisions rooted in beliefs and values. I felt comfortable within evangelical, conservative Christianity because of what it offered me. I felt comfortable joining the Marine Corps, because it provided me with both a sense of honor and a challenge.

And maybe I was afraid of rejection, too. I didn't want to be seen as a military derelict—a reject—let alone a Christian failure. There was some trepidation, but certainty is its own comfort. Jesus saved me so I could defend America. Terrorists were infidels; I was the strong shield of the Lord—just not the first shield.

3. Snot and Scabs

If I was mildly conflicted, then my bunkmate, Recruit Mobile, was all Kool-Aid. He craved the United States Marine Corps. According to him, he was destined for USMC greatness. He was also one of the platoon's lost causes. He was consistently quarter-decked. To this day, whenever I think of Recruit Mobile, I see a skinny southerner with snot running down his scabby nose. He spoke with a thick drawl, had boils on his face, and couldn't finish a three-mile run in the Marine Corps' allotted time—twenty-eight minutes or less, practically walking. But because Recruit Mobile couldn't run, Recruit Mobile was quarter-decked, which translated into me being quarter-decked, because, the DIs reasoned, I was his bunkmate and so I must be a sickly southerner, too. Well, I wasn't. And I resented Recruit Mobile for being a *shitbird*. Whenever Beelzebub was in a fit, he usually found his way to our bunk to ridicule Recruit Mobile.

"What the hell, Mobile? You were three-minutes behind on your run today," Beelzebub would say as he shoved his hands in Mobile's face.

"Recruit Mobile apologizes—" Mobile would begin before being abruptly cut off by a coughing fit.

"What the hell is wrong with you, Recruit?" Beelzebub, standing inches from Mobile's face, would sneer at Mobile's boils, scabs, and snot. "Recruit!" Beelzebub would shout, "Do you have AIDS? Are you a faggot, Recruit?"

Mobile's coughing fit would momentarily subside. "No, Drill Instructor, I don't have AIDS."

"Oh, shit, but you are a faggot? Well, call the President!" Beelzebub would turn his head to me and then back to Recruit Mobile. "Recruit, get on the quarter-deck."

Mobile would trudge to the front of our squad-bay. As Beelzebub turned to follow, he would call over his shoulder, "You too, Peters. Bunkmates live and die together."

Shit.

Lying in bed one night—Mobile had the top bunk, I had the bottom—I whispered up to Mobile. "What the hell is wrong with you, man? You're sick, go to sickbay."

"I can't. I have to finish Recruit Training. My Dad was in Vietnam."

"Well, yeah, sure, you'll finish, but you'll be a few weeks behind. There isn't anything wrong with allowing yourself to heal up first."

"I hear you, Peters, but I can't handle much more of this. If I go to sickbay, then they'll prolong my training by three maybe four weeks. That sound like something you'd do?"

I stared at the wooden slat holding the bunk above me. I had no answer. Beelzebub was breaking me down. He was teaching me to live like a Marine by pounding the "reset" button on my life. He was teaching me how to piss, tie my shoes, dress, march, shave, obey orders, PT, and kill. But change breeds fear. In my case, it was the fear of what I'd become mingled with the fear that I'd fail to become it. I was training to become a soldier—a man who could kill. The idea, when stripped of glory, is repulsive. But, within the bounds of duty, the temptation is alluring.

I realized, staring up at Mobile's bunk, that though a part of me despised the Marine Corps for its difficulty, I loved it, too. For both honor and renown, I had dreamt of wresting Grendel's arm from his body. I wanted to be a warrior. I wanted to reach out and pluck that fruit from its branch—I wanted to taste killing.

"No. I guess not."

"Well, there you go, then."

We slept.

Two weeks later Recruit Mobile dropped. He had bronchitis, red-eye, and a stress-fractured shin. The man was broken. I don't know if he ever finished Recruit Training.

4. C.O.D.

THERE ARE TWO PLACES on the West Coast where Marine Corps' recruits are trained: Recruit Depot in San Diego and Camp Pendleton, which is about an hour drive north of San Diego. Camp Pendleton is a sprawling Marine Corps Camp that houses the First Marine Division and where recruits learn to use an M-16, bivouac, and hike—lovingly referred to in the Marine Corps as "humping." This is also where the Crucible takes place, the final challenge in becoming a Marine. The Crucible culminates in a five-mile hump up a mountain called "The Reaper." In total, Recruit Training lasts thirteen weeks with each week highlighting a different aspect of warfighting. A platoon progresses through PT Week, MCMAP Week, Marine Corps History Week, Team Week, Drill Week, Range Week, Field Week, and the Crucible Week. As if Recruit Training isn't difficult enough, there is the added stress of a "final exam" at the end of each phase. You pass, you continue; you fail, you drop to another platoon. No one wants to drop.

Our day-to-day training was a predictable routine. We would wake early, eat, drill, eat, PT, practice MCMAP (Marine Corps Martial Arts Program), drill some more, PT some more, and then sleep. We were like ninjas in training. We lived and breathed the Marine Corps. As Ambule had said, we were property of the United States of America.

And when he wasn't harassing us, Beelzebub was teaching us Close Order Drill, the art of marching in formation and handling arms for ceremonies. We drilled to practice the invaluable military skill of instant obedience to orders. If we obeyed during drill, the logic went, then we would obey in combat. Imagine a marching band. Now replace the instruments with M-16s. This is drill. And in Marine Corps Recruit Training, recruits drill about 50 percent of the time. We would drill on the parade deck—an asphalt expanse in the middle of the Depot—in the barracks, and on the Depot's streets. We would drill to PT. We would drill to the chow hall. Beelzebub didn't discriminate. He loved drill, and he would drill us anytime, anywhere, for however long he wanted. This usually resulted in endlessly practicing a drill move called Column of Files. The goal in Column of Files is to maneuver an entire platoon from four-squads into one long line, or file. It sounds simple, but in actuality it's difficult to accomplish, especially with strung-out recruits.

When Beelzebub was in a mood to drill, *nothing* could stop him. He would call out, "Column of Files!" We would begin our steady mutation from ranks to file. Inevitably, one recruit would screw up. "Get back," Beelzebub would yell. We would, once again, assume our platoon formation and start the process over. This would continue for hours.

"Permission to speak, Drill Instructor," some poor recruit would interrupt.

"Speak."

"Permission to use the head, Drill Instructor."

"Hell no, Recruit," Beelzebub would say. "Column of Files! Left—left—left—right—left." This was followed by the sound of breaking water, the splash of a recruit urinating in his pants.

I didn't succumb to such indignities. I endured. I sought respite from the physical punishment of drill by escaping the confines of my body. I daydreamed. I dreamt I was a great scholar and writer. I dreamt I had a library filled with books and leather. I dreamt I smoked a pipe, drank scotch, studied, lectured, and wrote (not necessarily in that order). My mind would wander for hours as I created elaborate realities for my future self. I would marry, have kids, and teach. In another daydream, I would take my Marine Corps training and work for some private intelligence firm—like James Bond, but better. In yet another, I would finish college before continuing to a PhD program. I would be a scholar, a man of intelligence. I would—

"Get back!"

5. *Lesser Mortals*

Four weeks into Recruit Training our DIs had the opportunity to drown us. It was "Swim Week." Bravo Company trained at an indoor Olympic-sized swimming pool, so that if we were ever on a Navy ship, fell off, and were lost at sea, then we would know how to survive. We charged through water—angry and unafraid—in camouflage utilities with full combat-ready backpacks and M-16s. We practiced swimming, treading water, and dropping off a twenty-foot high dive. Our DIs assured us that if we ever found ourselves in the unlikely situation of having to use this particular training, then we could pull our collars around our mouths and blow. "Your damn cammies," they would shout, "once inflated, will act as a flotation device." The thing is, it didn't work.

Swim week wasn't that bad for those of us who knew how to swim. For those few who didn't, it was less than ideal. Recruit Jersey, a black recruit from the northeast, was a rock—he couldn't tread water, let alone swim. Beelzebub made it his mission to drown Recruit Jersey. I guess it was easier than teaching an eighteen-year-old to swim.

Our last day of swim week was *qual-day*—a "final exam." There are four levels of Marine Corps swimming: one, two, three, and four. At level four you can execute every major stroke, as well as the Combat Survival Stroke, in full gear. For the exam, our DIs would arrange us facing the short width, rather than the length, of the pool. Our swimming instructors, who wore short, canvas swim trunks like the movie stars of the 1950s, would stand over us, looking down from atop their lofty perches. They would call out a stroke, and we would swim across the pool showcasing our talents. If any of us, according to our instructors, couldn't properly execute a stroke, then our DIs would haul us out of the water. A recruit who made it through all four of the strokes, however, would be designated a level four swimmer, making him Recon authorized. Any recruit who failed would be dragged out of the water and assigned a number between one and three. We all aspired to level four because we all held onto, in some fashion, the romanticism of being a Recon Marine—the hardest Marines, the Special Forces. Even if I never tested for Recon, I had to admit, I at least wanted the option. During these training weeks, rumors spread throughout our platoon at nights when we thought Beelzebub was off duty. We heard tell of different Recon tests, trainings, and missions. Supposedly, a recruit in Alpha Company had been so "hard" that he'd been ushered out of Recruit Training and into the hallowed presence of SOCOM. It was enticing. What young man hasn't, at one point in his life, desired to be a god among lesser mortals?

"Survival!" an instructor shouted. The final exam of Swim Week had begun. A whistle blew, and the first wave of recruits jumped into the pool and began the survival stroke. The instructors, circling like hawks, began pointing at recruits who were failing and needed to be removed from the pool. The second wave began their swim, then the third. I was in the fourth wave. I stepped up to the edge of the pool; Recruit Jersey was next to me. He looked over at me. I saw fear.

"You'll do fine," I said.

He looked back at the pool. The whistle blew and we jumped. I was halfway across the pool when I heard screaming. It was Recruit Jersey. He was flailing about, choking in gurgles. I stopped midway and watched as Beelzebub jumped in after Recruit Jersey.

"You want something to yell about?" he said as he swam over to Recruit Jersey and dunked him. "Suck it up, Recruit!" I entertained swimming back, decided against it, and continued on, exiting the pool. I watched from a distance as Beelzebub nearly drowned Recruit Jersey. He was slamming him down and screeching with his strained, scratchy voice. Recruit Jersey, frantically, was calling for help. He thought he was dying. Beelzebub, finally, swam to the edge, leaving Recruit Jersey in the middle of the pool floating face up. Breathing but unable to move, he was defeated. Beelzebub climbed out of the pool and threw Recruit Jersey a life preserver. He paddled to the pool's edge, crawled out, and hobbled to sickbay.

"Breast," our instructor said. Wave one began, then two, three, and four. Halfway through the swim I felt a DI tap me on the shoulder. I was done; level two. I was unworthy of testing Recon. I left the pool, walked to the locker room, and dried off. Wearing my uniform, I marched outside to wait in formation until the other recruits finished their test. I don't know what happened to Recruit Jersey. As part of our unwritten code we never talked about broken recruits or what Beelzebub had done to them. We marched back to our barracks and continued our training, one recruit short. When Beelzebub breaks you, it's hard to recover.

6. *Unforgivable*

One of the joys of Recruit Training was the Marine Corps' obstacle course, a rope and monkey bar strewn jungle gym. Every recruit toed the starting line thinking he could conquer the Marine Corps' playground. Every recruit was humbled. One day, before the halfway point in our training, Beelzebub decided to run us through the obstacle course. He said that the day was special though, because we would attempt what was called a "combat course." We were to break into our squads and run the course with five ammo cans—fifteen to twenty-pound containers filled with ammunition. If any of us died, and he assured us he would let us know if we'd died, then our squad was to fire-carry the dead squad member through the rest of the course. The first squad that finished didn't have to join the other squads in the pit for a platoon quarter-decking. I wanted to finish first. Once we were broken into our squads and lined up, he provided us a few minutes to discuss strategy.

"Peters, Lopez, Duncan, Phoenix, and Dallas," our Squad Leader said, "you carry the ammo cans. Rodriquez, Chicago, LA, Smith, and Lee you follow directly behind 'em. If they die, pick up their ammo cans and keep going. The rest of us'll be ready to fire-carry the dead. Okay?"

"Do not say, 'okay.'" Lee was a thinly framed Asian. "You are the Squad Leader, command us."

"Shut up the fuck up, Lee. Everyone ready?" We nodded. "Alright, let's win this. I'm not getting quarter-decked because of you fuckers."

I picked up my ammo can.

"Alright," Beelzebub said, "first done won't get killed." He paused for dramatic effect: "Kill!"

I ran—hard and fast. I didn't wait for my squad. I figured they'd survive, but I didn't want to be the reason we failed. I pulled out in front. Not only was I in front of our squad, but I was in front of the whole platoon. I low crawled, I climbed over logs, and I carried my ammo can across rope bridges. Halfway through the obstacle course, as I was struggling up a wooden wall, Beelzebub sprinted over. "You're dead, Recruit," he said. "Don't ever, and I mean ever, leave your squad like that. You finish together or don't finish at all." He looked at me. "As a matter of fact, get your ass off the course. You're not fit. Ambule," he shouted, "take over for me. I gotta teach Recruit Peters a lesson." He turned to me. "To the pit, Recruit."

I followed.

In between the endless push-ups and mountain climbers, Beelzebub proceeded to lecture me on the nature of war and platoon maneuvers. He said that for one man to assume he could complete a mission on his own was selfish. A concerted effort is always better than an individual attempt. I was selfish and needed purging. Combat, he said, was about groups of people working together to accomplish a mission, something greater than any one individual.

If I wanted to be successful, then I would have to unfetter my selfish ambition. I needed to assimilate. "You want to be a Marine?" he bellowed. "You want to be a killer? Fuck you, Peters. You're not shit, and you never will be. Discipline, Recruit, discipline is what you need."

This continued for some time.

I didn't respond. I couldn't. I just counted off my leg-lifts. *Bullshit. The act of killing is selfish. How is what I did any different? I was laying my fucking life down for my brothers.* Beelzebub, however, was preparing us for the unforgivable, where there'd be no "do overs," no "second best." We had to instantly and perfectly execute our orders, or Marines would die. He was changing us. He was teaching us to function in high stress environments, to remain calm under fire, and kill the enemy without question. Beelzebub embodied the Marine Corps' slogan, "Pray for War." He wanted us to embody it as well.

7. Marine Academia

Recruit training was not all rifles, exercise, and drilling. We also attended our fair share of classes. We had classes on military bearing, uniform care, finances, first aid, Marine Corps discipline and conduct, and, my favorite, Marine Corps history. Our classes were held in a small auditorium. We usually had one instructor per class. After our DIs harried us into the classroom, our instructor would bark out instructions: we were ordered to sit up straight, keep our heads forwards, refrain from talking, and, if we felt like closing our eyelids, we were ordered to stand in the back of the classroom. Our instructor told us if we broke any of his rules or fell asleep in class, he would call back our DIs and allow them to wake us up before continuing. He would then proceed to lecture for the next two hours. He told us things like: the Marine Corps was founded in 1775, and in the beginning Marines used to sit in the crow's nest of old ships and shoot down at people who boarded, like pirates. Officers would wear a hat with a special design on top so Marines wouldn't shoot their own. He told us about Tripoli, Belleau Wood, the Japanese, Guadalcanal, Chesty Puller, Vietnam, Snipers, and Marine Corps Medal of Honor winners. According to our instructor, the United States Marine Corps was the only reason the Allies won World War II. "If it wasn't for us Devildogs, then the world would be speaking German now, errah?"

"Errah," we growled in unison. Our instructor had taught us this was the appropriate Marine grunt of call and response. He said it was an ancient Scandinavian war cry.

We had tests in our classes too, but to my knowledge everyone passed. Our instructor made sure no one failed; after all, there was no need to drop someone for being stupid. As long as we stuck to answers that shined a heavenly light on the Marine Corps, we would pass. In this area, we all excelled.

The same auditorium in which we attended classes also housed the Protestant church. If we had a "light" morning, then it was typically Sunday. We would wake, shower, clean our squad bay, and then have the opportunity to attend the church service of our preference: Catholic, Protestant, Jewish, Muslim, or Wiccan (to name a few). Our training would commence after lunch.

I attended the Protestant church service. After being marched to the auditorium, we would file in and sit down. A worship band would play evangelical pop-Christian songs. Some recruits would stand and sing, others would sit and reflect. I often found myself sitting during these rare breaks from training. After worship, a military chaplain would stand in front of us and sermonize. "Jesus," he would say, "offered himself as a sacrifice. You too, are offering yourselves as sacrifices. You have chosen to set aside your personal desires in order to embody freedom. God is just. And we must be just in our imitation of God. This means obeying the authorities, those ordained by heaven, for the authorities are responsible for the good. The good you have chosen to uphold. In this way, your sacrifice is used by God." He would smile at us before continuing. "You are God's instruments. Right now, I know it is difficult to see that. You are living through trials and tribulations. You are tired, weary—struggling." He paused. "Come to Jesus. Find your rest."

When he finished, we were quickly ushered outside and marched back to our barracks. These Sunday morning marches were led by fellow recruits, and as such, were silent. The chaplain's words, beating in line with our treading boots, pounded in my head. *I don't feel like an instrument.*

8. Spring Cleaning

Halfway through Recruit Training we moved from the San Diego Recruit Depot to Camp Pendleton. Before we moved, however, we had to complete Team Week. During Team Week our platoon was broken up into fire squads—groups of about four to eight people—to work throughout the base. Some recruits were assigned to the chow hall to prepare and serve food, others were assigned to the headquarters' office to make photocopies and clean, and others were assigned to the camp janitorial services. Three other recruits and I were commanded to stay behind and "spring clean" our barracks. This was the worst posting because whoever was in the barracks had to work with Beelzebub. I was hoping for an escape, but instead received rampant intimacy. All week long we cleaned, ran errands for Beelzebub, and got killed.

The other two recruits on barracks duty were Recruit Juarez and Recruit Portland. Juarez was a gangly Mexican. He enlisted to gain his US citizenship. Portland, on the other hand, was a stoner using the Marine Corps as a rehabilitation facility.

"Can you believe we're stuck with this shit?" Portland asked. The three of us were in the shower room. It was our first day on barracks duty and we were scrubbing the bathroom's floor. Beelzebub had said he wanted to see the reflection of his ass when he came back. We were doing our best to accommodate his request.

"I was hoping for chow duty," I replied. "I heard those recruits eat donuts."

"Bullshit," Portland said. We were silent for a time, scouring the floor with steel wool. "What's the first thing you'll do after Recruit Training?"

"I don't know. Eat a hamburger, I guess. You?"

"I'm gonna sleep—for a week."

"What about you?" I asked, turning to Juarez. He was scrubbing the floor next to us, humming softly.

"He won't answer."

"Why?"

"He'll only speak English with a DI—shitty English at that. I doubt he even knows what you're saying." Recruit Juarez stopped polishing the floor and looked at Portland. "Can you understand me?" Portland asked, taking care to enunciate. Juarez stared at Portland for a few seconds more before returning his attention to the bathroom's floor. "See? Dumb as a rock."

One afternoon while we were mopping our barracks, a shout exploded from the DI's office.

"Peters, get in here!"

Shit.

It was Beelzebub. He was sitting behind his desk, legs kicked over the top. His shaved head was glowing under the florescent lights. He smelled like *Bulldog*, a Marine Corps cologne. I walked in and stood at attention. "Recruit Peters reporting as ordered, Drill Instructor."

"At ease."

I was nervous.

"Why the hell are you here, Peters?"

"Drill Instructor?" I didn't understand the question.

"Why the hell are you here?"

"You called for me, Drill Instructor."

He shook his head. "I mean the Corps, Recruit."

I hesitated. "To serve my country, Drill Instructor."

"Really?"

"Yes, Drill Instructor."

"Hmm." His brown eyes bored into me. "I looked over your file, Recruit. It says you have two years of college, that you even played college football. Again, why the hell are you here? I wouldn't leave that."

"To serve, Drill Instructor."

"Yeah, bullshit, no one's in the Marine Corps to serve, Recruit. We're all running from something. What's your something?"

I stared at a spot on the wall behind Beelzebub's head. I wouldn't answer that question, not for him.

"Recruit?"

Silence.

"Alright, then tell me this, why not finish school and join as an officer?"

"The Marine Corps enlisted, Drill Instructor, they're the best and bravest."

"Oh! *Semper Fi* and all that, right?"

"Yes, Drill Instructor. Honor, Courage, and Commitment."

"Look at the little bird sing."

"Drill Instructor?"

"But you're not a Marine, are you? You're a reservist. Even if I hadn't seen your file, I can smell it on you. You reek of it."

"Of what, Drill Instructor?"

"Half-ass bullshit. You're not in this, not really. You think you've an escape." Beelzebub looked down at his desk. "Dismissed, Recruit."

I stood at attention, saluted, about faced, and went back to mopping. I didn't dwell on it; in the morning they were bussing us to Camp Pendleton. *Six more weeks. I can do anything for six weeks.*

INTERLUDE

"How are you?"

"I'm fine."

Trent smiled, fatherly. "We both know that isn't true."

I chewed my cheek.

"I'll tell you what," he sighed. "Why don't you start somewhere easy. Tell me about your return from Iraq."

I can do that.

"I remember peering up this flight of stairs at DIA. I had flown in from California. I didn't know what to expect. When I landed in California, the active duty Marines were greeted by coworkers, family, and friends. I was a reservist, and so I awkwardly fumbled through the crowds, seeking a bus to take me to base. I didn't know anyone, and no one knew me." I breathed. "For two weeks, I waited in California. I ran and read. I had nowhere to go. It was a strange feeling, after months of accountability. I was free, but it was a useless freedom. I didn't know how to spend it."

"Why was that strange?" Trent interrupted.

"I don't know. I guess . . . I was like an institutionalized prisoner freed from incarceration. There's both fear and a looming question: What next?"

"Hmm," he grunted. "Go on."

"The days were long, waiting for Denver."

"Is that where you're from?"

"No, my family's in Portland. I grew up in the Northwest."

"Why didn't you visit your family?"

"As a reserve I had to demobilize at Camp Pendleton first and then return to my reserve unit in Denver. It's a paperwork thing. I had to wrap up my deployment before I could visit my family."

"I see."

"Hours before, I remember thinking: I'd been wrapped in a sleeping bag, stuck in a combat zone. And now, here I was, comfortably tucked into a safe bed. I was in the United States, you know? But I had to constantly remind myself of that. I couldn't sleep. I expected mortars in the distance and nearby howitzers exploding into action. I expected to wake at seventeen hundred hours and row on a rickety machine in the middle of Ramadi. I expected war and death—and adrenaline. But my expectations were stupid. It probably wouldn't have been so extreme, except that . . . I was home, right? But I was alone. Most of the Marines in my reserve unit were still in Iraq or on their way home. And somewhere along the way, on the active duty side, I'd been lost in the shuffle. To them, I was already a civilian."

"At the risk of sounding like a counselor," Trent broke in, "how did that make you feel?"

"Life lost its luster. For me, the war was over. My living moment of history had passed. I'd thought that I would embrace my return. But I didn't. After war, everything else was bland. I felt empty, I guess." My last words hung in the air.

Trent waited for me to finish.

"And there I was," I said, circling back, "staring at a flight of stairs in the Denver airport. I didn't know what I'd find on the other end. Family? Friends? Reservists? Would there be waving flags and patriotic bands? Or would I be an anonymous face in a bustling airport? I don't know why that image sticks in my mind—those longs steps stretching up into the distance. Or why it's so important. I took a step, then another, and finally crested the top of the stairwell. The foyer was empty. It was after midnight. No one was there. I fought in *our* war and there I was, home and alone."

"And what did you do?"

"Found a shuttle. Lugged my seabag to the front of the airport. Rode through a dark and snowy Denver."

Trent was filling his notebook. "And where did you go?"

"To a hotel near Buckley, where I'm stationed."

"I see. And?"

"The following morning I contacted my reserve unit's gunnery sergeant, Gunny Bravo. He picked me up and drove me to Buckley. Before deployment,

I'd been allowed to store my truck on base. There was an exchange of papers. Gunny handed me the keys to my truck. He told me to take the rest of the week off, relax, and report back the following Monday. I'd have to keep living like a Marine for another few months, he'd said, until my orders officially ended."

"And you wanted out?"

"I didn't know what I wanted. I knew I would be starting seminary in the fall. Other than that?" I stopped. "At the hotel, I remember dumping out my seabag and looking around the room. It was sparse. A queen-sized bed, a desk . . . a box television. I only had a few civilian clothes; three or four books; a laptop. That was my life. I remember thinking how small it was. I crawled into bed and slept."

Trent glanced at his watch. "I think that's all we have time for today. Can we do next week? The same time?"

"Yeah, that'd be great."

9. Weapons of Opportunity

During our myriad training sessions it was customary to respond to our instructor by screaming, "kill!" This was most common throughout our painful MCMAP lessons. Each recruit would face a partner while our instructor sagely discussed weapons of opportunity. A weapon of opportunity, we learned, was anything that could kill or maim an opponent, or anything that might provide a fighter with an advantage. In the Marine Corps, in war, he told us, there was no such thing as a fair fight. When the fight was over, you needed to make sure you were the one standing. "So," he said, "I want your partner to start choking you, kill?"

"Kill!"

"Then I want you to break the choke hold using the MCMAP techniques that I've taught you, kill?"

"Kill!"

"Then, after you've broken the choke hold, kill?"

"Kill!"

"I want you to grab a weapon of opportunity and break your opponent's skull, kill?"

"Kill!"

"Alright, recruits, kill!"

And we would begin.

At times, a scratching whisper would break through my subconscious, posing questions of rebellion. I would see the recruit in front me. See him as my enemy, my responsibility. I would then envision his head crumpled and rotting at my feet. I had to do this. It had to consume me. There could be nothing else. Only the dead. If I waivered, then it would be me lying at his feet.

"Kill!"

They also taught us, as our Drill Instructors phrased it, "to put a bullet in Habib's head." Of course, my ability to place a bullet in one of Habib's eyes from five-hundred yards was not an inborn skill. It was a learned skill. During our seventh and eighth weeks at Recruit Training, we were schooled in the art of the long-distance snipe: "One shot, one kill." In week seven, we learned how to take apart a rifle, thoroughly clean it, put it back together, and perform a function check. We also learned the science of windage knobs, trajectory, sighting, breathing, and locking-in. The latter was the exercise of switching between the prone, kneeling, and standing positions while aiming our weapons at a 50-gallon barrel and dry firing. As the sun set behind Camp Pendleton and the cars on interstate five sped by, we honed our skills.

I-5. I sighted in my M-16. *One thousand miles to the north is home.* I had lived in Denver such a short time that I still associated the Northwest with home. The rifle clicked as I squeezed the trigger. *I wonder what Dad's doing?* There was a lot of divorce in my family, and, as such, the childhood memories of my father were few. I didn't really meet him until I was fourteen. Before that, he was a vague presence two thousand miles away. He lived in Dallas and I had lived with my mother in Portland, Oregon. Before my freshman year of high school, he moved to the Northwest. I moved in with him. We had done our best to rectify a lost relationship, but he traveled for work and I was an egocentric football player. I joined the Marine Corps feeling the weight of national responsibility, but with an eye on clarifying my father's ambiguity. I knew he was proud of the decision I had made. And his pride was my pride. It was my father who I was thinking of as I pulled the bolt back, breathed, and paused. *I bet he's watching TV.* Click.

"What the fuck?" Beelzebub roared. "What are you doing, Recruit?"

One of the Canadian twins stood. "Nothing, Drill Instructor. Locking in, Drill Instructor."

"Bullshit, Recruit. What Squad are you in?"

"One, Drill Instructor."

"Oh shit. Recruit McDougal, get your ass over here." My old roommate jogged towards Beelzebub and stood at attention.

"Recruit McDougal reporting as ordered, Drill Instructor."

"Do you know, Squad Leader, that one of your Recruits was sucking down a donut when he was supposed to be locking in his weapon?"

"No, Drill Instructor."

Beelzebub smiled. "Follow me, Recruit." Beelzebub grabbed a scrub brush and forced McDougal to push it around the concrete perimeter of camp. Recruit McDougal's ass was handed to him because he had failed to police his own. It lasted for some two or three hours. When I saw McDougal later that night, I thought he was dying. I tried to catch his eye, but to no avail. He was spent.

A week later my platoon mustered outside of our barracks. It was five in the morning. Beelzebub formed us, left-faced us, and rhetorically sought to motivate us. We were to test at the rifle range. Those of us who passed with a score of two-twenty or better would move on with their training; those of us who failed would drop. We all wanted to pass, if for no other reason than because we didn't want to prolong our training. No one wanted to face defeat.

"Today you will test your skill in shooting," Beelzebub started. "Your score, and the score of your platoon, is a direct reflection of me. If you fail, I will kill you. Do not fail. Remember, your weapon is your bride. Love her, care for her, and she will please you. Do not, I repeat, *do not* embarrass me. Right—face—move—out. Left—left—left—right—left."

If you've never heard a DI march his platoon, then you might hear Beelzebub's commands as either crass or harsh. A good Drill Instructor, however, doesn't bark his marching orders, he sings them. And a really good DI doesn't just sing his commands, he caresses them.

Like a sonnet in the hands of Shakespeare, Beelzebub marched us from our barracks to the range.

Seven recruits failed that day. We never saw them again. Though we never found out what actually happened, it was rumored they re-tested and picked up with a platoon a few weeks behind us in their training. I imagined them returning home broken, humiliated, feeling like failures. Or, at least that is what Beelzebub wanted us to imagine. As for me, I passed with a two-forty-eight. There are three levels of Marine Corps shooting: marksman, sharpshooter, and expert. With my score, I was an expert. In the prone position at five hundred yards, I could shoot your temple.

To reward us for our good shooting, Beelzebub took us Island Hopping. In World War II the Marine Corps was assigned to the Pacific Theater. The Marine Corps, consequently, "hopped" from island to island in an effort to push the Japanese back. Later, Marine Corps Drill Instructors appropriated the name, Island Hopping, in an effort to teach wide-eyed recruits Marine Corps history. DIs would take their platoon from one PT pit—a sand trap the size of a basketball court—to another, slaying the platoon all the while. There are somewhere between twenty and forty Island Hopping pits on Camp Pendleton. In celebration of our shooting acumen, Beelzebub took us to every Island Hopping pit in the Camp. He called this our Island Hopping Tour. By the end of the day, I was both delirious and an expert shooter. I could shoot from five hundred yards or thirty: lying down, sitting, or standing. I could do this while running with a donned gas mask. I could do this in a driving wind. Those of us left in our platoon had succeeded, of course. But Beelzebub was punishing us for those who had failed. For, as he reasoned: platoons either lived together or died.

10. If Shit

MY LAST HURDLE IN becoming a Marine was called the Crucible. The Crucible is a fifty-four-hour combat scenario. In the Crucible, DIs push recruits to their limits. It is a test of endurance, teamwork, and combat skills. This scenario includes obstacle courses, day and nighttime marches, night infiltration movements, combat resupply scenarios, and casualty evacuations—all on minimal food and sleep. During the Crucible, I was put in charge of a small platoon of recruits. It was my job to ensure they all passed. One recruit continually held us back, however. His name was Recruit Bane. He cried, dragged his feet, refused to train, and bitched. At one point during a ten-mile nighttime march, Recruit Bane fell behind. Drill Instructor Beelzebub stalked over to me. "Recruit, what do you plan on doing with Recruit Bane?"

"Leave him."

"Fuck that, Recruit. We don't leave shit behind, even if it is shit. You do whatever it takes to get Recruit Bane through the Crucible. You hear me? Whatever—it—takes."

I'd never hit a human. But I hit Bane, as hard as I could. I hit him, grabbed him by the collar, and dragged his ass to the front of the column.

Who the fuck just did that?

I was near the end of my training, and I no longer recognized myself. Bane was not human in my eyes; he was part of a larger machine, a machine that had no margin of error. He was a broken cog I needed to fix. I was callous and unsympathetic. I wanted to be the best. I wanted to serve my country and defend freedom. I wanted to impress the Devil.

The Crucible's final trial was a grinding hump up a vertical beast called the Reaper. It was during this hike up the Reaper—early in the morning—that Sergeant Beelzebub crept up behind me.

"Recruit."

"Yes, Drill Instructor?"

"Do you disagree with my leadership style?"

I was befuddled. I had no idea how to answer this question. I assumed this was fallout from the Recruit Bane situation, but never had a DI been so straightforward with me. I was afraid of any repercussions that would come from speaking my mind.

"I asked you a question, Recruit."

"Yes, Drill Instructor," I said. "I might. A Marine should be motivated by respect, not fear."

"Really? Is that so?"

We were both breathing hard as we continued to pass through the sagebrush that lined the Reaper.

"You think Recruit Bane would have finished the Crucible if you hadn't feared him into it?"

"I don't know, Drill Instructor." I stared, head down, lest I should look Beelzebub directly in the eyes. "But, fundamentally, I have to believe a Marine who truly admires and respects his commander is more apt to follow him in a charge than the Marine who fears his commander."

"Hell, Peters, that's crazy talk. These recruits are birds, lost pigeons floating in life. They have no structure, no discipline, and they sure as hell don't have any fitness. We have a job to do here, and respect ain't gonna cut it. What's needed is fear. What's needed is dehumanization. You have to strip a man down—humiliate him—before you can begin the process of rebuilding 'em." He paused, looked up the mountain, and continued. "You have the makings of a good non-commissioned officer, Peters, but remember this: nothing motivates like fear. When you're in Afghanistan and some *hajji* is staring you down, it's not about hearts and minds recruit, it's about bullets in bodies. If one of your Marines ain't up to the task, well then, there's only one way to make 'em up to it. Scare the shit out of him."

"Yes, Drill Instructor."

He nodded his head and was off again, barking like mad at some other poor recruit struggling up the Reaper. That was the only time Beelzebub talked with me as an equal.

11. Graduation

My family flew from Portland to San Diego for the graduation. They watched as Sergeant Beelzebub pinned the EGA on my collar. After, my father hugged me and said he was proud. My mother and stepmother told me how well the uniform fit. My sisters and brothers took pictures.

"Congratulations, you did it."

"You're gaunt," my mother said.

"Yeah, what'd they feed you?"

"Can you kill me with your pinkie?"

I'd never accomplished something so difficult.

As families from all over the western United States milled around the Parade Deck, Sergeant Beelzebub found me.

"You're a fine Marine, Peters," he said, shaking my hand.

I looked him in the eyes for the first time. "Thank you."

After graduation my family and McDougal's family ate at the Hard Rock Café, San Diego. It was the first real food I'd eaten in thirteen weeks. It tasted delicious. As our families sat around the table—McDougal and I in uniform—we told them our tales of Recruit Training. We did our best to stay true to the events. But who can say with any honesty that, after Recruit Training, they remember it perfectly? I certainly don't. But I remember the truth of it. It's like war that way. Those of us who have experienced Recruit Training and war remember the strangest things. Like the way an M-16 feels against your cheek or the way a head looks without a skull.

Before graduation, in our last week at Recruit Training, Beelzebub decided we should join the hazing of a week-one platoon's Black Sunday. He ran us up into their barracks and called us to attention. The other platoon's recruits were standing next to their bunks, their gear in front of them. Beelzebub commanded us to choose a new recruit and stand nose to nose with him.

We did.

"Pick up their seabags, Recruits."

We did.

"Turn it over and dump it out, Recruits."

We did.

"Now, put all that shit in the middle of the squad-bay, and mix it up nice and good."

We did.

It was a mess. The issued gear of seventy recruits was strewn across the floor.

"Now, kindly remove the sheets of these new recruits' beds."

We did.

As I passed the recruit whose bed I had destroyed I whispered, "It gets easier."

I lied. I figured it wouldn't hurt.

"Get out, Recruits," Beelzebub ordered. "Hit the parade deck and form it up."

We did, but not before we heard the other platoon's DI remark: "Recruits, I have you for twelve long weeks. I doubt you have what it takes to become Marines. Yet, it's my job to train you, to turn you into fierce machines—machines that kill. Do you understand what I'm saying? In twelve short weeks, you'll be a different person. You'll be a Marine. As such, you'll have a duty to defend this great nation. You're the first and the last, Recruits. I'll teach you honor, courage, and commitment. I'll teach you to always be faithful—*Semper Fi*. Till the day you die, you *will* remember me. May the Devil spare your souls, because you're mine now. You have two minutes to sort through this gear and make my squad-bay shiny. What the hell, Recruits? Do it now, move!"

My platoon formed up on the parade deck and marched back to our barracks.

"Halt," Beelzebub said. "Get inside and get on line."

Our squad-bay was on the third floor. As I made my way up the stairwell I began to walk. *We graduate in three days. What can he do to me now?*

It was a poor decision. Beelzebub saw, he always saw.

"What the hell? Recruit Peters, are you walking?"

I was caught and I was graduating in three days. "Yes," I said.

Beelzebub took me to the quarter-deck and slayed me one last time.

He died two years later in Fallujah.

12. San Angelo

It was hot when I arrived. I had completed Marine Combat Training—a four-week course in the skills of the general infantryman—before landing in San Angelo, Texas. Leaving behind the Marines I had trained with for the last five months, I was traveling to Marine Corps Intelligence Training at Goodfellow Air Force Base. My military occupation specialty was Intelligence. I was in uniform, standing on a curb in the humid mid-day sun. Trickles of sweat rolled down my back. With one seabag full of gear, I was boot green.

"Hey!" a cabbie yelled. "You need a ride, Marine?"

"I'm headed to Goodfellow."

"Hop in."

I'd never ridden in a cab before. I shut the door. My alphas, a Marine uniform consisting of a green coat, green trousers, and a khaki shirt with tie, were tight and uncomfortable.

"I make this trip two or three times a day," the cabbie started. "It seems the Marines and airmen are always comin' or goin.'"

"Oh." It was hot, and I didn't feel like chatting.

"Now, by the looks of you, you're comin' straight from combat school. You take that uniform off, and I'll get you outta here—not a word to anyone."

I looked at the cabbie in the rearview mirror. Our eyes met. He had greasy dark hair and stubble. "No," I said. "But thanks." We rode the rest of the way in silence.

When we pulled up to the Marine Corps Detachment building on the airbase, a young Private First Class was waiting for me. I exited the cab, paid my fare, and grabbed my seabag. The cabbie didn't say anything as he pulled away.

"You, Peters?" the PFC asked.

"*Lance Corporal* Peters? Yeah, that's me." I had been promoted during MCT

"Sorry, Lance Corporal. I meant to say that. Lance Corporal Peters, then?"

"Yep."

"I'm PFC Mexico. Let's get you checked in." PFC Mexico was shorter than me. He had a crew cut. His uniform was cared after.

All I see is a uniform and a haircut.

We walked inside to a blast of air-conditioned coolness. A muscular sergeant was standing behind the desk.

"Orders."

I handed him my folder. He signed my papers and checked me in. Both Mexico and I stood at attention.

The sergeant ignored me. To him, I was paperwork. "You're in barracks 3–307. Supply has your bedding. Go to medical tomorrow and turn in your records. PT is at zero five-thirty." He didn't look up. "Don't be late. The PFC will show you around." He went back to his work.

Mexico and I walked out and into the Texas humidity. "We're roommates," he said.

I nodded. "Well, let's get moved in, then."

As we made our way to the barracks Mexico turned to me. "What did you think of MCT?"

I was beginning to sweat through my alphas. "It was okay, not that much different from boot I guess. You?"

"It was alright, Lance Corporal. I liked running through Pendleton, playing war games. Shooting the fifty cal' was pretty cool, too. I can't believe you have to strap yourself in to shoot it. It had a fucking seatbelt . . . or something."

We found our barracks and climbed the stairs to the third floor. Sweat was pouring through the thick cotton of my dress uniform.

"Actually," Mexico continued, "when we were on the range shooting the fifty cal', a buffalo sauntered right out of the sagebrush, moseyed over to the tank we were lighting up, and just started eating. I wanted to shoot the fucker, but our sergeant called a 'ceasefire.'"

"That's pretty crazy," I said. I set down my seabag and opened up the door to my new home. It was a ten-foot-wide by fifteen-foot-long room that contained two beds, two chairs, two closets, a mini-fridge, and an old television. The walls were an off-white color, which were gently highlighted by gray office carpet.

"Well, it's not much, is it?"

"No, I guess not," Mexico said.

I would be living here for the next six months while I was schooled in the art of "imagery analysis," which is Marine-speak for "bomb dropping" and civilian speak for "shock-and-awe." Mexico and I were not only racking together during our military occupational school, but we were to be stationed together at the same reserve unit back in Denver, Colorado.

"Alright, Mexico. I'm getting outta my alphas. It's hot. You know when we start our school?"

"Next Thursday."

"Errah, Devil." *Devil*, short for *Devil Dog*, can be used in one of two ways: one, as a term of endearment or two, as a term of loathing.

"Errah."

13. Gradual Release

The Marine Corps subscribes to a gradual-release training method. Recruit Training is a high intensity experience coupled with high discipline. All the recruits that graduate on a given day progress to Marine Combat Training together. MCT is similar to Recruit Training in its intensity, but not in its expectation. Students are no longer Recruits, but Marines. They are, therefore, provided more freedom. During MCT, Marines cannot leave Camp Pendleton, but they can, with a weekend's liberty, rummage through the PX—the military's version of a Super Target. If Recruit Training is for teaching civilians how to shoot and hump, then MCT is for teaching Marines how to perfect those skills. After MCT, each Marine then travels to a non-infantry Military School, though all infantry Marines bypass MCT for their MOS training, which is Infantry School. During MCT Marines learn how to throw grenades, use a compass, and dig foxholes. The culminating experience is a weekend-long war game.

Throughout MCT, I was still with my "buddy," McDougal. We both enjoyed crawling through overgrown gullies in full combat gear—our faces painted drab green, our boonie covers donned, and our fingers trigger-happy. McDougal, who had purchased a disposable camera, often called us to break from our low crawling so we could snap a few self-portraits. We were two young men dipping tobacco, having fun, and playing war. Though the fighting in Afghanistan had commenced, actual war was the furthest thing from our thoughts. We had struck the delicate balance of becoming warriors while holding onto the most important aspects of our civilian identities. For us, both Recruit Training and MCT were a hiatus. We were reservists. War was for "real" Marines.

After we graduated from MCT, each Marine in my original platoon was handed their MOS orders and placed on a bus bound for the Los Angeles airport. Because we were traveling to different parts of the country, we spent the majority of our day in an airport lounge drinking beer and saying our goodbyes. One by one, we went our separate ways. I had spent the last five months with these Marines. We had experienced both Recruit Training and MCT together. It felt strange walking away from those experiences. When it was McDougal's turn to leave—bound for Virginia—I hugged him before saying goodbye. "How'd you ever convince me to enlist?" I asked.

"Me?" he laughed. "It was your idea."

‡ ‡ ‡

It was weeks before Mexico and I started our MOS training. Our gunnery sergeant kept us busy in the interim. And so we PT'd, drilled, and studied our basic Marine Corps history. We did this for two reasons: first, we were receiving a paycheck and needed to keep up the illusion of busyness, or as Gunny said, "readiness." And second, we were vying for a coveted award, Marine of the Quarter. Young, enlisted Marines like myself longed for this prize. It conferred both distinction from one's peers and leniency from the top. Mexico and I studied together between our PT sessions and our nightly cavorting in San Angelo.

We studied the answer to questions like: *What is the max effective range of an M-16? In what order would a LCPL, Captain, GySgt, and Major embark? In what order would they exit a vehicle? What are the General Orders?*

It wasn't exactly fun material, but there wasn't much else to do in San Angelo. We had weekend liberty, and so we spent some time exploring the city. During those long months of waiting, I purchased a Trek road bike and started biking for exercise. The East Texas highways were long and straight, wide-open landscapes perfect for solitary rides.

Weeks turned to a month and on a Wednesday in June the Marine-of-the-Quarter board was called to order. I had dry-cleaned my dress alphas, paid for a haircut—buzzed on the sides, short on top—and shaved twice. Once dressed, I marched from my barracks to the board, trying not to sweat despite the beating Texas sun.

"Lance Corporal Peters, report," barked Gunny. He was a stout man of middling height. He had a military mustache and a flattop haircut. He sat at a long table, flanked by both our captain and sergeant.

"Lance Corporal Peters, reporting as ordered, Gunny." I marched, stood at attention, and popped a salute.

"About—face," the captain ordered.

I about faced. They were looking my uniform over, checking for any inconsistencies. I had expected this.

"About—face."

I spun around.

"Sit down, Peters," the sergeant said.

I right faced, marched over to the closest chair, left faced, and sat down—back at ninety degrees, elbows slightly bent, hands resting on my knees (thumb and forefingers tightly affixed).

Gunny stared me down. "What," he asked, "is the max effective range of the M-16 service rifle?"

I stared back. I had no idea. Apparently, my study sessions with Mexico hadn't been that productive. I wasn't worried, however. The key to these boards was to appear both calm and confident. "Sixteen hundred yards, Gunny." I snapped my head to the captain, as if to say, *I nailed your question, try something harder.*

"When did the United States Marine Corps first adopt the Quatrefoil?"

"1837." Again, I had no clue. I turned my attention to the sergeant.

"Detail a proper function check."

Without taking a breath I reeled off the details: "Break the weapon apart, pull out the pin, release the bolt, pump the arming mechanism twice, insert the pin, connect the weapon, and send the bolt home." I was lying.

"Stand," barked Gunny.

I stood.

The captain looked me over. "Dismissed."

I saluted, about faced, and marched out of the boardroom. Mexico was waiting for me in the lobby.

"How did it go?"

"I have no idea. I didn't know the answers to half their questions. I guessed."

"Seriously?"

"Yeah, the max effective range of an M-16, who knows that shit? We're in Intel for a reason."

A few days later Gunny found me hanging over by the barracks. "LCPL Peters, congratulations! I wanted to be the first to tell you that you earned Marine of the Quarter."

I shook his hand.

"I'll tell you though, you didn't answer a damn question right, but you said the answers so convincingly I had to double check the manual after you left." He was chuckling to himself. "I figured if any Marine could get me second guessing my knowledge, then he deserved Marine of the Quarter. There'll be a banquet next Thursday, so get your dress Blues ready."

"Yes, Gunny."

"Oh, and tell Mexico you both start school on Monday. Congratulations, Devil Dog, you're about to become an Intel Marine. Don't let me down."

14. Class 070502

On the first day of class, Mexico and I arrived at the schoolhouse fifteen minutes early. It was six o'clock when our other classmates arrived. The intelligence school was a joint command, and so our class consisted of airmen and airwomen, as well as Marines. There were ten of us in class—five Marines and five Air Force pipeliners (the slang term for an airman or airwoman who has recently graduated from boot camp). In the military, service men and women are segregated by both officer and enlisted, and rank. The rank structure is simple. Officers are O-1 through 9; enlisted men and women are E-1 through 9—the higher the number, the higher both the pay and responsibility. In San Angelo, all of those students from the Air Force were E-3 or below; but on the Marine Corps side we had two E-5s, or sergeants. There was Airman Rat, a short skinny guy with a shaved head and a weak mustache; Airman Louisiana, a tall and thin black woman; Airman First Class Hobbes, a mid-thirties balding man looking for a second career; Airman First Class Church, the son of a pastor from Virginia; and Airman First Class Nevada, a cute girl in her mid-twenties. On the Marine Corps side there was me; Mexico; and Sergeant Indiana, a hardworking Marine who was not only our class leader but also capable of the things Marine Corps commercials advertised; Sergeant Dick, a mid-forties stall-out (a Marine whose next promotion has eluded him or her) who was constantly cheating on his wife; and Corporal Jacksonville, a black man with a dripping jerry curl and manicured nails.

Our class was named after the day we started our training: 070502. Our class advisor, Staff Sergeant Wilberson, was tall, gangly, and pasty. His forehead was enormous, and he had the annoying habit of covering his mouth when he laughed. He was a lifer in the Air Force whose specialty was imagery analysis. In his mid-thirties, he was married with two kids. It was six-fifteen in the morning when he walked into our classroom.

"Atten—tion," Sergeant Indiana barked. We all stood upright and jerked to attention.

"At ease," Wilberson said, "Jesus. I might be your advisor, but I'm still enlisted. Cool it." He chuckled while covering his mouth.

After four months of training with the Marine Corps, our advisor's nonchalance was jarring. Mexico and I gaped at each other before hesitantly relaxing.

"Better," Wilberson said while eyeballing Mexico. "Remember, this is an airbase and you Marines are attending an Air Force tech school. This isn't combat."

I noticed Wilberson wasn't properly shaved and was horrified by this maleficence. *Should I say something?* I didn't. Sergeant Indiana would speak up if necessary.

I sat down as Wilberson continued his introductory lecture.

"You are here to learn. You are here to learn how to learn. And throughout this learning process you will become a more intelligent service member capable of autonomously learning."

What?

"070502 will be the best class I have ever advised, because I will it to be so." Wilberson stopped and looked each one of us directly in the eyes. I tried not to laugh. "If you need anything," he continued, "ask me. I want this to be a successful journey for you. The next six months will be both academically rigorous and physically challenging. Now—" he stopped talking.

We waited.

He bowed his head and left the room.

"What the hell was that?" Sergeant Dick asked.

"Welcome to the Air Force, sergeant," Hobbes said.

"Everyone can't be a locked-on charger," Sergeant Indiana said. "We'll continue to do what we do—as Marines," he was looking at the Marines and refusing to acknowledge the airmen and airwomen.

"Jarhead," one of the airmen said.

Sergeant Dick stood up and pointed his hands, forefinger and thumb perfectly aligned, at the Air Force pipeliners. "You will only speak when spoken to, Airman. Check?"

Silence.

"Do you follow?" Sergeant Dick's face was turning red and splotchy.

"Sit down," Sergeant Indiana said. "Don't waste your time."

He sat.

Twenty minutes later the instructor of our first section came into the room and started her lecture. It was on the art and history of both imagery analysis and intelligence gathering.

Our new life had begun.

15. *Jus in Bello*

We had eight sections of study. Each section was capped with a three-hour final. You passed, you moved on; you failed, you picked up with the class behind you. We studied everything from Russian air defense to the technological capabilities of the American DOD. We practiced gathering intelligence, stripping it down to its bare essentials, drafting reports on our findings, and briefing our classmates both on our research and our predictions. As weird as Staff Sergeant Wilberson was, he was right about one thing: they were teaching us to draw logical conclusions, often times from disparate sources. In this way, we were learning to think, make connections, and venture semi-reliable courses of action.

Just as our progression of study was predestined, so too was our daily schedule. We woke each morning at five in order to PT with our Marine platoon. From there we showered, ate, and arrived at the schoolhouse at six-thirty. Class, thereafter, commenced until eleven-thirty. After a break, class restarted at one. The day usually ended somewhere between four and four-thirty. Our nights were spent studying, unless for security reasons we weren't allowed to take the classified material out of the schoolhouse. On those occasions, we'd hang around the barracks.

Our weekends, however, were considered liberty. I had a cousin, William, who lived two hours away in Lubbock. That summer *Texas Monthly* ran an article detailing the top fifty things to do in the state. William and I figured we'd try them all. We road tripped to Luckenbach, ate at Cooper's in Llano, and swam in the Colorado. We sang "The Eyes of Texas are Upon You" in the state capital. We visited our grandparents in Hillsboro. We even touched Willie

Nelson. Well, not really. But almost. The summer sped by, and, with it, so did my MOS training.

Every so often the Air Force would hold an all-schoolhouse briefing. One hundred and fifty of us would cram into a small conference room and listen to our captain wax on about the need for intelligence in a twenty-first-century military. During one such meeting, the captain showed us a video of Marines bombing insurgents in Afghanistan. It was a grainy video taken from an unmanned aerial vehicle being flown remotely via laptop. We heard the radio conversation of the intelligence analyst who was flying the UAV

"Fuckers, I see 'em," the radio cut out to static, *qushhh*. On frame, six or seven individuals were moving from a truck to a building. The color was washed out; the camera was bouncing. This particular UAV had the capability of firepower. The intelligence analyst flying it would pull the trigger.

Qushhh. "You have the go ahead," *qushhh*, a disembodied voice said to the pilot.

Qushhh, "Targets locked," *qushhh*.

UAVs are not quiet planes. The targeted Afghanis took notice and ran for cover.

Qushhh, "Fire," *qushhh*. The screen erupted. Fire engulfed the Afghanis.

Qushhh, "I hit 'em! Fuck, I hit 'em!" The pilot was chanting over and over.

One of us laughed.

"Excuse me?" the captain said as he turned off the video. "Do you find this funny?" He was asking this to the whole room rather than one derelict service member. "Please, enlighten me, what's so funny about what we do?"

Silence.

"What we do, professionally, is terrible. What we do is a horrendous necessity. But what we do is never funny." He paused. "Are we justified in this war? I'd like to think so. We were provoked and we have the proper intentions in fighting Al-Qaeda. We will win this war, and we will help the people of Afghanistan rebuild. It's who we are; it's what we do. Before that, however, we will conduct ourselves with honor. *Jus in bello*. Justice, even in war, is necessary. To laugh cheapens our role; it cheapens our justice. I expect you, all of you, to act with a certain measure of professionalism, especially when both the power and responsibility to destroy is only a keystroke away." He scanned the room before continuing. "If I hear another laugh, then the offending service member will be dismissed." He turned back to the screen and pressed play.

16. Wilberson's War

Before our final exam, Staff Sergeant Wilberson talked with each of us in regard to our progress. I walked into his office and stood at attention. "At ease," he said. "For the last time, this is the Air Force. Relax. Sit." I sat. "One week left until your final exam. How do you feel?"

"Fine," I responded. "There's a lot to study, but I feel prepared."

"And after?"

"I'll report to my unit in Denver. I'm a reserve, though. I think I'll go back to school."

He smiled. "School, huh?"

"Yes, Staff Sergeant. I plan on majoring in Communications."

"Not the Middle East?" We stared at each other. "You're a relatively new Marine, correct?"

"Correct."

"And you've never been to war?"

"No."

"How are feeling about that? Dealing death from a computer?" I didn't have an answer. "Wars happen, Peters. You're a war fighter now. It's best that you start thinking about yourself that way."

For a moment, I was honest: "I don't want to, staff sergeant." The moment I said it, I regretted it.

He laughed, covering his mouth with his hand. "No one does, Peters. No one does."

I passed my final exam and graduated. During 070502's graduation, Staff Sergeant Wilberson spoke on our behalf. "I have never," he began, "seen a class with so much drive and willpower. I attribute this to 070502's fine leader, Sergeant Indiana. Not all of you who started together finished together, but those of you who leave this place today, leave it proudly. Though, often times, we leave this schoolhouse and never meet again, I believe this will no longer be the case. When we meet upon the sands of the Middle East, may we remember our common bond: 070502."

Later that night, as I finished packing my car, I shook Mexico's hand and told him I'd see him in February. We had a month leave before we had to report to our new unit at Buckley Air Force Base in Aurora, Colorado, after which I would make the long, solitary drive to Kansas and Bethany College.

"Alright," he said, "take care."

"I will. You got plans?"

"You know me, Peters. I always got plans."

"Well, use protection."

I drove home to Portland. I spent Thanksgiving and Christmas with my family. It was cold and rainy. My dad and stepmom had their three-foot, fiber optic Christmas tree on display. My mom was busy with school, as she had recently decided to return to college. My brothers and sisters were growing up. We spent what time we could together before I packed up my 1990 red Dodge

Dakota and made the twenty-two-hour drive to Lindsborg, Kansas. Like my mother, I was returning to college.

It was snowing when I arrived at Bethany. I moved into the dormitory alone. Most of the students were absent because it was January and between school sessions. I hadn't been on Bethany's campus since I'd decided to drop out two years previous. I had originally chosen Bethany for two reasons: one, they offered me a football scholarship; and two, it was the farthest school from the Northwest offering said scholarship. I had wanted a fresh, new experience, free to learn and make mistakes. Bethany was a small, Lutheran liberal-arts college. I had signed my letter of intent with the delusional hopes of becoming a football star. Two years in, however, I was a tired and beat up third-string fullback. Where one dream died, another was birthed. Amidst Bethany's echoing halls ringing with choral melodies, I discovered learning and books and that pre-made molds were lies. I had dropped out and moved to Colorado frustrated with a broken football career, but had returned—after my hiatus in both Recruit Training and Imagery Analysis School—for the ingrained memories of passionate professors willing to invest in their students' growth. At Bethany I wasn't fitted; I was asked to become.

The spring term would start in February, which was about four weeks away. I wanted an early start, however, and so I enrolled in Bethany's January term, which, in my case, was a three-week crash course in advanced public speaking. Before my first class, I flipped on CNN while I dressed. The news was ominous.

"All signs point to an American troop buildup in Iraq by March," the reporter said in her British accent. She was wearing a drab-safari outfit. "The American Secretary of Defense is presenting his case to the UN Security Counsel by week's end, and my sources tell me that Secretary Powell's goal will be to convince the world that Iraq has not only begun the process of enriching uranium, but is already in possession of weapons of mass destruction."

"Thank you—" the anchor replied and moved onto other news. I left the television and turned on the shower.

I spent a week researching and prepping speeches. On Friday I drove the six hours to Aurora, Colorado, a suburb of Denver, for my first reservist-drill weekend. I slept at an Embassy Suites, woke up at four, dressed in my camouflage fatigues, and drove to Buckley Air Force Base. My truck was not yet registered, so I parked next to Buckley's gate and went into the Military Police Officers' hut to register for a weekend pass. It was a frigid Colorado morning, and I waited in a line of ten other services members who were also waiting to register their cars. The serviceman in front of me was a Marine. He was taller than me by three or four inches. His uniform was finely pressed. His shave was close. He turned to me. "You fucking believe this shit, Devil?"

"Yeah," I said, not knowing what he was talking about. "It's pretty cold."

"Shit, well, it won't be for long."

It was already February. "How's that?"

He turned and looked me over. "Who are you?"

"Lance Corporal Peters."

"You Bravo Company?"

"Yes," I quickly glanced at his collar, "Staff Sergeant."

"Nobody called you?"

"Am I late, Staff Sergeant?"

"Fuck man, we got the call, Devil."

"Oh," I was stumped. "That's . . . great."

The line was moving. He started filling out paperwork for his car's registration. When he was done, he walked out past me. "See you at Bravo."

I registered my car and drove to the Marine Corps headquarters.

Tucked away in the northeast corner of the Air Base was the Marine Corps detachment, which housed both Alpha and Bravo Companies. Alpha was an artillery detachment. Bravo was an intelligence detachment. This was the first time I had visited the unit. The building was two stories high and contained a gym, a shower facility, a cafeteria, numerous offices, and, of course, a military display case. Alpha Company was downstairs; we were upstairs. We in Bravo never mingled with our lesser counterparts below.

I went to the main Marine Corps Administration office, which was situated between Alpha Company and Bravo Company. I had to check in and hand over the paperwork I had acquired during Recruit Training, MCT, and Imagery Analysis School. There was a tall Marine with a shaved head and thick mustache behind the counter. "What can I help you with Marine?"

"I need to check in, Gunny."

"Alright, let me see that." He pointed to my paperwork. Ten minutes later he walked back to the counter. "You're in Bravo. It's upstairs. You'll want to check with Gunny Bravo. He's a good Marine. He'll help you with all that's comin' up."

"Coming up, Gunny?"

"Shit yeah, Marine. You acting like no one called you." He shook his head. "Get upstairs, Marine."

Bravo Company headquarters were in disarray: Marines were running about, phones were ringing, officers were yelling. I moved to a corner. I figured it wouldn't hurt if I disappeared until the chaos died. A few minutes later, in walked Mexico. I nodded to him. "How you doing?"

"Good," he said while looking around. "What's going on?"

"No idea."

"How was your Christmas?"

"Good. Yours?"

"Yeah, it was good," he said. "My pops and I went to Mexico to visit my grandpa. He owns a ranch in the southeast. Well, over the years my grandpa has been donating money to the local church. In return, they decided to honor him. So we went down for the celebration."

"What did they do?"

"His money bought the church a new stained-glass window, so we went to watch 'em install it. We had front row seats, Peters."

"Cool," I said. "How long—"

"Who the hell are you two?" a gruff voice inquired.

I stood at attention. "I'm Lance Corporal Peters and this is Private First Class Mexico," I glanced at the speaker's collar, "Gunny."

"Alright," the Gunny said, "and what the hell are you doing in Bravo Company?" The Gunny sported a flattop haircut, glasses, and an extra fifty pounds.

"We're new reservists, Gunny. We graduated from the schoolhouse in November. We checked in downstairs."

"Fu—king—shit," he said. "And nobody called you, right?"

"No, Gunny. I guess not."

He shook his head. "Iraq, gentlemen. We're going to Iraq. We leave on Thursday."

INTERLUDE

"Where did we leave off?" Trent asked.

"I fell asleep in my hotel room."

"Right. What happened next?"

"Weeks came and went. I requested leave. It was granted, and so I flew home to Portland. My mother hosted a picnic. My dad and stepmom were there. I caught up with my siblings."

"Was it good to see your family?"

"Yeah, it had taken nearly a month, but I felt like I was home, if only for a time."

"Did you ever . . . struggle, being back?"

"From the war?"

"From the war. Humor me. Be specific."

I bit into my cheek. "One afternoon, while in Portland, my mother and I went shopping at Safeway. We were strolling through the produce aisle when I heard an incoming mortar. I screamed, reached for my gas mask, and jumped on the floor. I was wide-eyed and sweating when I realized that my mother was shaking me. 'You're home now,' she was yelling, 'you're home!' I tried to clear my head. The store's manager came running over. It hadn't been a mortar. Water had been running through overhead pipes to spray the fresh produce. I stood up and apologized. My mother started to tell him I had recently returned from Iraq. I looked at them both. They were far away, like looking backward through a telescope. I rushed out of Safeway and waited for my mother in her car."

"Did she ask you what had happened? Did she talk with you about it?"

"Yeah. I told her it was nothing, that she didn't have anything to worry about. And she said: 'I'm your mother, Benjamin, I'll worry about it.'" I started to laugh.

Trent was smiling, too. "Go on."

"I told her that I wish I had an explanation, but I didn't."

"Do you know what that was, Benjamin?"

"Yeah, a flashback. I could've sworn I heard a mortar."

"And did you see your dad during this time?"

"Yeah, I was home for two weeks. I saw him quite a bit."

"And he was recovering from his open heart surgery?"

"Yeah."

"How was that coming?"

"Fine. He looked well. He had lost weight. He was walking most days."

"That must have been hard to lose your grandfather right before your father's health was in question."

"And the looming war."

Trent nodded. "And the looming war."

I gnawed on my cheek. "It was. It is." I breathed. "It was good to see him though. He told me he was proud of me."

"Did you hear that often growing up?"

"For sure. My parents were always good about telling us they loved us. It was just . . . you know . . . the war. Losing friends, dropping bombs . . . I . . . I didn't do anything to be proud of, you know? I'm no hero. But he kept pushing it, challenging me. 'Someday,' he'd say, 'you'll be proud. Trust me. You accomplished something great.' It made me mad. So I shot back: 'And what was that?' He stopped trying to convince me."

"Do you believe your father loves you?"

I nodded. Trent jotted in his notebook. "After you visited your family, what then?"

"Five months sped past. Back in Denver, I drilled with my reserve unit by day and lived out of a hotel by night. We weren't allowed to return to our regular lives until our demobilization papers were approved. So, I did what Marines do best. I waited."

"That's it?"

"Well, yes and no."

"Yes and no?"

"I met someone."

Trent raised an eyebrow. "Someone?"

"A girl . . . I mean, woman. She's a teacher."

"Does this someone have a name?"

"Natasha."

He smiled. "And?"

I rolled my eyes. "And I like her."

"Okay, okay. We'll leave it there today."

I stood up to leave.

"Benjamin," Trent called after me.

"Yes?" I turned.

"Next time we'll have to talk about the war."

I grasped for the door handle. "I know."

17. Rhizome

As a reservist, I explained to Gunny Bravo that he must be mistaken. He told me to shut the hell up, after which I informed him of my recent move and enrollment. He said I had until Tuesday to drive to Kansas, drop my classes, gather my belongings, and return to Buckley. "Unfortunately," he said, "you'll lose your tuition." By way of consolation, he shook his head and mumbled. "Someone really should've called you."

The world was frozen. It was February. Interstate 70 cut an ebon path between the crystal plains. I drove with no music, no radio—only thoughts. In five days I would be leaving for war. Where was the ticker tape and beautiful women? It didn't feel right. I wasn't part of the Greatest Generation—I was a nobody caught in the arbitrary gyrations of history. I didn't want to die, but I didn't want to be a coward. A flood of questions I'd hoped to never confront rushed my mind: *Do I believe in war? How should 9/11 be answered? Would the world be a safer, better place if I died in the pursuit of a free Iraq?*

The plains were quiet. Snow fell. The sky darkened.

My anxiety acquiesced to anger. *What right do I have to kill?* I could destroy a bull's-eye at 500 yards. I could target an enemy remotely and decimate him or her with a keystroke. *Could I actually shoot somebody?*

When I was home for Christmas, I asked my pastor, Marcus, about Christians serving in the military. He answered by posing a question: "If our neighbor is being slaughtered, do we stand by and do nothing?"

Marcus' question didn't soothe my concerns. Rather, it birthed a slew of subsequent questions.

"It's the love of both neighbor and enemy," Marcus said, "as depicted in the Good Samaritan, which prompts the church to use force." Excited, he started waving his hands. "It's how *we* stop wrongdoing and *God* punishes wrongdoers. War, in one sense, is the Christian form of charity and justice. Really, it's a matter of human dignity. We protect the innocent from gross injustice and evil."

"Through force?" I asked.

"Through force."

"And Jesus is okay with this?"

Marcus leaned over his desk. "Absolutely."

‡ ‡ ‡

It was past midnight when I arrived on campus. I couldn't sleep. I packed my things and loaded my truck. It was light when I finished. I fell asleep on my dorm room's couch. When I woke, I found my advisor in her office and told her my situation. She confirmed my tuition wouldn't be refunded. She apologized. I stood up to leave.

"I'll be praying for you," she said.

I turned to face her. "Why?"

She narrowed her gaze. "Truth be told, I don't believe in this war."

"*This* war?"

"Some might be just, but this one—who can say?"

"A pastor once told me that, as a Marine, I'm God's instrument." I paused. "Do you believe that?"

She was quiet before answering. "Sometimes even the smartest people legitimize that which they don't understand. I don't know that God sanctions violence. I'm fairly certain he doesn't."

"What should I do?"

She shrugged. "I wish I had an answer for you, Benjamin. I don't. I'm sorry."

Two days later I found myself in Bravo Company's gymnasium, which was being used as a staging area, sitting in an ocean of seabags. It was five in the morning. There were forty Marines in Bravo Company—Alpha hadn't received the call. We were attaching to the First Marine Division, First Intelligence Battalion, Camp Pendleton, California. Buses would soon arrive to deliver us to Denver International Airport. Family members were mingling, saying goodbye to their loved ones. My family was absent. Mexico was with his family. I sat on my pack and read.

Once in California, we were bused to Camp Pendleton. We drove through the front gate. I had been to Camp Pendleton twice before, both times on the recruit side of the Camp. I was an official Marine now, and so what followed was a month of administrative paperwork, training, and typical military dormancy. We were staging for a war that hadn't yet been declared. President Bush and company were doing their best to sell a war to the international community and, until they closed the deal, we had nothing to do but wait.

And wait we did.

Most days were spent "police calling"—picking up trash—the parking lot of our barracks. On the weekends, however, freed from the chains of Marinehood, Mexico and I would work our way down to San Diego. We saw Pete Yorn in concert. We ate at the Spaghetti Factory. We discussed war, politics, and women. We drank some beer, too. Mexico was promoted. He was no longer Private First Class Mexico, but Lance Corporal Mexico. We were equals. I congratulated him. "If nothing else," I said, "it's a pay raise."

We shipped out in late February. The war had not yet started, but the systemic powers saw fit to transfer us overseas. We flew, M-16s stored under our seats, on a commercial airliner contracted by the Department of Defense. From Los Angeles to Frankfurt and then from Frankfurt to Kuwait City, we anxiously defied gravity. It was a long journey, and my first international flight. At Frankfurt, for fun, our staff sergeants made us disembark and shave. They didn't want us to arrive in Kuwait unkempt.

For security purposes, our plane landed at night. We staged our gear and waited for the Kuwaiti buses to pick us up and take us to our final destination: Camp Commando.

"Smells like shit," Corporal Quixote said, sitting on the tarmac. "This whole country smells like shit." Quixote was a real-estate broker in Denver. He was in his mid-thirties, married, and had two kids. He was responsible for me, Mexico, and Lance Corporal Salt Lake, a young Mormon who'd joined the Marine Corps to pay for college. Corporal Quixote was our fire-team leader, which was in squad one. Our squad leader was Staff Sergeant Wessen, a Denver police officer by trade but dickhead by choice. He was short and pale with a flattop haircut affixed to a fat face. I'm certain he joined the police force for the power it afforded him, rather than answering a call to uphold civic principles. In fairness, he didn't enjoy my company either.

"It's a different culture, Corporal," Salt Lake said.

"What the hell's that supposed to mean?" Quixote asked.

"It means respect, not disrespect. It only smells of feces because you do not know any better. Conversely, they would say the same of you."

"Shut the hell up, Salt Lake."

"Hearts and minds," Mexico chanted.

The buses came. We loaded our gear and caravanned to Camp Commando. The bus was blacked out and the curtains on the windows were snapped shut. We couldn't see Kuwait, and Kuwait couldn't see us. After a time—forty-five minutes or so—we stopped. Staff Sergeant Wessen exited the bus. "Sit tight, Marines." A few moments passed. "Alright," Wessen said, climbing the bus steps. "Welcome to Camp Commando. Grab your gear, grab a rack, and grab some shuteye. Tomorrow's coming at zero five-thirty.

"Peters," he called out.

"Yes, staff sergeant."

"You're on fire watch."

18. Glowing Sea

THE MARINE ON FIRE watch was responsible for his fellow sleeping Marines. He made sure nothing was either burned down or stolen and nobody tried to kill anybody else. I hated fire watch—who didn't?—and after a twenty-four hour global hop, all I wanted was sleep. It was two-thirty in the morning, yet duty called. I walked off the bus to the sight of canvas tents sprawling over the Kuwaiti desert. The only light leaked from yellow, insect-swarmed lamps perched atop wooden poles. I found my seabag and tossed it on a rack before assuming my post outside our tent.

It was a long night.

At five in the morning, the dark night sky turned gray and then amber. Cradling my M-16, I started to pace back and forth in an effort to stay awake. The air was cool and crisp. Our tents—perfectly aligned in columns and rows—cast somber shadows as the soft, golden light quietly filled the camp. Next to the tent was a small table. I crawled onto it for a better view. The desert, bathed in gold, surrounded me. A red-hazy tip peeked over the curvature of the earth. In the midst of its slow ascent, the sun splashed the sky with bright, shocking oranges. It was vast, a giant disk swallowing the desert.

I am small.
The world is a glowing sea.
I am at war and expendable.

The air warmed as Marines stirred. I climbed down from the table.

19. Kuwait

THE FIRST DAY CONSISTED of check-in and paperwork. We were officially assigned tents and racks, fire watch duties, and working hours. Camp Commando was a large Kuwaiti military base about forty-five minutes outside of Kuwait City. During our tour of the base, we learned the Kuwaiti army was stationed on the south side of the base. We rarely came in contact with the Kuwaitis. Our side of the base was comprised of Americans, Brits, and Aussies. It was a coalition force. All of the structures on the coalition's side were tents. We had bunk tents, chow hall tents, gym tents, recreation tents, and work tents. Most of the tents had canvas tops and sides and wood flooring. The sides were tightly fixed to the floorboards in order to keep any critters out, especially the dreaded camel spider, a spider that was bigger than a dog—in my imagination—and could spit in your mouth and chew off your arm.

After finishing our paperwork and tour, we visited the camp's doctor. He told us about chemical attacks and injecting ourselves with 2-PAM. We then received the smallpox vaccine. This was followed by lunch with our squads and a check-in at our assigned work tents.

I was placed in a small tent with nine workstations that were networked into a large computer that was connected to the military's secret Internet. I was to work days, from seven to seven. My watch chief was a salty Staff Sergeant named Sparrow. His face was lined and leathery. He wore military issued glasses. He was a lifer. He loved both the Marine Corps and his job.

"Listen here, Marines," Sparrow began, "I know you're reservists. That means you're older, and hopefully wiser, than your average lance corporals and below. Act accordingly. Be on time. Work your full shift. Don't fuck around. Any questions?"

We shook our heads.

"Alright, this is Sergeant Nascar." Sparrow gestured to a Marine on his left. "He's not only an expert in our field, but he's also our IT guy. Over the next few hours he's going to walk you through what we do here. Pay attention. Your shift begins as soon as he's done. Welcome to Camp Commando, Gentlemen." He turned and walked through the tent flap that separated our general working quarters from his office.

"Howdy, Marines," Nascar said, dripping with Mississippi. He was tall and skinny and sported a wispy mustache. His bottom lip was bulging with Copenhagen. In his hand was a twelve-ounce spitter.

He started by explaining that we were to be the hidden hands of shock-and-awe. Our job was to draft as many targets as possible before the war started. When it did start, our job was to conduct battle-damage assessments. We would assemble bombing packets, brief the pilots on when and where to bomb, and assess the overall success of the bombings. Nascar had a unique way of lecturing, but after a time we understood both what he wanted and how he wanted it. A few hours passed, he left the tent, and our shift began.

When you're working twelve-hour shifts seven days a week, time has a tendency to slip. A particular shift might be dreadfully slow, but not the days. One day melts into another, which melts into a week, a month, months, a season. Two months passed this way. We built targets, prepped pilots, and slept. We PT'd when we could; we practiced gas mask drills when we had to. The war was not yet real. In many ways, it felt as if we were still playing war rather than preparing to conduct it.

Outside of our tent was a hollow concrete barrier buried in sandbags. Whenever the camp sounded an incoming alarm we would run to the closest bunker, dive in, don our gas masks, and wait for the all-clear. We also received haircuts from local Kuwaitis who had established shops on Camp Commando, which was my first interaction with someone of a different race and culture. They were dark skinned and smelled of rice and curry. As they cut my hair, I imagined killing them as an extension of Christian charity. *It's the right thing to do. It doesn't even contradict my faith.* But I was never able to consummate the death. If I was an instrument of God, then I was out of tune.

It was early March when nearly all of the Marines on Commando crammed into one of the recreation tents to watch Secretary Powell plead his case before the U.N. Security Council. We had been waiting for this moment. Most of the Marines wanted the war to start and believed it would not start until Secretary Powell presented his findings. We turned the TV to Fox News. A hundred eager Marines surrounded me. The atmosphere was electric. Across the screen an eagle flew. It morphed into an American flag. "The Ultimate Sacrifice" scrolled across the screen. Pictures of service members who had died in Afghanistan followed. The tent was quiet, solemn. "Fuck the Army! Let's get this shit started."

"Kill bodies!"

"We eat burnt babies!"

All was pandemonium until Secretary Powell walked onto the screen and sat down opposite the U.N. panel.

We quieted.

20. Certain Clarity

Secretary Powell spoke with certain clarity. Iraqi was guilty. War was necessary. His words sparked within me the youthful desire to experience combat. I left the recreation tent knowing that war was imminent.

In the center of Camp Commando was a large concrete tower. At the base of the tower there was a padlocked door. Mexico and I were walking past the tower after Secretary Powell's speech. "You know what I heard about that tower?"

"Huh?" I responded.

"When Saddam and his ilk came tearing through here back in '90, they stormed Commando and killed a bunch of Kuwaitis."

"And?"

"Well, I heard those they didn't kill they tortured, and whenever they finished, they hung 'em from the top of that tower."

"Damn."

"When the U.S. finally got to Commando the bodies were still hanging. They were all mangled and shit. That bitch is haunted."

"Who the hell told you that?" I asked.

"Salt Lake heard it from a translator who heard it from a *Hajji*."

"Go in and find out."

"Funny. I'm not going anywhere but my rack."

"What'd you think of Powell?"

"I think this shit's gonna kick off before we know it."

"You ever think you'd be fighting a war?"

"Why do you always ask such stupid fucking questions, Peters?"

I didn't answer, which prompted a belated response.

"I never really thought about it."

"I don't mean to pry, but what about your daughter? She's what? Three-months old?"

"Yeah," he said, "three months."

"How could you not think about it, then? War, I mean."

"Some of us just don't give a shit, Peters. You know? It's a job. I get paid. When I'm done, I'll get the GI Bill. It's a win, right? I'm giving my daughter a better life."

"A win? Yeah, I guess. So you don't have any problems with it? No reservations?"

He laughed. "Are you kidding me? Bush is fucking crazy, and I don't give a shit about Saddam. It's like I told you, it's a job. Either way, we're damned if we do and damned if we don't. Right?"

"How?"

"Starting this war is gonna piss the entire Middle East off, but what happens if we don't? We'd be weak. We'd get attacked all the time. As far as Bush is concerned, this shit's a loss."

"But it's nice for you?"

"It's a job, Peters. A tax-free job."

Back at our tent the lights were out. I had the bottom rack. The Marine above me was an active-duty Marine. His name was Corporal Johnson. He was a slightly overweight IT Marine who had perpetual bags under his eyes. As I slid into my rack, I noticed a soft glow drifting down from Johnson's rack. I leaned my head out and whispered. "Johnson, hey, what the hell you watching?"

"Sex. You want in?"

"No. I'm sleeping. Turn that shit down."

"Fuck you, Peters."

I fell asleep to the wafting grunts of erotic love.

21. Scuds

NAMES FADE, FACES BLEND, and dates blur. What never obscures throughout the passing of time, however, is your first taste of combat. It's pure adrenaline. Pure fear. Pure drug. You're scared shitless, but you want more. It's the illusion of being wholly aware, wholly present, and wholly alive—an experience mundane life never supplies. One moment you're caught in the grips of history, the next you're behind a florescent lit desk, faced with the terrifying banality of life.

Three days after Powell's speech, I was in one of Commando's gym tents, extending my triceps in Marine issued workout clothes: silky green shorts (very short), a green t-shirt, and a pair of camouflage "go-fasters." *Grsh-grsh-grsh.* I glanced at my gas mask lying on an adjacent workout bench. *Grsh-grsh-grsh.* I dropped the dumbbell on the floor and caught the eyes of the other Marine. *Grsh-grsh-grsh.* The base's alarm sounded.

Time stopped. Frozen.

Shelter!

The other Marine moved, shattering the moment. I grabbed my gas mask, my M-16, and ran out of the tent into the stunning light of mid-morning. People were running every which way, seeking the closest scud bunker. We had practiced this numerous times. I was working out at a different gym than normal, however, and didn't know the closest scud bunker. I followed the crowd. We ran en masse.

Explosion.

The ground shook.

Concussion.

I donned and cleared my gas mask. Sprinting now, I passed a scud bunker. People were shouting and waving their arms.

Caught in the open.

I ran back to the scud bunker and dove. Marines moved aside. I curled into a ball. *Grsh-grsh-grsh.*

Explosion.

Another alarm.

I waited. Sweat trickled down my forehead, obscuring the view out of my plastic mask.

Why me? I'm good. Why would anyone want to kill me? If Saddam and I could only sit and talk, we could figure this out—find a solution.

More time. More waiting. More sweat.

"Bullshit, no one's in the Marine Corps to serve, Recruit." Fuck Saddam. I hate him. I hope he dies.

More time. More waiting. More sweat.

The view from the bunker was dry and bare. I closed my eyes. *Why am I here?*

‡ ‡ ‡

The all-clear sounded. I jogged to my work tent to check in with Staff Sergeant Wessen. He told me a scud missile had directly hit Camp Commando. A corporal in our reserve unit had been next to the blast. He was alive, but shook up. Wessen told me to change into my fatigues and start working. The war had begun.

22. Mirror

I WAS STARING AT my workstation, in shock.

Another alarm sounded. We stumbled over one another in an effort to vacate the tent and occupy a nearby scud bunker. The all-clear was given. This was followed by another scud alarm, which was followed by another all-clear, which was followed by another alarm—a repeating pattern that continued for forty-eight hours.

We didn't sleep. We didn't eat. We didn't shit. We ran back and forth from our work tent to our scud bunker. Pilots were conducting America's shock-and-awe campaign as we tried our best to provide them with a constant flow of both fresh targets and BDAs.

People were dying.

Marines were preparing to push north.

After wearing the same fatigues for forty-eight hours in the heat of Kuwait, I stunk. I needed the bathroom, but scud alerts were coming in fifteen-minute waves. I didn't want to risk my life for a trip to the porta potty. Yet, after debating both the pros and cons with Mexico, I decided I would rather die than defecate on myself. I made a run for it.

I sprinted through a ghost town.

There was an eerie calm pervading Commando. Marines throughout the base were in their respective bunkers, hunkered down. I was the only one in open space. I found a porta potty, closed the door, and sat down. A smudged mirror was affixed to the door, hanging inches from my nose. I was haggard. I hadn't shaved in days. Dark circles hung underneath my eyes. My hair was slick with sweat and grease.

A mere forty-eight hours of war had elapsed, and all I wanted was for it to end. The days of my youthful naiveté were over. Through war, I saw a version of the truth. I was no hero, no knight. I was scared, a coward forged in war. My pre-war visions were shattered.

"What now?"

No one answered.

I finished and jogged back to the bunker. The alarm sounded. I quickened my pace.

"How was it?" asked Mexico when I crawled back into the bunker.

"Good. I look like hell."

"I can see that."

"What are we doing here?"

"Repaying the atrocities committed on 9/11," Salt Lake said. "Given that we are at war with terrorists, I hardly think your question appropriate."

I stared at Salt Lake through my gas mask. "Sorry."

"Get some," Quixote shouted.

"Errah!" another Marine yelled.

There were fifteen of us crammed into the bunker. Being a small, cement shelter covered with sandbags, Commando's scud bunkers were the coolest place on base. If nothing else, then it was at least a reprieve from the heat.

"We're bringing the fight to them," Quixote asserted. "I'd rather fuck 'em here than get fucked at home, you know?"

"I'm not sure Iraq could or would invade America," Salt Lake pointed out. "But, yes, your position is sound."

Quixote turned his head to Salt Lake, "Goddamn, son—you're a wooden idiot."

The all-clear sounded.

"Alright," Wessen shouted. "Back to work."

23. *Borders*

Once the initial onslaught of shock-and-awe had passed, it was time to move north. Intel Marines would be attached to Marine Recon units as they crossed the Iraqi boarder into Basra, after which they would continue to push into Nasiriyah, Najaf, and ultimately Baghdad.

Neither Mexico nor I traveled north. He was disappointed. I was relieved.

I was terrified of the border, of looking someone in the eyes and pulling the trigger. I craved the experience but was horrified of the outcome. *Could I do it?*

After living in bunkers and eating MREs for three weeks, Mexico and I watched television footage of Saddam Hussein tumbling down in one of Baghdad's city centers. "You think it's over?"

"I don't know," Mexico said.

"This has got to mean we're going home soon."

"It's history."

"Yeah, and we watched it on CNN like everyone else."

"That's the Marine Corps, Devil."

"Errah."

A week later a corporal in our reserve unit came riding into camp. He had been chosen. He was dusty, unshaven, and unkempt. His hair was in disarray. He looked tired, but exuded calmness. Mexico and I were sitting outside of our work tent drinking Folgers when the corporal came to check in with Wessen.

We stood up. "How was it, Corporal?"

He looked at me. The sun was setting. Half his face was aglow, the color orange.

Mexico laughed nervously and pounded the corporal on the shoulder. "Hey, you alright?"

The corporal turned to Mexico. "Yeah. It was okay." He ducked into the tent.

"What the hell? He's jacked up."

"Yeah, well, so is this coffee." I dumped it out.

In the Marine Corps, there is a mysterious hierarchy of "Devil Dogness." If you've been directly shot at, then, congratulations, you're "king of the mountain"—a salty, hard Marine. If you've only had bombs dropped on you, however, though better than state-side Marines, you're hovering somewhere near the bottom. Not only were Mexico and I lowly Lance Corporals, but we were also floundering on the metaphorical leatherneck meter. We would return to the States as frauds, lauded, but not shot at with AKs. There would be no combat action ribbon for us, not yet.

24. Gray Water

INSIDE THE TENT I saw that one of our Gunny's was watching the news. He was leaning back in his chair and sipping coffee. A leather handgun chest-holster was wrapped around his body. He peered over his shoulder at me. "Peters, how you doing, Marine?"

"Good Gunny. You?"

"Hanging in there." His eyes focused on my hair. "You a rock star now, Peters? That's some wild shit."

"Yeah, Gunny." I smiled.

Wessen was standing behind me. It was all he needed to hear.

"What the fuck, Peters? The Gunny said get a haircut. Why are you smiling?"

"Are you serious?" I was taken aback.

"Am I fucking serious?" Wessen's eyes popped out of his head. "Fuck *yes*! Get the hell out of here *shitbird*. Get a haircut! And don't come to work tomorrow, asshole. Go straight to guard duty. Work there for a week and let's see if that don't change your attitude."

My mouth was agape.

"Move, Lance Corporal," he whispered between clenched teeth.

"Yes, Staff Sergeant."

I was angry. I didn't mind the haircut, which was of no consequence, but guard duty was reserved for the dregs of the Marine Corps. It consisted of watching the *hajjis* who came on base each morning. Some *hajjis* built tents. Some worked in the chow hall. Others cleaned out the porta potties. Guard duty was a twelve-hour shift, and it was boring as hell. I hadn't had to pull guard duty yet and was hoping to avoid it all together.

I had my hair cut, and I reported at the guard shack the next morning in full battle gear. They assigned me "gray water" duty, as they euphemistically called it. I would be sucking shit out of toilets for a week. It seemed Wessen had called in a personal favor.

I waited for the truck to stop. My presence was meant to intimidate. My fully loaded M-16 said: "You might drive the truck that sucks the shit out of our nasty American toilets, but try anything funny and I'll kill you." I opened the door of the diesel-sized truck, grabbed the handrail, and hopped into the passenger seat. The driver was a dark-skinned, middle-aged man. He looked more Asian than Middle Eastern.

"Hi."

"Hello," he replied. "George Bush." He thrust his thumbs into the air.

I nodded.

"I come from India." We were driving to our first stop.

"You speak English?"

"A little," he said in a Punjabi accent.

"What brings you to Iraq?"

"Both my children go through medicine school. I give them money. So I come here to drive. You know, I good driver. They pay me to drive this truck and clean the toilets. I do this for family. It is a good thing. George Bush." He waved his thumbs.

"Doctors?"

"Yes, very proud."

"Are you married?"

"Yes. Many years. So happy."

"Do you ever see your children or wife?"

"No. I send money." We pulled up to the first set of toilets. "Okay, I work now." We exited. I shadowed his movements. He pumped the shit into his tank. It was pungent. We climbed back into the truck.

"Okay," he said, "now we dump. Then come back."

We drove off the base and into the desert. After twenty minutes of driving he stopped the truck at what passed for a dumping site. It was a lake of feces. Feral hounds prowled. The smell was unbearable. We shooed the dogs away and emptied the truck. We drove back to base and to the next station of toilets. We continued this pattern for twelve hours.

I guarded the Indian all week. We discussed, as much as we could, life in America, life in India, and life in Kuwait. He was lonely. He lived in Kuwait City. He had a small flat, and from what I could gather, he shared this with five or six other drivers of differing nationalities. They were all in Kuwait so they could send money back to their families. Before the Indian had moved to Kuwait, he'd been a sergeant major in the Indian military. He'd worked in supply. This, he told me, was where he'd learned to drive a truck. He hadn't seen his family in eight years. Before Iraq, he drove in Saudi Arabia.

One day during lunch he invited me to eat with him. We climbed down from the truck and crawled into a scud bunker to escape the heat. He pulled out a fresh tomato, an onion, and a lime, some couscous, flat bread, and a few mangoes. He chopped the tomato with a small knife (one I hadn't known about) on a cutting board. He mixed the couscous with the tomato and onion and then squeezed the lime into the mixture. The Indian handed me half of the concoction scooped onto a piece of flat bread. We reclined as best we could in the bunker, ate our meal—followed by a dessert of mangoes—and talked about his hometown. Hiding from the noonday sun, he told me that when I married I should honeymoon in India because of its unparalleled beauty.

We're the same. Asian. American. All we really wanted was to live our lives and make our own decisions. Granted, I wanted to live mine with less curry.

And the Red Guard? Didn't they have families, homes, and hobbies? Didn't they have dreams? If I could befriend an Indian, couldn't I also befriend . . . *No, they're the enemy.* The Indian and I had found common ground. I couldn't do the same with an Iraqi.

My last day with the Indian came. He wrote down his cell phone number and told me to call him when I arrived in the States.

I never did.

INTERLUDE

A SOLITARY LAMP SPLASHED light across Trent's desktop. A mixture of whites and grays washed the room. He had asked me to discuss the war. Opposite him, I was sitting on his couch. It was big and soft. I tried to talk about Iraq. I *wanted* to talk about Iraq. But I didn't know what to say.

We sat in silence.

"You'll have to process Iraq eventually."

"I know." I nodded. "But, it's weird. I can't find the words. I saw death. I dealt death. Yet I don't know how to understand it. It's frustrating. There's a foolishness and guilt, I think, because I bought into it, you know? I chose it."

"What do you mean?"

"I feel like I was duped. I enlisted after September 11th, like everybody else. We were young and patriotic. We had to join. We had to answer the Towers. Then we invaded Iraq under the pretense of finding weapons of mass destruction. We didn't find any, though. Now, most nights, I ask myself: does that invalidate the war? And if it does, then what does that make me? A murderer?"

"Why not a soldier?"

"What's the difference? One is state sanctioned. The other isn't? It's a thin line."

Trent nodded and wrote in his notebook. "Yes," he agreed and lifted his head. "But you're sharing logical arguments with me. I need you to process your emotions."

I sighed, biting my cheek. "I'm angry, okay? I'm angry at Bush, Saddam, conservatives . . . myself."

"Why are you mad at yourself?"

I told him of drafting targets and dropping bombs from a computer screen. I spoke of wielding death as if it were a video game. I had killed, yes, but I had no idea as to how many I had killed. I talked of collateral damage, of bombs hitting schools instead of insurgent hideouts. And the stress, the unimaginable stress. "At one point, my hair started falling out in clumps."

He nodded and scribbled. "And how are you assimilating into civilian culture?"

"I sleep on the floor."

"Excuse me?"

"It's strange. Since I've been back, I haven't been able to sleep on a bed. I sleep on the floor of my hotel room between the bed and the wall."

"Why?"

"I have no idea," I said, biting my cheek. "I'm also addicted to Iraq War documentaries. I watch two or three a week."

"Are you trying to stay connected to the war in some way?"

"I want to know what we did and what we're doing is paying off. That it wasn't a waste."

Trent glanced at his watch.

"Times up?"

"Time's up."

I stood.

"Actually, how are things with Natasha?"

I smiled. "Things are progressing. Why?"

"Well, you've been together for, what, four months?"

"Six."

It was his turn to smile. "And?"

"We'll see."

25. Sand

AFTER MY WEEK OF guard duty I reported back to the work tent. It wasn't much of a work tent, however. "Mission Accomplished" had been proclaimed, and our rotation was coming to an end. Wessen, nonetheless, found great pleasure in finding things for me to do. His favorite assignment was to make me sweep the sand that surrounded our work tent. He claimed that sand should be uniform. I did what he told me. This lasted for weeks. Our war was over, but we had no date of departure. So we PT'd, marched, trained, and swept sand. We still checked in at our work tent each day, but no longer did we draft targets or battle damage assessments. We were reserves who had fulfilled our purpose and were waiting to leave for home. We had been in Kuwait for four months.

Wessen was adamant about providing us with learning opportunities. Another two months passed. I resigned myself to Kuwait. I was no longer a prime mover—life was happening *to* me. I would never leave and Wessen would always be my boss. I was tired of Kuwait and the Marine Corps. War was ugly, it changed people, and I wanted to extract myself before it was too late. In my better moments, I dreamt about the future, of returning to Bethany College and graduating.

On one laborious occasion, Wessen had us caravan in Humvees across the desert with nothing more than our intuition and a compass. We were supposed to be looking for an airbase. At this airbase we would swap some Predator film with the Air Force. There were two Humvees. I was in one Humvee with Quixote and Salt Lake. Mexico was in the other with Wessen. We drove around for a few hours and practiced roadside scanning maneuvers, ever vigilant against the odd, stray camel. It was a waste of time.

Salt Lake was a pack-a-day smoker. I tried one of his Marlboros and then some of Quixote's Skoal—anything to kill the boredom. Salt Lake garrulously detailed his love affair with BYU football, which he only talked about when he wasn't discussing the finer points of his wife's ass.

"It's weird," I said. "I don't want to know about your wife's cheek."

"Yes, but she's rather delectable."

"Look," I turned around. I was in the passenger seat, Quixote was driving, and Salt Lake was in the back. "I'm sure your wife is beautiful, but she's *your* wife. It's really not that hard—"

"Fuck it, man," Quixote cut me off. "You got pics? Pass that shit up here." Through the swirling smoke, Salt Lake handed him a few sweaty and crumpled pictures. Quixote kept one hand on the steering wheel while he flipped through them with his other hand. "Damn. That's crazy." He shook his head. Salt Lake was grinning in the back.

"Creepy."

"It's not, actually," said Salt Lake. "I love my wife. She is beautiful. If I had a wonderful landscape brushed by Poussin—an equally eloquent work of art—then would you think me queer for sharing it thusly? I think not."

"I don't know what you're talking about," I said. "But, and trust me on this, Salt Lake, you're fucking weird and it's making me uncomfortable."

As we drove through the endless sands, three camels crested the horizon and plodded towards us. "Look at that," Quixote pointed.

"Remarkable," Salt Lake said. "Equally remarkable." He grinned.

On another occasion, Wessen told our fire team to don the one set of civilian clothes each of us had brought. We would be riding into Kuwait City to provide security, James Bond style, for a local contractor. I dressed in khakis and a blue button-up shirt. We each checked out a handgun from Commando's armory. I tucked my handgun between my belt and my back.

The contractor was a fat, greasy-haired American from the northeast. His face was red and splotchy. It looked like he was in a perpetual state of working out. Our job was to drive him around the city and guard him while he did whatever he wanted. We were to shoot anyone who attacked him. He ate at a Burger King. He went to the mall. He drank Starbucks. At the mall we stayed a safe distance behind him—so that we could survey the area—while he sipped coffee and read the Times, surrounded by women in Burkas. After he filled his face with meat and coffee, we drove him to a small shady house on the outskirts of the city. "What are we doing here, Sir?" Wessen asked.

"None of your fucking business, Marine."

Wessen clenched his jaw.

The contractor exited the SUV and turned around. "This won't take long," he said, slamming the door. No one said anything. We waited outside the house. The contractor returned after a few minutes. We drove back to base. Wesson was driving. Mexico and I were in the back seat.

"What the hell was that?" I whispered to Mexico.

"I don't know."

"A brothel?"

"Your mind's running wild, Peters. Who knows what it was."

My eyes grew wide. "An opium den."

"You read too much. It could've just as easily been a bar."

"I doubt Wessen would've questioned him if it'd been a bar."

The next day, on Commando's dirt parade deck, the concrete tower looming overhead, the Operation Iraqi Freedom Marine Forces General spoke. He told us we had displayed an excellence in war fighting that no other country could boast. He was proud of us, and otherwise doted on us like a mother. The road ahead was long, he told us. That was true, but, according to the General, we were prepared to fight terrorism wherever it lay. We would root it out. After he finished, a Korean Marine contingent performed a traditional Korean kung-fu show. Later, *hajjis* set up a bazaar on the parade deck. We looked at their local wares, ate their Kuwaiti barbecue, and listened to a cover band play classic rock. It was a festival. I think the commanders of Commando knew we were restless, and restlessness isn't a desirable quality for a military force in a combat zone.

Life went back to normal the next day. There was still no word on our ship date. A few weeks later our work tent was completely broken down and packed for shipment. Wessen, even Wessen, stopped trying to create the illusion of work. After breakfast each morning our fire team, minus the staff sergeant, would find a cool scud bunker to occupy for the rest of the day. Every now and then we would break our routine and play a game of pickup football on the parade deck. It was always Bravo Company versus Staff Sergeant Sparrow's active-duty fire team. We usually won. At nights, when Kuwait cooled off, we would sit outside and stay up late. We discussed the war and, well, sex. Every once in awhile Salt Lake would bring up Mormonism. He quit talking about it after I told him I wouldn't convert, no matter what he or Joseph Smith said.

It was a time of waiting.

We wanted our lives back. I wanted my life back. "Mission Accomplished" or not, the war was raging north of us while we were trapped in the doldrums of the south. My thoughts turned homeward. As best I could, I arranged to return to Kansas and Bethany College. It meant having to commute to Denver once a month for Marine Corps reserve weekends, but at least I wouldn't lose any credits while transferring schools. If I had learned anything, then I had learned that neither the grunt work of being a Marine nor selling civilian mattresses was for me. I wanted my degree. I wanted to make my own choices. I was tired of being told what to do or not do, what to believe or not believe. There was no Christian charity in war, only Marines killing enemies in order to keep other Marines safe. I wanted to write my own story.

A few weeks later we were sitting in our bunker during the heat of the day. We had eaten lunch. Mexico and I were on one side of the bunker, Salt Lake and Quixote were on the other. Salt Lake was smoking a Marlboro waxing eloquently about his wife. Quixote had his boonie cover pulled down over his eyes in an effort to both sleep and ignore Salt Lake. Mexico was watching a movie on his laptop. I was reading *1984*.

"Shut it, Salt Lake," Quixote mumbled.

I looked up from Orwell.

"I will talk when and wherever I choose," responded Salt Lake.

Quixote tipped his hat. He looked Salt Lake in the eyes before quickly slapping him across the face.

I laughed.

"What do you find so humorous?" Salt Lake asked me.

"C'mon, that was funny."

"Bitch," Mexico offered.

Salt Lake struck back: Quixote and he rolled out of the bunker while screaming profanities and slapping each other.

"*Hey!*" yelled Wessen, materializing from nowhere. "Break it up, *shitbirds*." He pulled off Quixote, who was solidly atop Salt Lake. "Act like a corporal, you hear me?"

"Yes, Staff Sergeant."

"Good. Now, pack your shit, we're leaving first thing tomorrow."

26. Powers

"BENJAMIN," SHE SAID, "YOU have a phone call."

"Thanks." I strolled into the office. It was summer. I was in Estes Park, Colorado, working at a sport and mountain adventure camp called Camp Pine. I was on the leadership staff and responsible for eight counselors. I was also in charge of music and entertainment. I had been home from Kuwait for a year, and in that time I had nearly graduated. To do so I transferred in twenty-eight Air Force Community College credits and then took eighteen-hour semesters. It was difficult but necessary. I would graduate with a degree in Communications. The last requirement was my senior internship, which I was currently fulfilling at Camp Pine. "Hello," I said, grasping the phone.

"Corporal Peters?"

My heart stopped. I knew what this was. I'd been following the news. I didn't want to respond. I wanted to hang up, run away. "Yes."

"This is Sergeant Pullman from Bravo Company. We've been recalled, Devil. You have twenty-four hours to report to base."

"Yes, Sergeant."

"Gear up, Corporal. You're headed to Fallujah."

I fit the phone into its receiver. In three weeks, Camp Pine would shut down for winter. I had to tell the camp director that I would be leaving early. My internship would end. I knew I would have to return to Iraq; I'd followed the news, but I'd also worked hard in the hopes of graduating before my next deployment. Over the past year, I had decided I wanted answers, or more specifically, I wanted my faith to answer. How could Christians, me included, be resigned to war? So I'd applied and been accepted into a master's program at Denver Seminary. If I couldn't graduate, however, my plans would unravel.

I stumbled into the main lodge and found Camp Pine's director, Joseph, pouring over receipts and paperwork. Over the summer we had developed a friendship. He lifted his head. "What's wrong?" he asked, worried there'd been an injury on the premise.

"The Marine Corps called. I have to leave."

This news, at first, didn't register. "Wait . . . what?"

"They're sending me to Iraq, Joseph. There's nothing—" I stopped, breathed.

"I'm sorry. Is there anything I can do?"

"No." I thought for a moment. "Can you tell everyone for me? I need to pack my things."

He nodded.

I spent the next few hours packing my bags and saying goodbyes. I called my advisor at Bethany College and explained the situation to her. She allowed me to turn in my senior internship paperwork early. This meant I was *officially* a college graduate, a holder of a Bachelor of Arts in Communications. "Do you have to report?"

"You're asking if I can go AWOL?"

She thought about it. "More like . . . protesting."

"It's Iraq or prison. I don't have a choice."

"We always have choices, Benjamin."

She was right, of course. I did have a choice. I could conscientiously object and be jailed by the U.S.M.C. But my advisor wasn't a Marine. The path of imprisonment was the path of a coward.

Things moved quickly. I drove to Denver and checked in with my unit. We drug tested, signed paperwork, and PT'd. I called my parents. They were distraught. My dad was mad at America and its wars; my mom was certain I would die. Only soldiers know the strangeness of this moment, of being called to war and comforting their parents.

I caught up with Mexico—I hadn't seen or talked to him in a year. We'd both taken time off from drilling after our last deployment. Though our military bearing was a tad rusty, we were both fit. We knew the certain eventuality of a second tour and had trained our bodies in preparation. It was a burden that I carried throughout my last year at Bethany.

Our reserve unit, Bravo Company, tested us on all things Marine Corps. We trained in MCMAP. We discussed the Rules of Engagement, which, for Marines, are a joke. There are rules and there is reality. Marines never confused the two. If threatened, we were trained to shoot per the Marine Corps mantra: One Shot, One Kill—preferably in the head. We filled out forms vouching for our mental health. We polished our corroded bearing. We were as ready as we would be. After a week, we boarded a plane at the Denver International Airport and flew to Camp Pendleton, California.

After we landed, an active duty Marine greeted us on the tarmac. "Greetings, Marines. My name is Corporal Swift. I'm a 0231, an Intelligence Specialist. I'm here to orient you. Tonight, we'll get you checked in and accommodated in your bunks. Tomorrow we'll take you to the armory and check out your weapons. You'll be here for two weeks to process and acclimatize to Marine life. After that, you'll be attached to your field unit and fly to Iraq."

"Wait," Mexico interrupted. "Are you saying we won't be together?"

"No," said Swift. "Word is, you'll be farmed out to Recon units either in Fallujah or Ramadi." He took a breath before continuing. "You'll be in the shit, Marines. I know you're reservists, but it's time to put your old life behind you. Welcome to Pendleton."

Once situated in our barracks, Mexico asked: "You hear about Salt Lake?"

"No. I haven't talked to him in quite a while. Why?"

"Said he didn't want to deploy. His Mormon-ass said it was against his religion."

"Are you serious?" I protested. "That's why he's not here?"

"Yeah, he was dishonorably discharged."

"Against his religion?"

"That's what he said."

"You can do that?" I asked.

"What?"

"Not show up. Plead religious objection."

Mexico shrugged. "Apparently."

"What are you?"

"Me?"

"Are you religious?" I asked.

"Catholic. Well, my family's Catholic. I was confirmed. You?"

"Christian, Protestant. You ever think of saying it's against your religion?"

Mexico laughed. "Shit, Peters. I'm Catholic. We invented war. Who'd believe me?"

"Seriously though, you ever thought about it?"

He was quiet before answering. "No. I told you before. I don't care about this war, but it pays. I guess that's sort of fucked up, but it's true. You?"

"I had this Drill Instructor at Recruit Training. Beelzebub. If I dared plead religious concerns, I'm pretty sure he'd find me and slit my throat."

He laughed.

"I don't know, Mexico. I signed on the dotted line. Right?"

"Yep, which makes you a dumbass."

"Thanks." I took a bow.

27. Family

Two days later, Mexico and I formed up outside of our barracks. Bravo Company's captain, Captain Summers, pulled me aside. He told me that he'd received a phone call earlier that morning from Pendleton's Chaplain who'd, in turn, been contacted by the Red Cross. My grandfather had died. He asked me if I wanted to take leave for the funeral. I said I did. He told me he would try and arrange it.

That night, however, I received another phone call. It was from my brother. "Hey, Benjamin, it's Lyle."

"How are you?"

"Dad's in the hospital," Lyle said quickly. "He had a heart attack and the doctors don't think he's gonna make it. "

"Are you joking?"

"No. I'm sorry."

"Grandpa. Then dad. What should I do?"

"Come home, man."

I knocked on my captain's door an hour later. I told him that my father had been hospitalized and that, no, I wasn't kidding. Nonetheless, Captain Summers needed to verify the information with the Red Cross: he was suspicious that my family was fabricating or exaggerating both of these events so I could forgo my tour.

"Did your parents contact the chaplain, Peters? Are they seeking a medical waiver for your deployment?"

I admitted this had crossed my mind. But there was no way my parents would do that. His questions flustered me, however, and as a result I slid back into civilian speak. "What would you do? It's my dad. If I don't say goodbye, then I'll regret it forever."

The captain clinched his jaw. "*Sir*. You forgot to say, *sir*."

My grandfather had died, my dad was dying, and all Captain Summers could think of was military protocol. My anger flared. I met his gaze. "He's my father . . . sir."

The captain rubbed his temples and sighed. He wouldn't apologize. "I'll call the Red Cross, Peters. Let me verify this information and I'll see what I can do."

"Thank you, sir."

The captain nodded.

We'd all heard stories about enlisted men following their captain into the depths of hell. Captain Summers, though flawed, was that kind of captain. He was intelligent and honest. Most importantly, we all knew he cared.

The next morning I found myself in a car with Corporal Swift. He was driving me to the Los Angeles airport. The Marine Corps had decided I would fly to Texas for my grandfather's funeral before flying to Portland to say goodbye to my father. I had a week. In seven days, I had to report back to Camp Pendleton. Mexico and the rest of Bravo, in the meantime, would be flying to Iraq.

"It turns out," Swift said, "that I'll be taking your place. You were headed to an infantry battalion in Fallujah. Bastards are sending me instead."

"Sorry."

"No worries. I lost my grandfather a few years back. I understand."

"Where will they send me after I return?"

"Who knows? Most likely you'll stay at Division—Camp Blue Diamond. It's in Ramadi."

"Division?"

"It's better than battalion, believe me. At Division the worst you'll face is mortars being lobbed over the fence. The Battalion, though, that's the shit, you know?"

We had no idea what we were talking about.

"Sorry, Swift. Really, I am." In a way I was relieved, which was its own shame.

"Don't be. I'm an active duty Marine. You're a reservist. It makes the most sense. My mom was pissed, though. She hates that I joined. I needed the money for college. There was no way she was going to pay for it."

"You enlisted for the GI Bill?"

"Yeah. I figured I'd serve four years, get out, and go to college."

"What do you want to study?"

"I want to be an engineer."

"Really? That's great."

He glanced at me. "Was it hard—college?"

"After the Marine Corps? No."

We drifted into the departure lane. I shook Swift's hand and apologized one more time. I felt bad, sticking him with my initial deployment. I needed to be with my family. But, ever so slightly, that old desire was wakening. I hadn't thought about it for twelve months. I wanted to fight. I wanted to test myself. It was youth rearing its ugly head. I was less idealistic, to be sure, but the feeling, the challenge, lingered. I knew both my capabilities and myself. I was a man who was relieved to stay at division while others fought the war. But I was also a man who wanted the opportunity to prove himself stronger than his weaknesses. Kuwait came flooding back and, with it, a corporal's face cast in half-light. He was changed, different. But how and why, I didn't know. Part of me wanted to experience the transformation of combat—of staring a man in the eyes who strove to kill me—and part of me wanted to bury my head in the sand.

‡ ‡ ‡

My grandfather's funeral was sobering. *Death is final.* No matter how hard my mother or her siblings cried, no matter what was said or left unsaid, my grandfather had breathed his last. I was a pallbearer at his funeral. I hadn't really known him, but I was sad to see him dead. I was sad for both my mother and her mother.

After the funeral I boarded a plane and flew to Seattle.

My brother and sister greeted me, and we drove straight to the hospital. I arrived in time to see my father for a few minutes before he entered surgery. We said our goodbyes. He was a cyborg, living via connection.

Hours passed.

We waited.

‡ ‡ ‡

A week passed. I found myself, once again, at the Seattle airport. My mother, who was divorced from my father, had driven me. She pulled the car alongside the curb. I opened the door. "We love you. You know that, right?"

I stopped and turned back to her. "I know."

"Will you be okay?"

"It's war, Mom." I shrugged. "What do you want me to say?"

She cried. I hadn't meant to wound her, but I was frustrated. She'd recently lost her father and was facing the prospects of losing her son. The last week had been difficult.

She shook her head.

I closed the door and boarded the plane. Three hours later I landed in Los Angeles. Swift was there, holding a sign for me. "I thought you were in Iraq, Swift."

"No, the reserves shipped out. Active duty Marines are flying out in a week or so. You'll leave with us."

"Does that make me active duty?"

He smiled. "You don't have what it takes."

"I know," I said. "Believe me, I know."

28. Swift

On the drive back to Pendleton, Swift asked me about my grandfather's funeral and how my father's surgery had gone. I told him both went well. I saw my grandfather off and my dad was still breathing—for the time being. Under the circumstances, our family was in pretty good shape.

I asked about his family. He said he had grown up in Iowa. His grandfather had been a farmer, as had his father. He enjoyed both Iowa and farming, but he'd always wanted to be an engineer—he thought it'd be fun. His mother was an elementary teacher. He had a sister, too. Swift laughed when he talked about her. She was younger, a high school senior. When they were kids, he said, they used to play hide-and-seek in the fields behind their house. She would sprint on her tiny legs, the wheat springing up around her, covering all but her bobbing head.

"You miss them?"

"I do."

"You think you'll attend school in Iowa?"

"I don't know. I like California, but Iowa is home. I was thinking I'd apply to a few programs and see which ones accepted me."

"Sounds like a plan."

"Oh, hey, before I forget," he said. "Master Guns said if you're shipping out with us, you should live like us. He moved your gear into an active duty barracks."

"Cool."

"Well, yeah, but the thing is, Master Guns Duke doesn't really like reservists. As a matter of fact, he thought it was bullshit you went home for the funeral and all that."

"*Bullshit?* It was my dad. He was sick."

"I'd ignore him if I were you. Keep clear of him. It'll be fine."

I trusted Corporal Swift. "Alright."

29. Cameras

I OPENED THE DOOR. The room was empty except for a few cabinets and two bunks. I heard the toilet flush. The bathroom door opened and out strode my new roommate. "What's up, Marine?"

"Not much," I said. "How are you?"

"Splendid."

"Which bunk should I take?"

He pointed to the one I was standing nearest. I started to unpack. My roommate was short and slim. He had closely cropped brown hair. He said his name was Corporal Dirk. He was a supply Marine. "Wanna see something?"

"Sure."

He opened his laptop and flopped onto my bed. "Check this shit out." His eyes were wide with excitement as he opened a video. He pressed play. The video started out black. After a time, I saw Corporal Dirk in what looked like our barrack's room. He was standing in front of my bed. He was naked and flexing. A girl was on the bed behind him.

"Right?" he asked while nodding his head.

"What's this?" I was nervous.

"It's my girl, Corporal, why?" The digital Dirk turned toward the bed.

"Hey, man," I protested. "I don't need to see this."

"I do some pretty awesome shit."

I had lost all military bearing. "Dude, are you serious right now?"

He stopped smiling and locked eyes with me. "Fuck yes, I'm serious. Do you have a problem?"

I stammered. "I just . . . you know . . . we're all entitled to privacy."

He laughed and slapped me on the back. "That's some bullshit, Devil!" He turned back to the computer. "Check out this one."

I was polite. After a few minutes, I excused myself. I wanted to walk.

"Where are you going?" he asked.

"I think I'll walk down to the PX. There's some . . . things I'd like to buy."

"I'll come with you."

"No," I said too quickly. "I'm good. You're busy. It's cool. I'll be back soon." I shut the door.

I ambled down to the PX while the sun sank behind the Pacific Ocean. It was a crisp evening. I was wearing military fatigues. I reminded myself if I saw an officer I'd have to salute. In civilian life I was a reserve, but here, at that moment, I was a Marine. I had to play the part.

I saw the PX and kept walking.

30. Knots

According to some versions of Christian theology, as I'd learned at Bethany, humanity was created in the image of God. Inside each of us a divine spark glows with the dazzling light of mystery. A truth both corporate and personal—the sacred is rooted in solidarity and the brilliant fire within. Acts of war, however, rob creation of this truer form and every person of his or her right to thrive. War is ugly. War is brokenness. Yet we have the freedom to act in accordance with either our baser desires or our higher selves, to respect creation or trample it with the boot of negligence.

I was no scholar or learned Rabbi. I was only a young Marine wrestling with the truth or non-truth of his actions. If I snuffed out the spark, then would I be held accountable? Grandfathers, fathers, Marines, we all die eventually. Maybe this was my time and in Iraq I would stumble upon finality. If hell were true though, would I burn for killing my enemy? The more I tried to untie the knot, the tighter it pulled.

31. Dawn

The crisp evening turned cold. I returned to my room. The battery of Corporal Dirk's laptop had dwindled. The lights were off and he was asleep. I undressed in the dark before crawling into bed and sleeping a shallow, dreamless sleep.

"Peters," Master Guns barked. "Where the hell've you been?"

I'd arrived at Intel Headquarters to check in. It was six-thirty in the morning. I was freshly shaved and wearing my Marine utilities. "Sorry, Master Guns, I'm not sure what you mean."

He tilted his head so he could absorb the expression on my face. He had a lazy eye. "You were to report at zero six-fifteen, Devil." He made a quick flicking sound by sucking at his teeth. "What the shit is your problem?"

Swift hadn't been lying. Duke didn't like reservists. I tried to answer him confidently, but I didn't know where to fix my gaze. His lazy eye was throwing me off. I finally settled on staring at a spot between his eyebrows. "I'm sorry, Master Guns. It won't happen again."

"Shit right," he said, sucking his teeth. "Do it again and I'll knock you down, Peters." He turned and strode away.

Swift crept up. "Don't worry, he's full of piss in the morning."

"Whatever, Swift. What am I *supposed* to be doing?"

"Sit tight. Master Guns said he would think of something for you." Swift gestured to a nearby chair. "Hang here. When I find out more, I'll let you know."

I waited.

A week passed.

Another.

I quit coming to the office. I was tired of sitting in one of Duke's chairs. Swift said it would probably be all right, but that I needed to hang around the barracks should he need to find me.

A week passed.

Another.

Swift found me one morning, a month after I'd arrived on camp. I was in Pendleton's gym lifting weights after a six-mile run. "Alright," he said. "Here's the plan. We're flying out on Saturday. Make sure you're gear is packed. We'll meet out front of Headquarters at zero five."

I nodded. He started to walk away before turning back. "A few of us are going out Friday night. You want to join?"

"Sure."

On Friday, Swift, a few other Marines, and I drove to San Diego. We found a small Irish Pub and ordered drinks. We swapped stories about Recruit Training. We discussed our coming deployment. We chatted about our families. At midnight, we drove back to Pendleton. I couldn't sleep, however. I stared at the ceiling and listened to the buzz of the fluorescent security light outside of my window. At four in the morning, I closed the door to my room and shouldered my seabag. I was waiting in front of headquarters when Swift found me. He nodded. We didn't say anything because there was nothing to say.

The bus eventually came. We boarded.

My life changed forever.

Part Two

1. Harem

We landed on a sprawling base in western Iraq. The air wing was stationed here, along with a generous PX and TV room. It was a bubble, a place of transition. Al Qaim was Marine purgatory. Instead of purging for the glories of heaven, however, we were purging our civilian selves for the lavish disgraces of hell. We had five days to acclimatize before the convoys would trail into camp. If, on the way to our final destination, we were hit with an IED, then we were to jump out of our seven-ton and charge headlong into the ambush. I didn't relish the idea. It felt too bare, too exposed in the open, sandy plains.

Mexico was already tucked into his battalion somewhere east of Ramadi, and Swift would be on a different convoy, a Humvee convoy headed to a small outpost near Fallujah. So when my convoy arrived, I was alone—a reservist among the active.

‡ ‡ ‡

Nothingness. No moon, no light. Visceral darkness. I was moving through undeveloped desert, crouched in the open bed of a seven-ton truck. Collectively rocking with the truck's sway, I was shoulder-to-shoulder with fifteen other Marines, exposed to a vast landscape. It was warm and dry. The air rushed over and through me.

A match in a blackout, a muzzle blast illuminating the desert: will I hear the AK before I feel the bullet?

The seven-ton rumbled along the thin-dusty road. There were no lights, no glowing blossoms on the horizon.

The convoy lasted for hours. We knew we were moving, but there was nothing by which to measure our movement. It was monotonous and uneventful.

We arrived at a large, solid structure. It was two in the morning. Electric lights from the hovering guard towers blinded us. We breathed a sigh of relief.

I had survived my first convoy in Iraq.

This wasn't my first sunrise in Kuwait. This was different, professional. We weren't entering a base on the edge of the wild; we were entering a population of trained and hardened warfighters drowning in the wilderness. Many came, but few left.

We heard Marines exchanging information on the ground.

A gate opened. The seven-ton lurched forward. The Marines around me, now visible in the weak light, were haggard but resolute. There was an air of electric excitement, like dogs loosed for the chase. They were fighters in a fight, poised and ready.

We were driven to a holding barrack where we were to wait the night.

Sleep eluded me and I was tired when morning came. I was jetlagged and on edge. A week ago, I'd slept in the confines of a Marine Corps barrack in California. This morning I would rise to the unknown.

A lance corporal, a woman, came to our holding barrack and led us to the chow hall. We had no time to change or shower. There was stubble on my face and dark circles beneath my eyes. I felt like a real soldier, a black-and-white Marine storming the beaches of Iwo Jima. We ate breakfast in an uneasy silence. After, the lance corporal delivered us to our new home.

I stood outside of a large marble structure. It was rounded on top. She told us that it had, at one time, belonged to a son of Saddam Hussein. "Apparently," she said, "he'd used it to house his harem. Now it's yours." We walked inside. There was a main room jam-packed with care packages, support for the troops. Each box was stuffed full of candy, beef jerky, and issues of *Sports Illustrated*. There were a few TVs. Couches were tossed about the room. From this common space, the Harem split off into three rooms filled with wooden bunks. The lance corporal led us to the room on the left. "Here it is," she said. "Pick a bunk and throw your seabag on it. I'll give you a few minutes to settle in before we head over to your work stations."

I'd be working in the CIC (Command Intelligence Center). The CIC was housed in a huge marble palace. It wasn't discrete, but the marble was mortar proof. Camp Blue Diamond, I soon discovered, was a base of palaces. Some of the buildings that constituted the camp were dilapidated from our shock-and-awe campaign the previous year. But the majority of them were not only intact, but also served as protection from insurgent attacks. The CIC was the biggest and, perhaps, the safest building on Blue Diamond.

The inner layout of the CIC was complex. There was an outer ring of offices divided by wooden slabs the Marine Corps had built, a maze of timbered cubicles. The inner chamber of the CIC, however, was one, large command center. In the middle was a horseshoe-shaped conference table, the hub of Marine Intelligence—a modern panopticon. Numerous TVs and laptops were scattered throughout the CIC, each reporting the news or airing a feed from a UAV. If one wanted to know what was happening in Fallujah, Al Anbar, Al Qaim, or anywhere else in Iraq, then this was where one went. The Marine Corps Commanding General sat at the center of the horseshoe, Zeus commanding his gods.

Riddled throughout the CIC were smaller workstations. Suits broken up by intelligence specialty. Intelligence gatherers were placed in one section, imagery analysts in another; operations were sectioned off to one side, communications huddled in the opposite corner. I was assigned a desk with the intelligence gatherers, which included the UAV operators. My job was not to operate a UAV but to collect data from the western provinces of Iraq. I'd work twelve hours shifts, brief the powers on the most important happenings in my assigned province, and turn my work station over to the Marine working the night shift. I was working under Master Guns and Colonel Washington. If I had any problems, I could to talk with Corporal Spain.

I nodded my head and grunted. I was tired. I had been traveling for seventy-two hours. I wanted to sleep. I was expecting to be dismissed before Master Guns strode into the CIC. His lazy eye zeroed in on me. "Peters, good to see you," he said. "You're working the first shift." He sucked his teeth. "Take a seat."

No sleep.

A Marine I didn't know, Lance Corporal Charleston, lectured me on how to collect the data I would need in order to compile my briefing. I did my best to stay awake. I drank coffee and slapped myself. Twelve hours crept along. Charleston said he knew how I was feeling and that I could cut out a little early. "No one will notice," he said. Charleston was tall and wore a flattop. He said he was from West Virginia and loved the Mountaineers. He was active duty. "I love the Corps, too," he said. He asked me if I shared his passions. I shrugged.

Ten minutes before my shift ended, Corporal Spain, a balding active-duty Marine with a Hispanic accent, sent me home. "Get some sleep," he said. "You'll need it. Be here tomorrow morning at seven. Don't be late."

"Yes, corporal." I stumbled to my barracks, found my bed, and fell asleep.

2. Shift Change

Though my individual shifts progressed slowly, time slid by in a blur. My previous life was a forgotten memory not easily recalled. It was unbelievable to me that people in the U.S. were working, vacationing, bar hopping, or attending church. These things were foreign, no longer compatible with my experience. *Shouldn't they be in mourning? Don't they care?*

Colonel Washington dictated our daily routine. He wanted everyone to PT regularly. I would wake, shuffle to Blue Diamond's aluminum gym, and row. If an insurgent had decided to lob a mortar onto the gym while I was rowing—aluminum makes for poor marble—I would've died on that damn machine. But Washington was obsessed with Blue Diamond's rower. He would set specific times and distances for each of his Marines. If we succeeded, he praised us; if we failed, he assigned us guard duty. I didn't want guard duty, so I spent my mornings rowing.

After a shower, I would eat breakfast and walk to the CIC. I would listen to the night shift's turnover briefing and then assume my role as the day-shift intelligence analyst of the Al Anbar province. Throughout the day, I would amass large quantities of data. This could be cell phone discussions, satellite imagery, or reports from returning patrols. I would sift through the information, decide what was germane, and create a PowerPoint stack that detailed both this information and my assessments of it. At the end of my shift, both Colonel Washington and Master Guns would stand before me in demand of a brief. If they heard anything of import, then they, in turn, would share it with the commanding general.

"At fourteen-hundred hours," I said during one of my first briefings, "a convoy to Al'Qaim was disrupted by an IED. A reactionary force was deployed, and a fire fight ensued. There were seven insurgents found dead. One Marine was KIA. After the battle, a search of the area revealed a large cache. This isn't surprising, as we heard a significant amount of chatter throughout the day revealing an insurgent buildup in the area."

"Not surprising, Marine?" Master Guns asked.

"No, Master Guns."

"So you knew this was going to happen and you didn't alert anyone?"

I shifted and looked to my lead sergeant, Sergeant Red, for support.

"Don't look at Sergeant Red," Colonel Washington said. "This is your task, Peters. Answer the question."

If I was certain of anything, it was that the Marine Corps wouldn't leave the fate of its troops to a twenty-five-year-old E-4. CNN knew more than I did. In fact, both Master Guns and the colonel knew my briefing before I even briefed it. With the difficult questions they posed, it was easier for me to stay quiet and take my beating.

"Answer the colonel, Corporal Peters." Master Guns' lazy eye rolled its socket, trying in earnest to pin me down.

"I sent an email to the watch chief, sir."

"But you didn't elect to tell your shift sergeant. Am I correct in that assessment?"

"Yes, sir."

The colonel sighed. "Forty-five on the rowing machine, corporal."

"Yes, sir."

"Continue," Master Guns barked. He sucked at his tar-stained teeth.

"That's all I have, Master Guns."

"Really?" the colonel inquired, leaning back.

"Yes, sir." My stomach sank. I had missed something. I wanted to yell: "If you already know, then why the hell am I doing this!"

"What about the riverboat fire fight on the Euphrates?"

"I'm sorry, colonel. I didn't know about it."

"What the fuck, Peters." Duke's lazy eye erratically swirled in its pit. "You're an Intelligence Marine, are you not?"

"Yes, Master Guns." I knew where this was headed.

"Well, goddammit, Marine! You sit there at your desk all day and read your damn books. Pay attention! You've a job to do." It was true; I read a lot. What did it matter if I gathered all of the intelligence as it came in or if I periodically assessed it throughout my shift? Apparently, it mattered.

"Add another thirty, corporal," the Colonel said, shaking his head.

I imagined saying: "You're an idiot." Instead, I dropped my head and answered, "Yes, sir." They both stood and walked out of the CIC.

"Awesome, Peters," Sergeant Red said. "What the hell's your problem?"

"They clearly have the information before I'm getting it, sergeant. That's obvious. How's that my fault?"

"First, watch your tone, Marine. I'll have you on guard duty if you don't check yourself. Second, it's your job to know."

"I understand that, sergeant. I do. But they are receiving information I don't always get, let alone that they know every damn thing before I say it. What's the point?"

Sergeant Red shook her head. "Readiness, Marine, readiness. Are you ready to lead if the opportunity presented itself?"

Today was an imaginative day: "I'm a reserve, so, no. I just want to go home." Instead, I complied. "Sorry, sergeant. I'll do better."

"See that you do."

This happened during most shift changes.

3. *Liberal*

In the chow hall after our shift—warm hamburgers, soggy fries, and a limp salad—Red asked me what I was planning after returning home. I told her about my acceptance into Denver Seminary.

"Whoa, you'd commit to being celibate?" Charleston, who was sitting next to Red, asked.

"Not a monastery. A seminary."

"What's the difference?"

"A lot."

Red chuckled. "You're Christian?"

"Yeah," I said. "Why are you laughing?"

"I thought you said you were a Democrat?"

"I am. Well, I voted for Kerry anyway."

"Then how can you be Christian?"

"Seriously?"

"Yeah, seriously."

"I'd like to know the answer to this, too," Charleston said.

I was a reservist with strange ideas. "I don't think that being a Democrat and a Christian is a mutually exclusive proposition—"

"What about abortion?" Red interrupted.

"Look, abortion sucks, right? But who am I to tell anyone what he or she should or shouldn't do? As far as I'm concerned, Christianity teaches a consistent ethic of life. If you're against abortion, then you'd better be against capital punishment, too. And, to be honest, this war."

"Bullshit," Charleston said. "You're in the Marine Corps. You can't be against war."

"I know you have education and such," Red said. "But the war we're fighting is just. No one questions that, goddammit. Jesus wouldn't question that. In war, it's perfectly fine to do what you have to do."

"What's Colonel Washington always saying? That the insurgents are freedom fighters. That they're patriots. Look at it from their perspective. We're the bad guys. Killing them isn't any more Christian than abortion."

"Yeah," Charleston said, "but they attacked us. I'd much rather bring the fight to them than sit around and wait to be killed."

"I doubt Al Qaeda would mount an attack on your home in West Virginia, Charleston."

"But they could. And if they did . . . " he let his statement hang in the air.

"I don't know. I just think . . . there isn't much of a difference between 'them' and 'us.' Maybe when Jesus said to love your neighbor, he meant those who were different: the enemy, the outcast, the despised. Is it so much of a stretch to think Christians are supposed to love everyone . . . including Bin Laden?"

Red's face was aglow with anger. "Don't say that again."

Before I could respond, Charleston asked: "But what's 'love?'"

"I don't know, Charleston. I don't have the answers."

"Well, you can kill someone and still love 'em. As a matter of fact, I got a boner for Iraq. I love this place. But these motherfuckers need to die. Shit, Peters, some people are better off dead."

"I'm not sure that embodies the spirit of the whole thing."

Charleston was shaking his head. "It's people like you, Peters."

"People like me?"

"Yeah," he said. "It's people like you who make this necessary. If we could just drop a-bombs and shit, this war would already be over."

I looked at Red. She was still angry. "C'mon, really?" I asked her. "You're going to take his side over mine? At least I'm rational."

"It's not about that, Peters. We've a job to do. We protect the innocent. If we don't, then who will? I need to know that—no matter what—you'll do it. How can I trust you if you think Jesus said the military is against Christianity?"

"I didn't say that." I was flustered. "But he did say to love your enemies, right?"

"He also says to live peacefully with all people—if you're able. We're not able, Peters. These people attacked us, remember?"

I took a deep breath. "You're right. I'm sorry. Let's finish eating." I picked up my fork.

"Kerry," Charleston mumbled.

4. Perfect Sense

Bush won his second term. I watched the election in Iraq. I was a corporal and only knew what I was told. I had no idea if the administration's intelligence was bad or if their WMDs were seen through oil-smeared lenses. Information in the Marine Corps, at best, was hierarchical and fractured. And though I was intelligence, I was nothing but a lowly analyst. I had unanswered questions and doubts, which transformed into anger. Conservative Christians had sent me to my death by voting for Bush. *Why did they re-elect him?* Not as an affirmation of Bush's foreign policies. No. *Because they despised abortions and queers.* They didn't give a shit about the war or those that fought in it.

I drifted to sleep, but was abruptly jarred awake. My room was shaking. There was a loud ringing in my ears. An alarm was sounding somewhere, but I could barely hear it. I was disoriented and struggling to rise when Sergeant Spain found me and started yelling. "Gas mask, gas mask! Don your gas mask." I rushed to obey. I thrust my hand underneath my bunk and rooted around for my gas mask. I found it and shoved it on my face.

"What happened?" I started to run outside before Spain grabbed my arm.

"Sit tight, Marine. We were hit by a mortar."

"A what?" The explosion, coupled with the gas mask, made it difficult to hear anything.

"A mortar, corporal. A direct hit. Those shit-fucks tried to blow the Harem."

I was shocked. If I hadn't been in a marble palace, then . . . Marines were congregating in the common room. I saw Charleston and Master Guns. There was some nervous chatter. The alarm was still sounding.

"See," Charleston said as he walked over to me. "They're trying to kill you, Peters. They're fucking cowards."

I nodded, dazed.

"How don't that make sense to you?"

I peered at him through my mask. "It does, Charleston. It makes perfect sense."

He continued, "I've been here for nineteen months—"

I cut him off. "What? Why didn't you go home with the last rotation?"

"Master Guns, the one before Duke, told me to go, Peters. But I requested to stay. I'll be here for three years before I see West Virginia again."

"Why?"

"It's not only a job to me, Peters. It's my duty. I'm making my country a safer place."

The all clear sounded.

I shook my head and went to bed.

5. Robot Monkeys

I WAS SITTING AT my computer and watching Fox News, the only news feed we were allowed to watch, when my inbox dinged. I opened the email. I was stunned. *Is this a joke?* "Sergeant Red, would you mind reading this email for me?"

"What's up, Peters?"

"You tell me."

She was silent as she read the email over my shoulder. "What the hell?"

"I know, right? Am I supposed to brief this?"

"I think you have to, Corporal."

I added the information to my stack of PowerPoint slides and dreaded briefing Washington later that evening.

"Anything else?" Master Guns asked. It was the end of my briefing session. I took a deep breath.

"One more thing, Master Guns, sir." I nodded to the colonel. "We intercepted a cell phone communication earlier this morning that might shed some light on the state of the insurgency."

"What's that?"

"One insurgent, talking to another insurgent, was discussing the nature of our capabilities. According to the first insurgent, the second insurgent needs to be on the lookout for America's robot monkeys."

"Excuse me?"

"Yes, sir. The first insurgent is under the impression that our CIA has deployed an elite fighting force of robot monkeys, in order to disrupt the insurgency." I paused. "Sir."

The colonel met my stare. "You're joking."

"No, sir."

"Well, shit, that's flattering. The insurgency thinks we're all kinds of awesome. What do you make of that, corporal? What should we do with that information?"

I knew he would ask that question and had tried to think of an answer, but I'd drawn a blank. "I have no idea, sir."

"You know that's something I hate to hear my analysts say, don't you?"

"Yes, sir."

"Good brief, Peters. You only owe me fifteen minutes."

6. *Homer*

THE HOLIDAYS WERE A difficult time to be deployed. Most of us tried not to think about what our friends and family were doing back home. And though my father was healing, I worked hard to bury my civilian life lest it snatch hold of my brain and corrupt me with comforting thoughts. The holidays required a double effort. Thanksgiving came. It was a melancholic day for me, as it also happened to be my birthday. We sat in the chow hall, eating bland turkey and raspberry sauce. For a surprise, we each received a shot of whiskey. It was nice. During my time overseas, I'd picked up the nasty habit of chewing tobacco—Copenhagen. In light of more pressing issues, it was a small indulgence. I sipped my whiskey, savoring every last drop, and spit my dip into a Dixie cup. It was Thanksgiving. I was twenty-six, at war, and fighting the insurgency in Iraq. I wished there had been more to drink.

"Peters," Master Guns said as he walked into the chow hall. "I've been looking all over for you, Marine."

I stood up. "Yes, Master Guns?"

"Your number's been called. You're on the swift-boat patrol tomorrow. It's headed up the Euphrates. You'll be riding with an Army QRF. They leave at zero four-thirty. Don't be late. Muster's in front of the CIC. I'll tell you what you need to know and do in the morning."

I nodded.

He slapped my back.

Tomorrow, whether I wanted to or not, I would experience a fire fight. My mouth went dry. *I can do this.*

I strode back to the Harem. *I wonder what dad's doing.* I didn't talk with him often, but I'd recently received an email from Lyle. Dad was mending. *Will his heart be able to handle my death?* The swift-boats were designed to root out unsavory activity along the Euphrates. Most patrols were ambushed, which resulted in deaths, but also coalition forces finding large caches of weapons.

I'm not ready. I was a reservist, an Intelligence Marine. *What do I know about combat?* I knew nothing. *I'm the good guy. I'm the good guy. I'm the good guy.* I chanted myself to sleep.

I rose early and stalked through Blue Diamond in the pre-dawn darkness. The season was turning. The air carried a distinct chill. I was wearing my battle gear. My clips were loaded. *Whatever happens, I will not die today.* I arrived at the CIC early. It was quiet. The surrounding palm trees swayed to a playful breeze. *Have those always been here?* I wanted to pray, but was lost for words. *Give me the strength to kill? Help me stay alive?* It all seemed shallow. *What do insurgents pray?* I'd never read the Qur'an. I had no idea what their sacred text claimed. I didn't really know what my sacred text claimed, either.

Corporal Spain strode towards me. "You ready, Devil Dog?"

"I guess."

"Look, I've gone out a hundred times. You'll be fine. Just remember, when the shots start coming, breathe. You're a Marine. One shot, one kill. These fuckers'll spray their damn AKs all over the place. Find cover, breathe, and squeeze. You got it?"

I shook my head.

"You'll do fine," he smiled. I hadn't talked to Corporal Spain much throughout my tour.

"Thanks."

"Cigarette?"

"Nah," I laughed. "I tried during my first tour. It didn't take."

He smacked the top of his pack before pulling out a stick and lighting it. "Not me," he said, taking a deep breath. "I love smoking. Keeps me sane."

"I understand."

We sat down. There was silence for a time as Spain's smoke swirled around us. The sky was starting to lighten. "What will you do when you go home?"

"Why does everyone ask me that?"

"You're a reservist," he said. "We go back to work on Pendleton. If anything, this is a break. But not you, you get to keep on living."

"I'm planning on getting a master's degree," I said. "Aren't you married?"

He shook his head. "I was. She left me. This is my third tour, Devil. She couldn't handle it anymore. I was pissed, at first. She took my son and just . . . left. What do you do with that, you know? I understand now, though.

It's as hard for them as it is for us, except they don't know what's happening. We do. She told me once that she used to watch the news every night, hoping she wouldn't see my name. That shit sucks."

"You're not bitter?"

He pulled on his cigarette. "No, no I'm not. Sad maybe."

We sat in silence.

"Will you re-enlist?"

"Yeah, probably. I don't really know anything else. I enlisted right outta high school. No one in my family's ever gone to college and I didn't want to slave away . . . like my father."

"What's he do?"

"He passed away. Was in construction."

"I'm sorry."

"Don't be. He was an ass."

"Oh."

"Peters," Master Guns barked. He'd snuck up behind us. We turned. "Call it off, Devil. The Army doesn't want an Intel Marine with 'em today. Don't ask me why." He turned to leave. "Make sure you get their report. You're responsible for briefing us on the patrol, check?"

"Check, Master Guns." Relief. Pure relief washed over me. Spain saw it. He smiled and threw his butt on the ground.

"Lucky, motherfucker," he said. "Someone must be watching out for you." He followed Master Guns back inside the CIC.

Later that day, I received the report. The patrol had been ambushed a click away from Blue Diamond. What would have otherwise been a routine fire fight had turned ugly when the boat capsized. Three soldiers had drowned because their gear was too heavy. Another was KIA. One soldier had survived the onslaught, and had been pulled out by Blue Diamond's QRF. It was bullshit that these men had to die for a damn weapons cache. *It could've been me.* But it wasn't. I was glad. I was alive.

Staring at my computer, Fox News chirping in the background, I read the patrol's report. *Meaning? What meaning is in death?* I searched for general, abstract answers as if I were in class at Bethany. Nothing. I substituted the abstract for the concrete: *I will kill you because I don't want to die.* Deep down that was all I really cared about. *Death is meaningless.* Most Marines, if they were honest, would say the same. No one fights for abstract ideals. No one fights for freedom. In the panic of combat, they fight because they don't want their spark snuffed—they might care about their fellow Marine. But that's not always true. If I'd died on that patrol, the sun would still rise and my parents would've been assured that I'd died bravely, defending my country. They would've been told a lie. I would have pissed my pants like the rest.

There was no meaning in that patrol. What we did—what I'd signed up for—was to champion a false ideal of heroism. I had believed the narrative. I had seen the television commercials and been seduced. Beginning that first day in Recruit Training, I'd been taught that Marines were heroes, like Achilles or Hector, and that there was honor in what we did. I had believed this. Or at least I had believed there was truth in it. But Achilles was sniped, and Hector was mutilated. Even then, the Greeks knew—no matter how much they dressed it up—war was hell. And in it, men do tragic things. *Is there meaning in war?* No. At least in Homer, heroes locked eyes and knew their killer for what he was. In Iraq, the enemy was mysterious. Whatever happened to the days of honor among rivals? Was there no longer a soldier's virtue: an understanding that we do what we must, but it was an abhorrent thing, rotten to its core?

Not in Iraq. In Iraq, there was nothing but bloodlust and carnage.

There can be honor and dignity in death, but not in the way *we* were fighting. There was too much anonymity. Marines were killed from all angles and at all times of the day. *I don't know you, I don't see you, but I'm going to kill you . . . and run.* That was the tactic of our enemy. *Is ours any different?* How many missiles had we fired out of UAVs only to watch the insurgents scatter on a bursting screen? Asymmetry perfected. We were able to kill, anonymously, and our enemies could never touch us. So they would lob mortars over our walls and detonate bombs on the side of their roads. It was a cycle of violence, a mechanistic and technological cycle.

We were neither heroes nor patriots. We weren't even human. We were animals, killing to survive.

And how could we not? Beelzebub had been right. In order to change a man, you had to dehumanize him, strip him down. *How could I drop a bomb on another human being? How could I put the forehead of an Iraqi man in the crosshairs of my M-16 and squeeze the trigger?* Easy. Turn them all into *sandniggers* and *hajjis.*

I read that report and I briefed that report, but I found no meaning in it. Dead words on cold paper. *People died. They die every day.* Who was I to judge?

I went back to the Harem and slept.

7. Fallujah

I woke to a CIC in motion. Operation Phantom Fury had started. McDougal, Mexico, and Swift were all on the ground, amassing before the city. *Keep them safe.* From my vantage point—a desk and an HP—nothing seemed real. The second battle for Fallujah was something you read about in a textbook, like Khe Sanh, not something you lived.

Horrific stories of Marines fighting from street-to-street poured into the CIC A battle of two opposing wills, Fallujah was an endless battle. This wasn't policy or politics. It was war—real and living, a life force all its own. I'd experienced both anger and disenchantment after the swift-boat patrol. Caught in the historical moment of Fallujah, however, all that fell to the wayside. In its place rose a drug-like emotion. The moment was alive and, embracing it, I was alive, too. The present was visceral—feeling, tasting. I loved it. The beating drums of Shakespeare's cadence measured existence: "And gentlemen in England now abed, Shall think themselves accursed."

Years later, my sister-in-law, who, through a strange twist of fate, had been a camper the year I interned at Camp Pine, would ask me what happened to "Camp Benjamin," the outspoken, fun-loving counselor. I would answer: "Lost in Iraq." This was that very moment when Camp Benjamin, pre-war Benjamin, slipped into the wilderness.

All of my training, everything Beelzebub had taught me, came to a head. I was no longer a civilian soldier, a reserve, or even a Marine. I was an anonymous killer who watched as we dropped bombs, reigned down fire from a laptop. Distractions were pushed to the periphery. They had struck out at me—ME!—with mortars and rocket-propelled grenades. I would kill them for it. I would watch them die from the cold confines of a computer screen.

"Corporal Peters," Sergeant Spain said.

"Yes."

"You're imagery, right?"

"Yes, sergeant."

"Check this shit out." He held up a picture and then pointed to the UAV video feed on his laptop. "Is that the right fucking building?"

I looked from picture to screen. People, insurgents or not, were scampering like ants. "It's right," I said. "Drop it."

Spain pushed a button. The screen, awash for a moment in brilliant light, revealed smoking rubble and limp bodies.

"Assholes," Spain said. "They shouldn't have fucked with us."

There was no mercy. If we should miss, if there was any collateral damage, well, let that be a lesson. A clarion call for justice: Do not challenge us, we will break you. I fought the only way I could. I forgot who I was. I killed for revenge.

‡ ‡ ‡

I broke away from my computer screen. Sergeant Red entered the CIC having returned from a patrol. She had crossed the wire with a Q.R.F. in order to interrogate an insurgent. She was pale and shaking. "What happened?"

"IED," she shouted.

"You okay?"

"What?"

"Are you okay?"

She pointed to her ears.

"Were there any casualties?"

She shook her head, "I can't—" She stumbled out of the CIC's mainframe.

I went back to work.

‡ ‡ ‡

As I was preparing my brief, the KIA list came through the CIC. I glanced at the names. *Please, please, please.* And there it was:

Staff Sergeant Beelzebub, KIA.

I was stunned, shocked.

He was invincible.

The Devil.

He was dead.

If he could die, then . . .

War cares nothing of lineage. The system churns. It kills in its wake. It's indiscriminate. *Who am I compared to the beast?*

I sat down. *Could McDougal die? Surely not. He's a reservist. What of Mexico? Or Swift?* I found it humorous that I'd assigned immortality to Beelzebub. But I had, and I had found comfort in thinking he would live forever.

The colonel and Master Guns came in and sat down.

"Report," the colonel cried. It was a sober and serious briefing. This is what they'd prepared us for. Spain, Red, Charleston, we didn't disappoint, not that night. We provided the pertinent information. We delivered it appropriately. We fulfilled our duty. Afterward, the colonel spoke:

"Today you participated in the largest American troop buildup since World War II. You wrote history. That may not mean much to you now, but in time, it will. I'm proud of each of you," he paused, looking at each of us in the eyes. "You will, undoubtedly, have known Marines who died today. Mourn, but mourn quickly. The war continues. Find your vengeance tomorrow."

We filed out of the CIC and went into the chow hall in silence. We ate. There was a low murmuring that ran throughout the cafeteria. I finished and walked back to the Harem. I crawled into my sleeping bag and flicked on my headlamp. I read for a bit, trying to forget the day's events, imagining I was anywhere but Ramadi. An hour passed. I dozed.

There was yelling. I sat up in my bed. Loud voices were shouting outside of my door. I climbed down from my bunk and walked outside.

"What happened?" Red was outside with Spain and Charleston. It was dark, past midnight. Red and Spain were wearing their PT gear, most likely having slept in it. Charleston was still in his utilities. Spain was holding up Charleston, who was weeping. He was drunk. I don't know where he'd found the alcohol. He was staggering and would have fallen if it weren't for Spain's support. "What—"

"Take him to medical," Red said. "Doc will know what to do. If you can't find anyone, then lock him up somewhere. And goddammit, take away his weapon."

"Alright," Spain replied.

"Sergeant?"

Red turned to me, but waited until Spain was out of hearing distance. "It was Charleston."

"Yeah."

"He . . . uh . . . he," she shifted, "we saw him put the barrel of his M-16, locked and loaded, into his mouth and squeeze."

"What?"

"It misfired," she said. "He should be dead."

I was quiet. "Why?"

She looked at me—angry. "He's been here for nineteen months, Peters. That's too long."

"Oh."

"He lost a friend today."

"Do you know who?" I asked.

"I didn't know him. They'd enlisted together."

"I can't believe he tried to . . . you know?"

"Can't you?"

"I thought he loved this shit."

She sat down. I sat next to her. "Did you know anyone who was KIA?"

"Believe it or not, a Drill Instructor of mine was KIA. You?"

"No. Not today." She stood up. "Marines don't kill themselves, Peters. It's not something we do."

I nodded. She turned and walked away.

I couldn't sleep. I shrugged on my Kevlar and went for a walk. I passed the gym and the chow hall; the makeshift range and the *hajji* shops. It was dark enough that I had to stop every fifty yards to find my bearings. My mind wandered over the interior hills of parents and siblings, life and death, war and killing. *Was the price too high?* Marines were dying. Iraqis were dying. We were killing humans—we were killing ourselves.

An hour later, I found myself standing in front of the Harem. The horizon was glowing. I dressed in my utilities and made my rack. I brushed my teeth and shaved in a tub of water. I walked to the chow hall and ate a breakfast of grits and bacon. I drank coffee. I walked through a red dawn. The palm trees swayed above. The CIC was quiet but busy. The night shift was ending. I listened to a turnover briefing. I chatted with the Marine in charge of my province. He told me that the robot monkeys were back. I laughed.

And then I sat down and went back to work.

Kill.

Kill.

Kill.

INTERLUDE

"How are you today?" Trent asked.

"Good."

"Your family?"

"My Dad's recovering. Getting healthier every day." I shifted and started to chew on the side of my mouth.

He stared at me. "And Natasha?"

"Things are going well."

He scribbled in his notebook. "I know that you're a seminary student, so, if I can ask, how is your faith?"

"What do you mean?"

"I think it's natural that one would question his or her beliefs after an experience such as yours. It's only natural that one might even lose his or her faith."

"Yeah, I could see that."

"Traditions are important though. They connect us to the past, make us whole, and provide scaffolding for our future. There are some things we shouldn't leave behind." He looked at me, waiting to see how I would react.

"I have questions, sure," I said. "But I'm not ready to give anything up."

"What's your biggest question?" he asked, leaning forward.

I chuckled, thinking about my thesis. "Am I justified in what I did? I mean, war's broken. Deep down, we all know it's wrong. Everybody's uncomfortable with it. But we do it anyway. So then I think: what the hell is God up to, letting us run around with M-16s and AK-47s? If it's not supposed to be that way, then how's it supposed to be?"

Trent scribbled in his notebook.

8. Grace

"You hear what happened up North?" Rutherford, a young lance corporal, asked. He was a Jets fan.

We were in the chow hall. Fallujah was over. We had won the battle and were establishing safe zones within the city, patrolling street-to-street. A week had passed since Charleston had tried to kill himself. I hadn't seen him.

"No."

"Check it out," he pointed to a small TV in the corner of the mess. I turned. It was tuned to Fox News.

There had been an explosion. A suicide bomber had waltzed into an Army chow hall and detonated himself. He was in paradise now, along with twenty-two American soldiers. I concentrated on the images of the dying and the wounded. Nothing I saw registered. Death was all around.

I turned my head and inspected Blue Diamond's serving staff. They were *hajjis.* I wondered if they were conspiring to kill us. "That's fucked up," I said, shoveling bacon into my mouth.

"Hearts and minds."

"What?"

"We give the *hajjis* jobs, right? It's good for their economy. And what the fuck do they do?"

"Boom."

"I heard," Rutherford started, "that if you work on an American base, Al Qaeda will track down your family and hold 'em hostage 'til you give 'em what they want." He was smacking his food while he talked. "Imagine that shit? You're trying to make ends meet, and some fucker kills your wife. So what do you do? You strap a bomb to yourself and blow up a bunch of soldiers—saves your kids, though."

"And what happens to them?"

"They enlist with Al Qaeda" He was pointing his fork at me. "Where else they gonna go, Iraqi Human Services?"

"Time for work." I stood.

"Who you got in the Super Bowl?" he asked while packing a dip.

We strode to the CIC. The NFL Playoffs had started. If I cared about the games, then I could have risen at three in the morning to watch. I didn't. I coveted both my sleep and the small amounts of free time that I had. I used to care. Before the war, I would have risen with the moon to watch a game. My father taught me to love football. In high school, early on Saturday mornings, he would throw open the door to my room while strumming his guitar and singing college fight songs. We would spend the day rooting for our favorite teams and lamenting the strategic ignorance of their coaches. It was important then. It was frivolous now.

I sat behind my workstation. The CIC was empty but for a few Marines. I was early. There was a captain working in the adjacent section. She was an imagery analyst. Her name was Captain Grace. She was rare. She was stunningly beautiful in a room full of ugliness. "Corporal Peters," she said. I jumped, afraid I had committed some terrible transgression. Captains, and in particular, attractive female officers in the male-dominated environment of the CIC, rarely acknowledged the inferior ranks.

"Yes, Ma'am?"

"I'm hitting the head. Tell Sergeant Lukas if he asks."

"Yes, Ma'am," I said. *Why me?* Oftentimes in the Marine Corps, simple requests have a way of backfiring for the lower-ranking party. She rose and walked outside.

Behind the CIC there was a row of ten portable toilets. They were draped with camouflage netting and surrounded with sandbags. The area was used both for smoking and pissing.

She'd only been outside for a moment when I heard an explosion. The CIC shook. It was made of marble. I was alive. An alarm was blaring. Someone ran into the CIC screaming.

I donned my gas mask.

"The Porta Potty," Rutherford yelled.

We quickly navigated the CIC's wooden maze and hurried outside, bursting out of the CIC and into the low dawn light.

Grace was dead.

What was left of her was strewn over the smoking pit.

I stared at the wall of solitary toilets. In a row of ten, she'd chosen the one on the far left. The insurgents had managed to directly hit her toilet.

Master Guns arrived with Medical. "Peters, Rutherford, clean this shit up." He sucked at his teeth.

"Master Guns?"

"That's right, Peters. You're gonna have to work today," he was unmoving. "After Medical gets her body out of here, I want you to scrub up the blood and shit. You got it?"

"Check, Master Guns," I responded, dazed. Taking off my gas mask, I watched as Medical disposed of her remains and then cleaned the area with Rutherford's help.

I wasn't supposed to be here, doing this. No human was; no human should. And yet, this was an everyday occurrence in the Levant. I couldn't resolve the death of Grace with my insulated American lifestyle. What I had in America was a joke, a mockery of the world. Death was the only real thing, not a whitewashed suburban sidewalk. *Welcome to reality*. And then, *How arbitrary? If she'd only waited a minute, then she'd still be alive*. What does war care of timing? *If she'd only chosen a different toilet*. But she didn't. One moment she was in the CIC, the next she was dead—torn to shreds. She was an officer of the United States Marine Corps. She was hard; she was fragile. She was alive; she was dead.

That night we conducted a memorial service in the CIC. Blue Diamond's chaplain presided from behind a makeshift pulpit and before a pair of boots draped with Grace's dog tags. He spoke of duty and honor, of fighting bravely and defending one's country. He talked of comfort and peace, and the justice of God. "In Christ," he said, "we find both the ultimate justice and ultimate solace . . . "

Captain Grace had died while taking a shit. There was no bravery, only a maddening randomness. *Goddammit, people are dying. Why are we still talking about Christ? Peace? Reconciliation? I see a world ripping itself apart. And for what? Oil? New Markets? Freedom? Oppression? Who the fuck knows.* I shifted in my seat as the chaplain droned. *We're all gonna die in this shit of a country. And for what?*

" . . . taught us to pray," the Chaplain finished. We chanted in response: "Our Father, who art in heaven." I lowered my voice and mumbled the rest. "Thy kingdom come, thy will be done." *Will someone please tell me what that means*? We finished our ritual. We said our goodbyes. The image of her lifeless body was fixed in my mind. I'd confessed my doubts. My soul felt small.

9. The Wall

CHARLESTON HAD BEEN SENT on an indefinite retreat to Qatar. Red relayed that Master Guns, after Charleston's near miss, decided to implement a rest-and-relaxation week for his Marines. If I behaved, she said, then I would also receive an opportunity for relaxation. I wouldn't hold my breath. But, at the same time, I welcomed the prospect of leaving Iraq. I needed a break. *But what about McDougal or Mexico or Swift?* They needed it far more than I did. I killed from a computer while they were patrolling the streets of Fallujah. They'd kill for an opportunity to leave Iraq—they had killed for the opportunity.

A few days later Master Guns found me. I was on shift, sitting behind my desk, and reading *A Conspiracy of Paper*. "Holy shit, Peters." He sucked his teeth while shaking his head. "Stand the fuck up, march your ass to the guard shack, and report. I'm assigning you to guard duty until you can figure out what the hell it is you're doing here." I kept my mouth shut. I wouldn't make any excuses for my actions. I liked to read. I liked to fill the spaces between debriefing and reporting with the words of other people. Maybe guard duty would provide the guilt-free break I needed.

It was December in Iraq. The weather was turning; chill filled the air. I was wearing a fleece underneath my camouflage utilities. The Marine in the guard hut was a gunnery sergeant. He looked me over. "You're a reserve, right?"

"Yes."

"Master Guns told me you'd be coming." He was wary. "He requested that I put you on the Wall. You know what that means?"

I didn't.

"You'll work the night shift, from seven at night to seven in the morning. Your shift'll mostly be comprised of assessing from which direction the constant stream of bullets is coming from. You think you can handle that?"

I was wide eyed. *Shit.* "Yes, Gunny."

"Alright," he said. "Get the hell outta here, get some sleep, and be back at eighteen hundred. I'll show you the ropes then."

I did as I was told.

The next two weeks passed without incident. I would rise to the desert's winter sun setting behind the Euphrates. I would shower, dress in battle gear, and report to the Wall. I would stand vigil throughout the night. Winter's grip had tightened, however, and during my shift the temperature plummeted. The sergeant on duty would drive the length of the Wall each night and provide us with a little comfort—warm coffee. "How you killing, Devils?" he would ask. And how, exactly, was I expected to answer that question? *Great. Splendidly. With pleasure!* I noncommittally settled for a grunt.

We received incoming on a regular basis, but the contact was sporadic and inconsistent. Donning our NVGs, we would peer into the night, seeking our assailants. If we could trace the origin of the bullets to a specific location, then we would call on Blue Diamond's artillery battalion to respond. It was a constant back and forth. They would question with AK-47s or RPGs, and we would answer with M-16s and howitzers. The Marine I was on duty with, Lance Corporal Jackson, was from Mississippi. A southerner to the core, he loved the south; and he loved to discuss it. I didn't mind his flapping mouth, however, because his chatter kept me awake.

During my time on the Wall, I didn't shoot anyone and nobody was shot. A Marine still died, however. In Iraq, the night's blackness is impenetrable. There was a strict "lights out" command. We didn't want to alert the insurgents to our activities any more than was necessary. Because of this, Humvees returning from patrol required a gate guard to lead them to their parking lots. The gate guard, wearing a florescent vest, would carefully direct the slow-moving line of vehicles. One night, while on duty, a gate guard was leading a string of Humvees through camp. The driver, talking with his passengers, neglected to see that the gate guard had stopped. He was crushed between the Humvee behind him and a seven-ton truck in front of him.

The Marines on the Wall were subdued that night. We rotated into gate guard duty—anyone of us could've been crushed. No one wanted to die, but if we had to exit, then at least we wanted to die while discharging our weapons. Killed by friendly fire in the form of a rolling Humvee didn't make for glory. *I'm pitiless.*

Yes, war was real. Yes, death was arbitrary and meaningless. And yes, I was scared. But there was something about war that made me feel wholly aware to the present. *The uncertainty? The history? The gravity?*

Master Guns found me while I was checking into the guard's hut at the beginning of my shift. I had been on the Wall for two dark and cold weeks. "Peters," he barked before sucking his teeth. "You ready to work, Marine?"

I stopped in the doorway and met his gaze. His head was smoothly shaved, as was his face. His lazy eye was rolling in its socket and his tongue was probing the gap between his front teeth. He was taller and heftier than me. His camouflage utilities were faded with use. He was a Marine cut from the pages of *Time* magazine. For him, this wasn't a job. He wasn't a warfighter because it paid well. At his age with his experience, he could've been making three times the money the United States government paid him by working as a contractor or as a free market mercenary. Rather, he was a Devil by choice. He chose the Marine Corps. Or maybe the Marine Corps had chosen him. Either way, I didn't like him but I wanted to please him. *Like Beelzebub.* "Yes, Master Guns. I'm ready to work."

He held on with his one working eye. He sucked his teeth. "Good," he said. "Report to the CIC tomorrow, zero six. You and Rutherford are flying to Qatar for a little R-and-R. You'll stay for a week. After, if I catch you reading your damn books in the CIC I'll break your fucking neck. Understand?"

"Check, Master Guns."

He turned. "Oh, and when you come back, you're working the night shift. No more days for you, Peters. Colonel's orders."

"Yes, Master Guns."

The following morning Rutherford and I boarded a Chinook twin-blade helicopter. The machine gunner smiled at us, yanked back the bolt, and opened fire into the Iraqi sunrise.

10. Caesura

"What the hell is happening?" I shouted to Rutherford. He shrugged his shoulders.

The copilot, leaning out of the cockpit, yelled at us. "We're taking fire!" Then, to assure us: "Happens all the time!"

The machine gunner was sweating with effort, maneuvering his weapon.

Ten minutes later, we'd cleared Ramadi and were well on our way to Al Qa'im where we boarded a C-130 and flew to the safety of Qatar.

"Check it out," Rutherford said, pointing to the buffet. We were on an Air Force base living like civilians. There were soups, breads, crustaceans, and pies. It was a world apart. We ate, we drank, and we slept. We had all the free time we wanted. We visited the PX and we ate at Chili's. We allowed ourselves to unwind.

Halfway through our retreat, we were provided with three different recreational options: we could visit the mall, ride camels through the countryside, or participate in a cultural cruise. We chose the cruise.

We drove into the city. Qatar was the nicest Middle Eastern city I'd yet seen. It was relatively clean and cared for; it was developed and organized. While my standards for what constituted a nice, civilized city had been lowered considerably during my time in Iraq, I was nonetheless able to appreciate that there were no bombed buildings, ranging dogs, or dead men.

Our van pulled alongside the riverfront. A boat was waiting for us and six other Marines. The captain of the boat wasn't ready to depart, so we strolled down the boardwalk. It was a cool evening. I was wearing civilian clothes for the first time in months. The slight breeze off the ocean was calming. Small kiosks lined the pathway. A man, small and round, walked out from behind his kiosks. "Ah, hello," he said. "You are American, yes?"

"Yes."

"Bush," he said while holding his two thumbs in the air.

"Yes." I continued walking.

"Stop," he chimed. I turned. "For you," he pointed to his kiosk. I followed him. He went inside. There was clanging. His head popped out of the kiosk's window. "Coffee," he said. "Turkish," he sounded out the word: "sw—eet."

I took the dish from his hand and lifted it to my lips. I wondered, briefly, if he was trying to poison me. *If he is, it's better than going back*. I drank.

It was terrible, like drinking condensed milk mixed with day-old coffee grounds.

I coughed.

The man laughed before extending his hand. I grasped it. "Thank you."

A siren began whirring in the background. The man nodded and hurried out of his kiosk. I followed him to a large open square near the boardwalk. Men gathered, formed themselves, and began their nightly prayer. They sat, kneeled, and stood. They chanted and prayed. I stood, watching, hands at my side. *Public worship?* I'd never experienced this in America. It was jarring. They were Muslims. But they weren't the enemy. *We're at war with Al Qaeda, not Islam.* But I'd come to associate the call to prayer with AK-47s. *Are these guys—these worshipers—going to shoot me?* I'd been trained to expect as much.

Yet, unmoving, I watched as they worshipped.

They were devout and unafraid. They weren't the enemy. Islam wasn't the enemy. Their culture, even, wasn't the enemy. Here, in Qatar, I was the alien, the foreigner. I was Western, a Marine. On the shores of the Persian Gulf, I was crass and unrefined. Their religion, their worship unmasked me. I was the soldier of an occupying force.

‡ ‡ ‡

We boarded the boat and sailed into the ocean. A wait staff served us Middle Eastern cuisine. We ate, drank wine, and smoked Hookah. The gulf's waves lapped against the schooner. "Crazy watching those *hajjis* pray, huh?" Rutherford asked, a little to loudly.

"Yeah," I said. The wait staff danced around us with their flat trays and pitchers of water.

A Marine to our left with a blonde, flattop haircut—I didn't know him—spoke: "Only good *hajji's* a dead *hajji*. Am I right?"

Rutherford and I turned to Blondie who was shoveling food into his mouth. A mustached Marine, sitting opposite us, said: "Show some respect."

It was difficult to decipher who had the higher ranking. Most of the Marines on the cruise didn't know each other, *and* we were dressed in civilian clothing. None of us knew if Blondie outranked Mustachio, or vice versa. It was a mystery. We had no way of knowing to whom we should defer. I remained silent. Mustachio continued: "The hearts and minds of a people are important. What you say here can either affirm or condemn us. You understand that, right? If for no other reason, then at least be courteous to the wait staff."

Blondie balked. "Fuck 'em!" he shouted. "They're *hajjis*. They can't speak English. Bunch a dumbasses. And who the hell are you?" Blondie was drunk, swaying with the boat.

"Lance Corporal Mustachio. One div., two four. You?"

"Staff Sergeant Blondie. You hear that," he was trying to enunciate. "Staff Ser—geant. So eat your food and shut the fuck up, Lance Corporal." Mustachio dropped his head and ate his tabouli, mumbling under his breath.

Outranked, we ate the rest of our dinner in silence.

11. The Craving

THE MACHINE GUNNER FIRED into the night sky with his fifty cal. We were back in Iraq. Like a subtle but addictive drug, the war beckoned. I might have left war for a time, but it was there, waiting for me, whispering.

The weeks came and went. Fallujah, on the whole, was subdued. Each intelligence analyst turned their attention back to their respective areas of concern. Mine was still western Iraq. I read reports, analyzed data, and told people when and where to drop bombs. I briefed Masters Guns and the colonel, and I rowed on Blue Diamond's machine. It was a predictable routine interrupted by the occasional mortar or death.

It was around this time that we started receiving pictures from the initial push through Fallujah. It was my job to synthesize the photographs into a cohesive narrative so that the Marine Corps could chronicle what had happened. I would open an intelligence email, unsuspectingly, and behold a picture of a man's head smashed open like a watermelon, or a weeping mother, or a dead child. These weren't fakes. They were human beings ground by an infernal machine. What I saw gave me pause, but only a beat. *Who the fuck is responsible for this?* Beelzebub would know. But that Devil was dead. Maybe I was too.

12. Epiphany

CHRISTMAS JINGLES FLITTED AROUND the CIC. Presents from well-meaning Americans were stuffed into every available corner. I was working the night shift. At eight at night on Christmas Eve, I called my parents, each in turn. They were fine. My father was on the mend; my mother was with her new husband. "Yes," I assured them. "I received your packages." They wanted to know how I was doing. I didn't have the worst job in Iraq so, all things considered, I was all right. It was Christmas, yes, but, presently, I wasn't being shot at. We said our goodbyes. I hung up the phone.

At my desk, I was reading a book in preparation for seminary, a tome titled *Integrative Theology*. I didn't understand most of it.

Red, who had also been reassigned to the night shift, called my name. "Peters," she said. "The candle light is starting soon, if you're interested."

I said I was. I closed my book and walked with her.

The stars were out, clear as that night two-thousand years ago. It was frigid. The service was held in the back of a bombed out palace. What once signified the oppressive power of Saddam Hussein was now being used for the dual purpose of worship and remembrance. I shuffled up to it, filled with awe. The roof was missing; two walls were destroyed. The palace, broken and beaten, towered over us, suffocating us with its hovering presence. *I did that. I dropped those bombs. Strange. It's Christmas in a war zone.*

According to Luke, God had incarnated and entered into human history. On this night, so long ago, the divine reclamation of the broken systems of the world had been set in motion. A child had been born into poverty and, later, a man revolted. He was killed. *I do the killing now.* Perhaps that was the lesson, precipitated ages ago. Saddam's marble palace, with its shattered walls and tumbled stones, was a reminder: empire wins—force triumphs.

The Chaplain spoke. We lit our candles. A soft glow lightened our faces. We were huddled together for warmth, but I was cold.

"Christ incarnated," the Chaplain said, "to save us from our own brokenness. His incarnation paved the way for our reconciliation—your reconciliation. Tonight, embrace that message. Find God through Christ's sacrifice ultimately brought forth by his incarnation." *That can't be all.* I wanted, I needed more than personal salvation. It wasn't enough for the world's present situation.

"Let us worship," the Chaplain said, "let us sing."

And we sang.

We sang like beings of celestial grace: *truly he taught us to love one another; his law is love and his gospel is peace. Chains shall he break for the slave is our brother; and in his name all oppression shall cease.*

The silence was broken.

In a world rife with violence and despair, destruction and malice, hate and intolerance—I remembered. We had been given an example of love and solidarity, of peace as a cessation of violence, of forgiveness of the oppressor by the oppressed.

What am I doing here?

In great mystery, Christ birthed the ideals of God: the end of oppression and the injection of hope into history for both the oppressor and the oppressed. There was another way. Even for me, the oppressor. Even for us, the occupiers. I perpetuated violence. And yet I sang a song of both justice and freedom from oppression.

Christ had forgiven Rome; Christ, too, had rescued Rome. Perhaps redemption was possible.

I blew out my candle.

13. Fingers

JANUARY CAME AND WITH it the Iraqi elections. Like so many, I watched the election results unfold on Fox News. I watched Iraqis line up in droves to cast their vote, to establish a parliament. For many Iraqis, this was their first experience with active democracy. They appeared both proud and honored, waving their ink-stained fingers as a proclamation of their vote.

But then came the night. And with it the insurgency.

Iraqis were no longer waving their fingers. Insurgents sought out those with stained hands and cut them off. It was a dark and sobering counterpoint to the West and its invading democracy. Those who had been provided a voice in the light of day were robbed and muted with the dying sun.

All throughout that day of voting, we collected data and reported. *Maybe this is why we're here*? The war started to make a bit more sense. And then the night came, and with it the screams of those with dark fingers. Hope was deflated. *Maybe we're only making things worse*?

14. Kids

A CONVOY TRAILED INTO Blue Diamond. They were F.O.B. Marines who'd been providing security for local election centers. They'd been busy. I was hurrying to the CIC when I heard a shout. "Corporal Peters." I looked around. The shout had come from the arriving convoy. I saw a familiar face caked in dust and sand. Recruit McDougal, my buddy, now Lance Corporal McDougal.

"Well look at you," I smiled. "All grown up."

He laughed. We hugged. It had been a long time. After Recruit Training and MCT we had gone our separate ways. I'd traveled to Texas to train in intelligence, while he had gone to Virginia to train as a military electrician. As

I saw him, however, he was in full battle gear with a loaded M-4. He was no electrician. "How long has it been?"

"Two and a half years," he answered.

I shook my head at how quickly time passed. "What are you doing in Iraq? It don't see any wire cutters."

"No." He sighed. "My reserve unit was called up to deal with security in Al Anbar. We've been working the elections." He looked over my shoulder at the CIC. "It's been crazy."

"I can't imagine. How are you holding up?"

He didn't answer. "You hear Beelzebub died?"

"Yeah."

"I couldn't believe it," he said. "He was indestructible."

"I know." I paused. "I need to check in at the CIC. How long you on Blue Diamond?"

"A few hours, why?"

"Can you grab dinner in the chow hall?" He nodded. "Alright," I said "I'll meet you in the mess."

I ran to Sergeant Red. She said I could be excused for a few minutes to eat. I left the CIC and entered the chow hall. I found McDougal sitting by himself, waiting. He was eating a hamburger with soggy fries. I sat opposite him. "Okay, really, no bullshit, how you doing?" I could sense both his desire to talk, but also his weariness.

"You remember when we decided to enlist?" he smiled.

"Yeah. Living in Denver, two dropouts."

"You were selling mattresses."

"And you, couches."

"That was a long time ago."

"Yeah, it was."

"Check this out," he said. "He pulled out a deck of cards. Our commander gave us these. It's a deck of insurgent cards."

"I saw those on Fox."

"It's weird, you know? We play cards with pictures of these guys on it and talk about how we're gonna kill 'em. You know, it's just . . . there are conversations I thought I'd never have."

"This place is doing strange things to me, too. You think we're really here for oil and all that?"

McDougal was chewing on one of his nails when he answered. "Could be, I guess. I hope not. I understand the government has different concerns, but, I don't know, I guess I feel better about making war if we're actually here to set the Iraqis free, you know?"

"Blue Ink?"

"Blue Ink," he agreed. "It was nice to see, even if a mirage."

"That's depressing." I laughed.

"I think I'll grab some coffee," he said. "You want some?"

"Sure."

He was gone for a few moments. As he sat down, he slid warm Dixie-cup coffee into my hand. "I heard you finally graduated."

"I did," I said. "I graduated a few weeks before I came out here."

"What's your degree?"

"Communications."

"Nice, Peters. What's next?"

"Working at Camp Pine I found out that I'd been accepted into seminary. After this, if I make it through, I'll start on a master's."

"No shit? You want to be a pastor?"

"I don't know. I guess . . . I'm a Christian, right? But I don't know what that means anymore. The Marines, the war, my dad . . . all of it . . . there's a lot of questions. I guess I want answers."

"And you think you'll find 'em there?"

"That's the plan. What about you? What's next, after all this?" I circled my hands in the air.

"After Virgina, I went home to Austin. I went back to school for a while, but I don't know. It wasn't for me. I met a girl, though."

"Yeah?"

"Yeah."

I shook my head. "And?"

"I like her." He was squirming.

"She okay with you being a Marine?"

"Yeah, her father was in the military. She knows what it means . . . sort of . . . I guess. I'm not sure what I'm going to tell her when I get home though."

"Meaning?"

"We were ambushed. Insurgents drove a truck into our Texas Barriers and starting spraying their AKs. I took cover, started shooting back. It was chaos, you know? Coming in from all directions. A van, out of nowhere, drives right down the middle of our damn fire fight. The driver must've been hit because he was driving like shit, swerving all over the road. I didn't know what it was though. Hell, I thought it was another car bomb. So my captain calls in a QRF to ease the tension and get us the hell out of there. He decided it was best to sit tight and wait, which we did, but while we were waiting, fending off the insurgents, a woman jumps out of the van—carrying something. So I start shooting, right? But as she falls to the ground, I hear this wailing. It turns out that she was carrying her damn son. So a couple of Marines run out there and drag this kid to cover. He was hit though, in the neck, bleeding out. My captain yells: 'Who the hell likes kids?' I said I did, so he hands me the kid who couldn't have been older than five. I take him, jam my finger in his throat, and start praying.

I'm hoping the blood stops and we can get him to a medic. Holding him tight when the QRF shows up, I crawl in the Humvee with him. I can feel his blood pulsating on my fingers inside of his throat—the whole time I'm thinking, holy shit, please God, don't let this kid die. But who the fuck am I, you know? I don't have power over life, just death." He chewed a nail, spit it out, and watched as it landed in a wet puddle on the chow-hall's floor.

"And?"

"And we drive through the ambush: insurgents are throwing their rounds down range, IEDs are going off—no one knows what the hell is going on. We finally get to base. I tell the driver to head straight to the Doc. He does, but by the time we get there, kid's bled out in my arms. I held onto him for a while. I didn't know where to put it, you know. The Doc finally came over and took it . . . *him* from me. It was fucked."

"Jesus, Todd," I said, calling him by his first name.

"I keep asking myself: whose bullet hit him? Was it the insurgents or ours? Who knows, Peters, maybe I killed the kid?"

I shook my head.

"Beelzebub never said it would be like this," he said.

"Do you have to tell her?"

"What?"

"Your new girl, the one you seem to like, you said you didn't know what to tell her?"

"Oh, right. I don't know. I feel like I should."

"I'm sure you'll make the right decision."

"This was your idea, you know?" An accusation lingered underneath the question. He was right. I'd talked him into joining with me because I didn't want to experience Recruit Training alone. I didn't have an answer for him, so I said nothing. "It's not your fault though," he continued, "it's no one's I guess. Life just sucks."

I nodded.

We walked back to the CIC.

"Next time you're on Diamond, come and say 'hello.'"

"I'll do that, Peters." He walked to his convoy as I entered the CIC. McDougal and I had known each other for a year before we'd enlisted together. He was from Austin and I was from Portland. September 11th had happened and our lives diverged. I turned back before entering the CIC and watched him close the door to his Humvee. He and I were friends, and in a truer sense, brothers.

It was four years before I would see McDougal again.

15. *Everything Changes*

Master Guns made an unexpected visit to the night shift. It was still early, however, and he'd brought most of the day shift with him. He asked us to muster outside of the CIC. We did. Sergeants Spain and Red were there, as well as Lance Corporal Rutherford. Charleston was still on hiatus. Once formed, Master Guns marched in front of us.

"There comes a time in every Marine's life when they gotta deal with the loss of a Marine, a friend. We're warfighters, and these deaths happen. They're a hazard of our job, which is to keep America safe." His lazy eye was darting back and forth, while his good eye settled on me. "We're Marines. The best. Tip of the spear. We're neither soldiers nor airmen, but *TeufelHunden*: 'Hounds from Hell.' It's as such that we conduct ourselves." He paused. "This'll come as a surprise to those of us who knew him, for he served with us in the states for three years." The Masters Guns was squinting, stoic, an immovable barrier against what he had to say. "Corporal Swift died last night in Fallujah."

There was a collective gasp. I'd only known Swift for a short time, before we left for Iraq, but those to my right and left had developed friendships with him. They were comrades, brothers in arms.

Master Guns, still eyeing me for some reason, continued. "He was manning the fifty-cal on a Humvee, providing security, while his fire team entered a house. An insurgent popped out of a nearby alley and shot him between his Kevlar. His fire team called for a medevac. It was no good." He sucked his teeth. "Corporal Swift bled out on the streets of Fallujah. I'm sorry. I'm sorry he was there."

It snuck up on me, because I had forgotten: Corporal Swift was in Fallujah for me. He had taken my place. I'd flown to my grandfather's funeral and then home to be at my father's bedside. The unit I would've been assigned to, Swift had been assigned to instead. He was with the Recon Battalion; I was bumped to Division. That was why, even now, Master Guns was staring at me. It was a slow realization, like the last light of sun disappearing behind the Euphrates—him for me.

He had died in my place.

I was speechless, emotionless. I stared ahead. Red was behind me, crying. I hadn't known it, but I learned later that Red and Swift had attended high school together. Their families were close friends, or so she told me. I glanced backwards. She, too, was staring at me, her eyes full of hate. They all knew. Swift, in so many ways, had been a sacrifice. *For what? Was his life less valuable than mine?*

His mother, Swift had said, was angry at finding out that he'd been deployed in my place. And his sister. She would be graduating in a few months, entering into a much larger world, a world without her brother. *What have I done?*

A normal day. Swift's mother would be making dinner. She would glance out her kitchen window. A car she wouldn't recognize would appear on the road, slow, and then turn into her driveway. She'd see it, put down the knife she was using to cut the carrots with and walk towards the door. The bell would ring. She'd make eye contact with either her husband or daughter. She'd open the door. See a man in uniform. Once, twice, she would cry out. Her hand would jump to her mouth. And then tears. Unending tears.

Who was I to deserve this? What story, down what path was my life now hurtling?

What was done could not be undone.

The Master Guns was talking. "We must honor the dead," he said. "But we've a job to do, Marines. Mourn tonight, but no longer. Tomorrow, we kill." He looked at me one last time before turning away and marching back inside the CIC.

"I'm sorry," I said, turning to Red.

"Shut the fuck up, Peters. You don't even believe in this goddamn war. And without that, his death is meaningless."

I stepped back. I wanted to hide, to curl in a dark corner. I wanted to be forgotten. "I'm—" I started before Red cut me off.

"Leave me alone," she whispered, dropping her shoulders. "Just leave me alone." Spain had come alongside her and offered her a shoulder. She took it and openly cried. I moved away, and Rutherford came with me.

We walked to the chow hall and sat at an empty table. "It's not your fault," he said. "It had nothing to do with you."

"It had everything to do with me."

"What did she mean, 'You don't believe in this war?'"

"It's something I said before. A conversation I'd had with her and Charleston."

"Don't you though? Believe in it?"

I lifted my head. "I don't know."

"Look, Peters, war is shit and people die. It's the way of the world. Swift's death was at the hand of some dumbass Iraqi, not you. Who can say what would've happened had you been there? Maybe you would've seen the insurgent and shot, maybe not. Maybe you would've bled out on the street instead of Swift. Either way, you're a Marine, reservist or not. This war is all you have. It's who you are, Devil."

I nodded. My life before—family, college, Camp Pine, graduate school—was nothing. All that was, was before me. War was life; life was war.

I was Beelzebub and I would die here—lost in Iraq. Rutherford was right. Empire wins. My soul was forfeit.

I stood. Rutherford stood with me. "C'mon," I said. "Let's get back to the CIC."

Dusk departed for night.

INTERLUDE

"Tell me about Swift," Trent said. We were in his office. The desktop between us was drowning in papers and books.

"What?"

"You've mentioned him before, but we've never really talked about him. I think we should."

"Talk about him?"

"Yes."

"There's not much to tell. We met, hung out a little, got to know each other. When my grandfather died and my dad's heart spasmed, I left California. Swift filled my battalion slot, which was stupid, because, actually, we landed in country at the same time. It should've been me in Fallujah."

"But it wasn't."

I was silent.

"Do you ever think about him?"

"What's to think about?"

"His death."

"I think about his family the most, I guess."

"Why?"

"It seems like a hard thing, losing a son. Especially like that."

"Meaning?" Trent probed.

"The medevac . . . a little longer and he would've been fine. Five minutes, that's all he would've needed." I paused. "I guess I do think about it—sometimes."

"What do you think about?"

"What would it have been like to lay there—a dusty street; garbage floating on the wind; dogs prowling the sidewalk—watching my blood seep out, pooling around me? Cold. Scared. At first, they would've been fast, you know? *Inandout, inandout.* My heart rate would rise as Marines scurried to save me. Eventually, you know, my breathing would slow. *In-and-out, in-and-out.* A frantic struggle to hold on, then . . . release. Letting go. Peace. And then—death."

"No light?"

"What?"

"Well, in most death stories, there's usually a light to guide the dying home."

"No. No light—just struggle."

"Do you believe in heaven?" Trent asked.

"No," I said after a time. "I guess I don't. It's difficult to get past reality, you know? The spiritual is a bit too ethereal for me."

"What about hope?"

Hope? Grace's lifeless body strewn outside a line of Porta Potties. "Where's the hope in delayed justice? My existence—our existence—overflows with suffering. Most people die a miserable death. And that's all Christianity has to offer? Paradise after the fact. That's bullshit. I think *we* participate in either heaven or hell—right here, right now."

"We?"

"There's no hope in the individual," I ranted. "Violence and war are systemic injustices. What can one person do?"

"And Swift represents . . . what?"

"A human being crushed by the powers." I bit my cheek. "And my own failures."

"So the individual comes into it somewhat?"

"Where responsibility is concerned, yeah."

"That's a hard line," Trent said. "Are you afraid of death?"

"No, I'm just tired of creating hell."

16. Scales

ONE NIGHT, NEAR THE end of my tour, I was following the chatter of a pilot flying a UAV that was gathering intelligence on a person of interest within my province—Abu Bakr. He was suspected of "wedding crashing"—a term describing an insurgent who kills large groups of Iraqis in order to disrupt the burgeoning control of coalition forces.

"Reminds me of San Angelo," the UAV's operator said through the chat window.

San Angelo. "Who is this?" I typed.

The answer was slow in coming: "Corporal Mexico."

I typed back that he was chatting with his old roommate, Corporal Peters. We couldn't chat long, and we certainly couldn't discuss anything in detail over the secret internet's chat server, but we did catch up. He said he'd been in Fallujah and it was hell. He asked me how my dad was and then gave me a hard time for staying at Division. For my part, I told him I was well, as well as could be expected, but that I was looking forward to home. He agreed. We said our goodbyes. I watched the rest of his UAV session, but came away knowing little of Abu Bakr.

I stood and stretched. My shift was coming to a close. At seven in the morning, after I finished working, I planned on eating breakfast, rowing for thirty minutes on the machine, and then reading myself to sleep. It was six-fifteen. I had forty-five minutes left on my shift when Master Guns strolled into the CIC. "Peters, come with me." Already standing, I trailed the Master Guns as he turned and marched.

I followed him to his office, which was buried deep within the CIC. I had only been inside his office once and was nervous at the prospect of being alone with him. Master Guns had recently shaved his head and the fluorescent light reflected in his brow. He motioned for me sit. I did. He opened a bag of sunflower seeds and started to methodically chew while sucking his teeth. "I have a series of questions the Commandant says I have to ask each of my Marines before we go back to the States. Check?"

"Check, Master Guns."

He picked up a piece of paper, sat it back down, and slid on his glasses before grabbing the paper once more. His glasses were resting on the tip of his nose. He looked old and tired. He peered at me over the top of his glasses. "How would you rate your experience in Iraq?"

"Uh," I fumbled. I didn't know how to respond. "Is there a scale?"

He sucked his teeth before spitting out a seed. "One to ten, Peters."

I wasn't sure how honest I wanted to be with Master Guns. I hadn't *enjoyed* my time here. Who had? "Two."

He sucked his teeth. "What is the state of your mental health?"

What? "Uh, I don't know—eight."

"So you would say that you're healthy and fit?"

"Yes."

He spit out a seed. "If offered a deployment extension, then, on a scale from one to ten, would you accept the extension?"

"Is one good or bad?"

"It's a flat refusal."

"One."

He eyed me over his bifocals and mumbled. "If you could leave Iraq today, then would you?"

"Is there a scale for this question?"

"A simple 'yes' or 'no' would do."

"Yes."

"If you could, then you would leave?"

I darted my eyes, "Yes." *Why is that so hard to believe?*

He set the paper down. "Most Marines say *no*, Peters. Most of us want to stay. But you don't. What do you think that makes you?"

I looked at him. "Human."

He sucked his teeth. "I'll see what I can do."

True to his word, he found me a week later in the CIC and told me that, within a month, I would be on a plane bound for home.

17. Return

I SAID GOODBYE TO Spain and Rutherford. They were glad I was rotating home, and said that they would follow within the month. We promised to stay in touch, but we all knew it was an empty promise. The night before I left, I sought out Red. She was in the plastic shed we called a "gym."

I told her I was leaving, though she already knew it. I thanked her for her work and her leadership. I apologized for all that had happened.

"You don't have to apologize. Nothing that happened was your fault. It's war, that's all."

"Well, either way, I know it wasn't easy for you."

She shook her head.

"What will you do after Iraq?"

"Me? I'll reenlist. I'll be a Marine as long as they'll let me, Peters." She smiled. "I heard you told Master Guns you wanted to leave."

"I did. Why is that so hard to believe?"

"It's not. I don't think anyone has ever been that honest with him though. He was raging." She was laughing now. "You should have seen his face when he told us during our staff meeting. I believe the word he used was *shitbird*. He wanted to send you out as soon as possible, but couldn't find a plane for you."

We laughed.

"Well, take care." I turned.

"Peters," Red grabbed my shoulder. "You still don't believe in this war, do you?"

The sun was streaming in the windows. It was a hot day. Around me, weights clinked. The air was humid with sweat.

"It's not that I don't believe in this particular war, it's just . . . should anyone *believe* in war?"

She thought for a moment. "As long as there are people who would strap a bomb to their chest and explode it in a marketplace, then war is necessary. You can't escape that fact, Peters. Not even you. You may not understand this, but I fight to protect the innocent. I'm a guardian; we're all guardians. Even you're a guardian, though you may not like it."

I nodded. "Goodbye, Red."

That night I boarded a Chinook helicopter bound for Al Qa'im, and a C-130 home. We took fire pulling out of Blue Diamond. The machine gunner lit up the night sky. The roar of gunfire blasted in my ears, metal filled my nostrils.

It was a short chopper flight. We soon landed in western Iraq. I bunked in a small hut. I woke early. Al Qa'im was a huge base in a relatively safe part of Iraq. The cement wall that surrounded the base was ten-feet tall. I found a flight of stairs that lead to an out-of-the-way guard tower and climbed to the top. I was alone. I stood and looked out over the unending expanse of desert. It was cracked and brown. Sagebrush spotted the landscape. The sun rose. *Where am I, among that?* Out there, somewhere, a different man roamed the wilderness.

I said goodbye.

An hour later, I boarded a C-130 and flew home.

18. Triadic

"The study of God is a study in three parts." My professor at Denver Seminary, Professor Burghard, started his lecture. He was tall and balding. His mild-mannered intonation was a welcomed relief. "It is the examination of God, creation, and of God and creation in relationship."

It was September. I had returned from Iraq in March. The leaves were a burning orange; the Colorado air, with each breath, was sharp. The atmosphere at Denver Seminary was both warm and welcoming. I had three years of weekend drilling and summer service ahead of me. I was in school, yes, but if the president were to order another surge, then I would be called upon to answer.

Professor Burghard continued: "This semester we will examine the latter, the study of God and creation in relationship. That is to say, how does the cosmos relate to God, and how do we, as humanity, both respond and relate to the divine? We will briefly discuss both God's attributes and actions, but only as they impinge on creation. Any questions?"

I had too many.

Before starting at Denver Seminary I was required to complete numerous personality assessments. The results were supplied to various assessment experts. I was called to discuss the results. As I sat down for my meeting, the counselor pulled out a stack of notes. He placed them on the table between us. "We have a problem, Benjamin."

I smiled and met his gaze. "Why's that?"

"I think you know why."

"Do I?"

"Tell me about the war."

"Ah, that."

He sighed. "My job is to assess your readiness for both seminary and the ministry. Right now, your mental state is dismal. You're clearly angry. You don't respect authority, and you're suicidal." He paused. "Am I right?"

Was I? I bit my cheek.

"You don't have to tell me what's going on with you, but you either need to start seeing a counselor, one who will report to me at the end of the semester, or I'll have to ask the dean to rethink your acceptance into Denver Seminary."

"I don't think I can afford a counselor."

"I know. We have a staff of counselors I can recommend. They'll provide you with a sizeable discount."

"Who?"

He scratched a number on a piece of paper and handed it to me. "His name is Trent. I think you'll have a lot in common."

Professor Burghard was lecturing. I was distractedly taking notes.

Angry.

So what? Most veterans were. And, yes, I disregarded authority because authority made me feel helpless. "Report to the Wall," authority said. "Get shot at." And how else could I respond, except by saying: "Errah, Devil"?

So I was mad at authority because authority had placed a hit on my life—a perfectly normal reaction. The revelation, however, had come when the counselor told me I was suicidal. *There's no way that's true.* What had once splayed a vivid luminosity—images of hope and joy—were now gray-washed replicas. Life was drab and listless, an exercise in monotony. But did I want to end it? *No.*

"When it comes to God and creation in relationship, we often wonder if God is sovereign. Is he overall? Does the divine control the departures and arrivals of airplanes or the death and birth of humans? To put it another way, does God control the gears of history or does the divine pull away, a watchmaker surveying her intricate machinery? This, of course, leads to another question, the root of our desire when studying the third part of Christian doctrine: does God care?"

He dismissed class with that question.

Walking to my car, I dialed Trent's number and set up a meeting for the following morning.

19. Mystery

"Before we start," Professor Burghard said, "I want to make something clear. Namely, the question of 'why theology?' What does theology do for us?" His eyes circled the room, searching for a reply. No one answered. He continued: "Theology done well is practical. That is, it informs, it must inform, the way in which we live. It has the power to shape us, to transform us. Theology, ultimately, can make us better humans. But, and this is important, theology is *mystery*. We cannot know all there is to know. This arena is full of uncertainty. We, however, must earn the right to claim mystery. That's why we're here: to work towards and for a better cosmos, and to earn the right to claim mystery. If we're lucky, then we might come to a better understanding of both God and ourselves. But that is neither promised nor guaranteed."

Hands, now, sprung up throughout the classroom. Students sought clarification for students desire certainty.

‡ ‡ ‡

"That's not what it means at all," Piper said. I was in the middle of a session with my discussion group for Professor Burghard's class. "Look," she continued, "if it's a choice between two options and the first is inevitable, but, after you pray, option two comes to pass, then that's what God wanted all along. He doesn't change and he certainly doesn't change his mind."

"It must be comforting to think that way," chimed Greg, a bearded second year student.

"I don't *think* that way," Piper retorted, "the Bible does."

"Easy peasy."

"It's right there, plain for anyone to see."

"And middle knowledge?" asked Samantha, a first year student from Des Moines.

"What about it?"

"Is it legit?"

"Yeah," said Greg, "ever heard of string theory? Multiple dimensions? Time travel? Theologians have known about it for years, it's called 'middle knowledge.' It's the theological equivalent of a black hole."

"Nerd," I said. The group turned towards me.

"You've been quiet," Samantha said. "What about you, Benjamin?"

The truth was, the conversation was over my head. My theological training had been minimal. In the last few months I had learned words like "supralapsarianism" and "anthropomorphic." I was struggling to keep up. I shook my head. "I don't know. It seems—" I bit my cheek. "Humanity perpetrates some pretty ugly things. I have a hard time believing either those things were ordained from the beginning or that God approves."

"That's sin, Benjamin," Piper clarified, "working the way it works." Certainty was her strong suit.

"Maybe. But maybe God takes a risk on creation, offering us something incredibly beautiful. It's our choice though, right? History seems too concrete if it can't change—like it's set in stone. That's depressing. For me, the story is unwritten. We're, you know, partners. Our actions can influence the outcome, both positively and negatively. And there's hope in God's response to our suffering."

"I would say the story is already written," Piper said. "Which might seem to change from our perspective, but not from God's. He's immutable. And I, for one, find depthless comfort in that."

How could war be divinely sanctioned? I shook my head. *There's no way McDougal would be okay with that.* "I don't know. But people die in war, famine, and poverty. There's too much suffering. Maybe it sounds like I'm throwing a fit, but I find comfort in knowing there's something I can do to affect change—real change."

"Of course," said Piper, clearing a stray, blonde hair from her eyes. "You can always pray. God answers prayer."

"I was looking for something a little more . . . solid, I think."

Piper's eyes widened. "What are you suggesting?"

"Nothing."

"That's free will," Samantha said. "God gives us the choice to kill, we kill. Take war. We make that decision; God wouldn't preordain war, would he? War has to be an instance of God turning us over to our desires. So we war, we kill, we commit evils, and not because God ordained it, but because we *chose* it."

"That's awfully convenient for God," Greg said. "The innocent suffer because God gave some dictator over to his evil desires."

Piper shook her head. "No. God did and does preordain war. It's all over the Hebrew Scriptures. War is part of life, and like everything else *he* created, he'll wield war as a tool to teach us a lesson or refine us."

"Piper, no offense, but that's stupid," Greg said. "Anyone who's experienced war would tell you that much. It's an abhorrent evil."

"Well, yes, it is, that's true, but who can understand the ways of God?"

"You seem to," Greg pointed out.

"In the end, either God is sovereign and you live out of that paradigm or he isn't and you burn forever in hell."

"What?"

"Just kidding," Piper smiled. "But seriously, God is sovereign. He has to be. That means, in some ways, he oversees war too. I don't pretend to understand what that means, but I know it's true."

"What about the state?" Greg asked, scratching his beard. "In war, if human beings have free will to make their own choices to fight or not fight, then what about the state? Are the actions of a state preordained? Does a state have free will to act? It seems to me that oftentimes an individual is obeying the commands of the state. Who's held responsible for that?"

"Romans 13," Piper said. "God ordained the powers and the authorities. We can't question the state, because the state is ordained by God."

"So you're saying," I probed, "if a state acts, then it acts on God's behalf?"

"*I* don't say anything," Piper said. "*Paul* says it. But, yes, in a way."

"In a way?"

"If the state is righteous, then we have nothing to fear, and as citizens it becomes our duty to act in accordance with a state's laws and edicts. If that means entering into a draft and fighting, then that means we're acting in accordance with God."

"Easy peasy."

"And if they're wrong?" I asked.

"Which does happen," Greg interjected.

"Then God will sort it out, but it's our duty to obey the proper ordering of things."

What? Outside, in the real world, the debate over Halliburton and Iraq's oil were raging. "Piper. You don't have a clue what you're talking about."

"Excuse me?" Her face reddened.

"I've been to war. You make it sound sterile. It's not. It is a living thing that indiscriminately kills. God wouldn't ordain war any more than he would ordain a government that perpetrates genocide. That's insane!"

"That's not what I meant," Piper retreated. "I only meant to say . . . God is sovereign, that's all. It's not our job to question, only obey. Sometimes God gives us incomprehensible tasks. It's a mystery, but we still obey. When a government like ours goes to war, then I believe the soldier isn't at fault."

"Why's that?"

"Because we're just."

"We're just?" I asked. "Have you seen the images streaming out of Abu Ghraib? Have you read the news? Last week some Marine killed an entire village—men, women, and children. Have you reviewed our reasons for getting into this war in the first place? It doesn't exactly fit into a nice and tidy just war theory, does it?" I couldn't stop now; I was committed. "At first, I wasn't sure why I came to seminary, but it's become increasingly clear over the last few months. I'm a Marine. I made a choice, and I can't change that. I'm also a Christian. I've bought into a religion that says, 'love your enemies.' I'm torn apart by opposites. Our government pats me on the back and says everything will be okay and that I'm some sort of hero. But people died; I killed them. I hated it and, yet, I craved it. The truth is: I've never felt so alive.

"And you want to know what haunts me every night? The question: was I justified in what I did? The government and the conservative right says, *yes*! The far left says, *no*! And moderate Christians don't have a damn clue either way." I paused. "But what I keep coming back to is this: someone, somewhere, has to be held responsible—me, the government, God, Christendom. I don't even care whom at this point. I just want to know."

The other three mumbled responses. The group dissolved. I said I was sorry.

Walking to the parking lot, Greg caught up with me. "Dude," he shouted.

"Hey."

"You were in the war?"

"Yeah."

"Oh. I'm a pacifist," he blurted. People varied in their reaction to finding out that I was a veteran. Some people shook my hand and said thank you; others stared suspiciously, like their children were in danger of being eaten.

"Cool."

"That's not what I meant," he tugged at his beard. "Look my wife and I are having some people over for dinner tomorrow night, you interested?"

Part Two

20. Natasha

"Sit down," Professor Burghard said. I was in his in office on the second story of the administrative building. Books, big tomes packed with superior knowledge, surrounded us.

"Thank you."

"Well," he breathed, "what can I do for you?"

The spring semester of my first year at seminary was coming to a close. At times, I felt like my own education was lacking and that I was a step behind my peers. But I worked hard. I felt I was slowly gaining ground. In an effort to continue progressing, I'd called an early meeting with Professor Burghard. I needed to settle on a thesis topic so I could both start researching and writing. I told him as much.

"What are you interested in?"

"I don't know. I'm really enjoying my Greek classes."

"Do you understand the thesis process?"

Nope. "Yeah, I think."

"Let me make a suggestion. Find something you'll never tire of, because the next two years of your life will be spent on it."

I nodded. "What about war?"

"What about it?"

"As a thesis topic?"

"You would have to narrow it down, obviously. Theses have to be extremely specific."

"Oh."

"Why don't you discuss it with Professor Kelwin. He's our New Testament scholar and might be able to steer you in the appropriate direction."

I said thank you and left Professor Burghard's office. I descended to the receptionist's desk and asked for Professor Kelwin's room number. I climbed the stairs, made two laps around the second floor, and finally located his office. The lights were out, but I could hear a faint clicking on the other side of the door. I tapped.

"Go away."

Shocked, I turned to leave.

The door opened.

"What do you want?" It was Professor Kelwin. He was taller than me. His head was a tangle of gray hair. He wore a mustache and a bow tie.

I explained my situation. Professor Kelwin snatched a book off his shelf and handed it to me.

"Read this." He shut the door.

I lifted the book. The title read *War: Four Christian Views*. I stuffed it into my satchel and drove home.

‡ ‡ ‡

We were downtown at Little India. Sitting across from me was Nastasha. We'd been introduced through a mutual friend. She was tall with both dark hair and skin. Her family's heritage hailed from Serbia. She was a first generation American and taught English at a large public high school. She read Fitzgerald, but loved Hosseini. She was smart and witty, beautiful and mysterious, balanced and grounded. She was the perfect bit of everything. I was outclassed.

As cars whizzed by outside, exotic music filled the space between us. It was our sixth date. The clinking dishware and chatting of patrons settled into a low background hum. The tabouleh was crisp. I asked her how school had been. She said it was good, but that she was looking forward to summer. I agreed.

"Did you figure out your thesis?"

"No. I have a long way to go. Professor Kelwin lent me a book."

"Which is?"

I assumed a professorial persona. "Until you have read thoroughly on your subject of interest, do not return. I will brook no half-cocked ideas." I pushed the imaginary glasses sliding down my nose back to their proper place. "'Might I suggest Romans. Now there is a book bursting with potential.' In other words," I continued, "my topic is, potentially, war."

"You make a great professor."

I shrugged.

"What about war?"

"I've always wondered if Christians should fight in wars. I might write on that."

"Shouldn't they?" Natasha asked, dipping her pita into the plate of hummus that rested between us.

Unaware that I was stumbling towards my thesis, I said: "What? War is totally against a Christian paradigm."

"Really? You believe that?"

"Yeah."

"Certainly it's necessary . . . sometimes? I mean, there are unjust wars and there are just wars, right?"

"No, I don't know, but . . . war is always bad. Even if necessary, it's still an evil."

"Unless you're using it for good?"

"Impossible."

"Whatever," she said. "You can protect the innocent."

"Nope."

"Isn't it dangerous to have formalized your position before either researching or writing?"

"Good point."

"You're just interpreting the Bible through your experiences."

"That's a bit callous."

"But true."

"Professor Burghard always claimed immutable, fourfold interpretation."

"Riveting."

I ignored her snark. "First Scripture, then tradition, then reason, and last, experience."

"You've moved the last to the first."

"I'm in good company."

"Funny. Very funny, Benjamin."

"Either way, yes, my experience has informed my reading. Everyone's does. But, I have a hard time believing that anyone who experiences war and combat firsthand can claim its purity. It's evil. It flies in the face of the Sermon on the Mount."

"Why don't you ever talk about the war?" she asked, changing the subject.

I let out a breath. "I want to. I feel like I can. I mean, it's not like I did that much. There were others who experienced far more than I did. I guess . . . I don't know," I shrugged. "What do you want to know?"

"Everything."

We talked late into the night.

INTERLUDE

"I HAD A MEETING with the seminary's spiritual formation director."

"And how did that go?" Trent asked. We were in his office. It was the armpit of winter—February—cold and snowing outside. I was sitting on Trent's couch, legs crossed.

"Fine, I guess. At one point, she told me that ministry was like war. She connected ministry and Paul's spiritual armor."

"I'm sure that went well?"

"It was ridiculous. I wanted to slap her."

Trent leaned in. "What's the real issue, Benjamin?"

I didn't have an answer. "I don't know, ever since I returned, I've seen how people try to relate to me because of the war. It's just . . . it's not helpful."

"How so?"

"C'mon! Ministry is war? That's insane. I knew a Marine who came home, made a go of it, but couldn't. He killed himself. Why? Because it was easier than living with the questions . . . the emptiness. How's that related to a minister, ministering?"

"Maybe she was trying to connect with you?"

"Maybe?" I crossed my arms. "It's these people, you know? They live in the suburbs and drive their Escalades. They come from affluent families and attend the best colleges. Their spouses are doctors and pilots and lawyers. And they want to talk to me about the war, like I'm some expert. They don't give a fuck. They just want to live their lives, sending minorities off to fight their battles. How am I supposed to come to terms with that? These people send me off to fight, and if I had died, they wouldn't have cared. They wouldn't have flinched."

"So you're mad at the wealthy?"

I thought for a moment. "I don't know. I hear all this talk about protecting American interests—oil, markets, or whatever else. I'm never going to see that. It doesn't make a bit of difference to me. It does to the rich, right?"

Trent scribbled before meeting my gaze. "Sometimes there is no easy answer, Benjamin. Sometimes life is gray. All we can do is meet people where they are."

21. Weekends

"MARINES," FIRST SERGEANT DILLON yelled. "Kill Iraqis!"

I was a graduate student, yes. I had been demobilized, true. But I was still a Marine reserve, drilling one weekend a month and two weeks each summer. This summer I was stationed at a military-friendly rifle range in Wyoming. My unit, Bravo Company, had recently acquired a new first sergeant. He was a Denver police officer and a Marine to the core.

We yanked our bolts back and fired, practicing on a combat range. I was in a foxhole with Sergeant Mexico (we had both been promoted). Targets were popping up at ten, twenty-five, and fifty yards. First Sergeant was trying his best to convince us that our targets were Iraqis. "Shouldn't he be saying, 'Insurgents?'" I asked Mexico between shooting off rounds.

"What the hell does he know? He's never been deployed, Devil. To him, this shit's all the same."

"It's weird though, right?"

"Kill."

"Police call!" First Sergeant screamed.

Mexico and I crawled out of our foxhole to clean up the rounds our unit had discharged. "How's your daughter?"

"She's great. Five, can you believe that?"

I shook my head. "No. Time is flying, Mexico. Wasn't it yesterday we were studying in San Angelo?"

He laughed. "Remember Staff Sergeant Wilberson?"

"Covering his mouth when he laughed."

"That reminds me," Mexico said. "I saw Sergeant Indiana in Fallujah. He was running a Predator."

"Really?"

"Yeah, he told me he was getting out soon to join some private firm—three times as much money, no bullshit."

"Like a mercenary?"

"Private contractor."

"Same thing."

"I'm thinking of doing it."

"What?"

"There's a company in California. I'd work in three-month rotations. Iraq, home, Iraq. I'd make sixty a rotation. That's a lot of money, Peters."

"Mexico the entrepreneur."

"You ought to join me. We're out in what, two years? That's enough time for me to finish my bachelor's and you your master's. Think about it."

It was a lot of money, which, as Natasha and I were hurtling towards permanence, would help us establish a life together. "What would we do?"

"Fly around and detonate IEDs. Not bad work."

I bent down, grabbed a few shells, and tossed them into an ammo can. "You have no reservations? What about your daughter?"

"She lives with her mom. And, no, I don't have any reservations. The insurgents are still bad and I don't mind making a cash load while fucking 'em up. I'd also be protecting the troops. It's not a bad gig, Peters."

"Form it up, Marines!" First Sergeant barked.

"I'll think about it."

22. Coterie

The summer was gone. It was a new school year. I celebrated my one year anniversary of returning from Iraq with Natasha. School, sadly, required both of our attentions and cooled our hot pursuit of one another. She was preparing to teach a full load with four preps, and I was scheduling my fall classes. I enrolled in a class titled, "Methods and Research," which did two things: first, it prepared me for my thesis. I would learn how to research, write, and draft a thesis proposal. Second, it would pair me with five other students in a kind of thesis coterie, the purpose of which was to meet twice a month and discuss both our research and writing. There was Andrew and Kiera, a married couple passionate for all things Slavic; Brian, a third year student from San Francisco; Karl, a second year student who had a love affair with canoes; and Greg, the thick-haired classmate and discussion group confidant from Professor Burghard's class.

"Nice to meet you," Andrew said, shaking my hand. It was our first official meeting. We had reserved a study room in the seminary's library. The room was fitted with a long conference table and a windowed wall. A coffee machine gurgled on the counter beside the conference table. "We should decide on a name for our group," he continued. "All of the thesis coteries, traditionally, have awesome names."

"I agree," Greg said. "I vote for 'Space Odyssey.'"

"That's ridiculous," Kiera said, who was tall, blonde, and, of all of us, the most likely to gain acceptance into a doctoral program. She was a genius.

"Ridiculous or not, I think we should go with 'The Canoe Boats,'" Karl said. "It's funny and it has meaning."

"Meaning?"

"Yeah, I used to race canoes in Minnesota."

"No," Brian said, who was in a hurry to start. "I suggest 'The Tinklings.' It's like Tinkle and Inklings, but compounded. Get it?"

"Funny," Andrew said. "It's got a ring."

"Agreed," Greg said.

"Done." Brian was quickly becoming our leader. "Okay, who's first? Who wants to discuss their thesis?"

"I'll start," I said.

"Let's hear it."

"Alright, so—" I took a deep breath. *You've studied this. You know this.* "So, as most of you know, I'm a Marine."

"Really?" Andrew asked.

"He's in the military."

"Cool."

"Anyway," I said. "I've always had this lingering question: was I, were we, justified in what we did?"

"Did?" Greg asked.

"Yeah, in Afghanistan and Iraq."

"Do you mean, unilateral invasion?" Brian asked.

"Yes and no. More basic than that. Is anyone, anywhere ever justified in fighting in a war? Being a Christian, I'm interested in creating a discussion for the Christian community, though my initial question isn't limited to Christians. Historically, both governments and individuals have used Romans to justify the authorities' power to employ war. So, if I'm to start anywhere, I wanted to start with a critique of Romans 12:14—13:7. What does it say, what doesn't it say?"

"Can you give us an example?" Greg asked, genuinely interested.

"Don't interrupt him," Brian said. "Keep going."

"That's okay. We can discuss this first part. Actually, it would be helpful."

"Cool."

"To answer your question, as far as I understand it, for the first three hundred years of Christianity this text was understood as a call to nonviolence, a counterpoint to the violence of the Roman Empire. It wasn't until after Constantine assimilated Christianity into the Empire that this passage was understood as a justification for the state to declare war. It's weird, really, because for the first three hundred years of Christianity, if you were a soldier and you wanted to enter into a Christian community, you would've had to renounce your enlistment."

"That doesn't really tell us anything," Kiera said. "Soldiers don't typically trip over themselves to join obscure religious communities."

She was on to something. I pushed back from the table, poured a cup of coffee from the machine, and then continued. "No, you're probably right. But it was still understood by the community that a soldier couldn't enter their ranks."

"Pun," Karl said.

"Anyway, to provide context, Paul urges his readers at the start of Romans 12 to be living sacrifices, which, for my purposes, is explained in verse 9 as embodying 'genuine love.'"

"Why does any of this matter?" Brian preferred a more direct conversation.

"Because most scholars would say that verses 14–21 are explanations of genuine love."

"So the community of Roman Christians is told to express genuine love, and verses 14–21 provide the details, right?"

"Yes. With that in mind, the essential question is: are these commands for those within the community, without, or both?"

"Does it have to be one over the other?" Karl loved a good paradox.

I sipped my coffee. "According to some scholars."

"What do *you* think?" Andrew probed.

It's so much easier to summarize other people. "Appropriate behavior within a given community should also be reflected outside of that community." I shrugged. "Treat others the way you want to be treated."

"Brain surgery," Greg said.

"Well, no," I said. "But this section does highlight the purpose of Romans."

"Which is?"

"Cohesion. Paul's overarching purpose is to teach the community—both Jews and Christians—how to live in community with one another and their non-believing neighbors. Anyway, there's one more thing to consider."

"Okay."

"Luke writes: 'But I tell you who hear me: Love your enemies, do good to those who hate you, bless those who curse you, pray for those who mistreat you.' Paul sort of, you know, paraphrases Luke in order to root his comments in the oral tradition: love all people, no exceptions, no distinctions—love your enemy."

"Yeah, yeah," Andrew said. "But if your enemy seeks to kill you, what's love?"

Charleston asked the same question.

"But that's just it," Kiera said. "Can I love and be aggressive or is my only option self defense?"

"Or is there another way?"

"There's another way, but that's getting too far ahead."

They booed. "Give it to us."

"I'll keep the suspense. Anyway, Jesus said to love your enemy; Paul said to bless the persecutors or, 'Advocate before God on behalf of those whom persecute.'" I stopped.

"So Paul ratchets up the command" responded Greg.

"How?" Brian asked.

"It's not some neighborly dispute or competing merchant," Greg said. "But the worst of the worst. Christians should love those human beings who flourish in oppressive and violent states, places that are anti-Kingdom." He tugged his beard. "Bless the Emperor."

"That's a shitty command," Andrew said.

"*Skubalon*."

"Yeah," I agreed. "Who wants to bless the Idi Amins of the world?"

23. Bread and Vodka

"Tear the bread," Andrew started. "Now chunk it." September was drawing to a close. The Tinklings had decided to take a break from their constant research and writing. We stacked our books and drove to Andrew and Kiera's for a dinner party. I invited Natasha. The scented candles on the table cast their long shadows. Outside it was dark and cool; inside it was warm and comfortable. Andrew was in the process of showing us how to make a traditional Russian dish, which he had picked up during his time studying abroad in St. Petersburg. "Then place the bread into your bowl like this. Simple." He grabbed a bottle of vodka and opened it. "Pour as much vodka as you'd like on the bread. Let it sit for few minutes so the bread can soak it up. Now eat it."

"That's just soggy bread?"

"Soaked in vodka. Eat it with a spoon."

"That's fantastically disgusting," Brian said.

"I want it in my mouth," Greg said.

"All yours." Andrew handed the bowl to Greg, who lifted the spoon and swallowed the mixture.

"Well," he mumbled with full cheeks. "It tastes like shit."

"In St. Petersburg, we ate this all the time." Andrew grinned. "For breakfast even. I've never understood the evangelical perspective: don't drink because it's a sin. That's just stupid. Eat your damn bowl of vodka and talk, you know? I mean, really talk. It's good for everybody."

"Talking or vodka?" Natasha asked.

"Both."

"What would Russians have said about Iraq?" I asked.

"Uh . . . can you say, 'hypocrisy?'"

"We believe a lot of things about our country," Kiera said. "But not many things that are honest. We call America a 'Christian Nation,' but we invaded another country so that we could exploit it economically."

"No one wants to compromise their standard of living," Andrew said. "So we kill. America is an empire that's convinced it's a sheep."

"That's a bit harsh," Brian said. "Saddam posed a threat to a lot of countries and people. I'm not saying I agree with the war, but I would, at least, call it gray. We couldn't invade; we couldn't not invade."

"Double negative.

"Eat your mush."

"Don't mind if I do . . . but that's a political view, maybe even a realistic view, but it's certainly not a Christian view."

"Blah, blah, blah," Brian said. "Christianity—being old—can't always inform the decisions we make politically—today."

"We all view the world through a culturally given paradigm, though. It might be religious, political, ideological, or whatever; it might be a paradigm soup, but when we make decisions, we're making those choices out of our paradigm, encyclopedia, *habitus*, or whatever you want to call it. So even if Christianity can't or doesn't speak today, it still plays a role in our subconscious, personally and culturally. The question is: are we aware of and able to critique our paradigms?"

"Even if we are, what difference does it make?" Karl asked.

"If the president says, 'Let's oust Saddam.' And you're like, 'Right on, let's kick his ass.' Well, what led to your agreement? Was it some sort of philosophical theory? A Christian, preemptive war stance? Your political beliefs? Was it an amalgamation? I think, before we can understand our choices, we have to first understand what comprises our paradigms. And only then can we seek to change."

"Yeah, but my paradigm conflicts with yours," Brian said. "You claim Christianity says one thing about the appropriate response to war, and I say another. In the end, have we come any closer to making a collective decision?"

"Well, funny you should ask—"

Greg stood up and slammed a hand on the table. "Nope," he declared. "No work tonight! Only vodka!"

Andrew pounded a fist to his chest. "I salute you, Greg!"

"Sit down," Kiera said. "We are who we are." She gestured for me to continue while Andrew refreshed Greg's bowl.

"Mutual affirmation leads to shared goals," I said.

"Nonsensical." Karl twisted his wedding ring.

"It's the communal hermeneutic: we interpret and create; we live and embody together."

"What does that have to do with Iraq?" Natasha asked.

"I think it's fair to say that no one prefers war to peace, right? Maybe that's our collective starting point. The teachings of Jesus seek to dampen violence. The community, in agreement, seeks to embody those same teachings. The community doesn't have to agree on every point, but it does have to seek to live out its common goal. In this case, creating peace over war."

"Blackwater," Brian said. "Blackwater prefers war to peace."

"Yep," Greg said. "As does entire the military-industrial complex."

"But not those committed to the social teachings of Christ."

"I don't know," Kiera said. "Wasn't it last week that Robertson called for America to assassinate Chavez?"

"Is he committed to the social teachings of Jesus?"

"Robertson or Chavez?"

"Exactly. Communities, acknowledging the humanity in each other, are able to unite in solidarity around a common goal, which, in this case, is justice."

"Justice?" Andrew asked, smiling. "Justice is shared in vodka!"

"Wait," Kiera said. "How does a community make peace over war?"

"It can't," Greg said. "That's why I believe what I believe. As a Mennonite, I don't participate in the Kingdoms of the World."

"For those of us not Mennonite?"

"Iraqis," I said. "It's our job—Mennonite or not—to remind the *polis* that Iraqis are not our enemies. They're not evil and they're not inhuman, even when they're killing us. We do that, we create a dissonance between the gods of patriotism and the teachings of Jesus."

"Enough!" Andrew said. "No more work. No more thesis. Tonight, we drink." He eyed me, daring me to question him.

"You'll hear no arguments from me." I held up my empty bowl.

24. Running

"THAT'S TOO FAR," BRIAN said. "Paul writes, 'As long as you are able.' We aren't able to live in peace with terrorists. They force our hand."

I've heard that before. "I hear you, really, I do. But my translation doesn't read 'As long as you are able' but 'As far as it depends on you.' It's not some escape clause. Paul's telling the Romans one can always *choose* peace over violence."

Brian and I were jogging on the Platte River trail that curved behind the seminary. It was cold and wet. Snow was falling, covering the trail in powder. Our footprints were splayed behind us.

"That's ridiculous! Where would it end? When we're all dead and rotting?"

"I didn't say it was easy. Quite frankly, I don't think Paul was a balanced guru. He's extreme. But after the Zealots, Paul saw the rising tide of revolution and cautioned the Roman Christians against it. Better to die pursuing peace than violently shaking your fist. Paul was making the case that we should always choose peace."

"And die?"

"That's the logical conclusion." My warm breath billowed out as it crashed into the crisp air. "What would happen if Christians flew to Iraq and stood between the soldier and the Insurgent? Would people die? Absolutely. But awareness would be raised, the global community would throw a fit, and people would start looking for peaceful resolutions to international disputes."

"That's the dumbest thing I've ever heard."

An Indian truck driver. A shared meal. "Maybe. But don't you think you'd have a different perspective if you lived and ate amongst the Iraqis? Not as their savior or anything, but in solidarity."

"I don't know. I'd probably be shot on sight. I seriously doubt the Taliban would welcome me with open arms."

I let out a long, slow breath. "I'm not saying I understand it. I just think it's the logical extension of Paul's message. Christians can't participate in violence. We forget Paul was trying to create a culture that was wholly opposite from the Roman Empire. One says: 'peace through victory'—*nike*, right? The other says: 'peace through loving and right action.' It's our job to feed the enemy, to overcome evil with good. In context, that can't be construed to mean overcoming evil with precision-guided bombs. It's a social program. One guy writes: 'Even a cup of water given to the thirsty becomes a means of expressing the love of Christ.' That's justice—social justice." I shrugged. "That's the gospel."

"Come on, Benjamin. There's more to the gospel than that." Brian, who was taller than me, was pulling ahead with his long strides. I was struggling to keep up.

"Is there? We twist the teachings of Jesus into some sort of self-help, self-actualization manual. But Paul is making a case that when the church ceases to care for the poor, protect the marginalized, and love its enemies then it's no longer the church. It was never about personal transformation, but rather communal transformation as way to both foster personal growth and challenge the systemic powers."

"I'm sorry. I can't go there with you. I think you're compromising too much." Brian bristled. "I'm not saying you have to buy into penal substitution or anything, but, come on, you're throwing the baby out."

We stopped running, having reached our destination.

"Are you saying that as a Christian or as an American? As an American, then yeah, penal substitution, personal transformation, protecting interests, and bombing the motherfuckers makes perfect sense. After all, they're terrorists. They're Muslims, right? But as a Christian? No, that's a different paradigm all together. You can't participate in the killing of the enemy."

"That's reductionist."

"It's where I am."

"Because of the war?"

Sure, make this about me. I was silent as I paced. "Don't discount my argument just because I've experienced it."

"You talk about theology the way you talk about Notre Dame."

"What?"

"Every year they're the best team in college football. Every year they're going to win the National Championship. You come up with all of these crazy arguments, but at the end of every season, you're proven wrong. They're just not good. Your arguments are irrational."

"War isn't college football."

"No, but to hear you talk, it's the same."

"You're an ass."

"That's why you like me."

"Whatever." We started walking towards our cars. "The hard thing is that there's so much money to be made in war. How can we know if our actions are altruistic?"

"Haliburton. Blackwater. They're people like you and me trying to make money."

"At the expense of others."

"All money is made at the expense of others."

That's a brutal outlook. "A friend of mine thinks I should take a job as a contractor after seminary."

"What would you do?"

"Fly around Iraq. Detonate IEDs."

"Do you think you'll do it?"

"Financially it makes sense; theologically it doesn't."

"You don't always have to do the virtuous thing, Benjamin. Money isn't evil."

Isn't it?

"Hey," Brian said. "What's going on with you and Natasha?"

"Changing the subject?"

"And I'm interested."

"I think I might propose."

"Seriously?"

"Yeah."

"Where?"

"Our first date was at the Boulder Book Store. I'm thinking of asking her there."

"When?"

"I have to ask her dad first. After that. A few weeks maybe."

Brian smiled. "Congratulations."

"She might say no."

"I would."

"That's funny." I unlocked my car.

"Does she know about all of your war stuff?"

I nodded. "Yeah. She knows."

"And she's okay with it?"

"I don't know," I said. "I guess we'll find out."

25. *Kelwin*

THE WALLS WERE LINED with books. A lamp casting low light stood next to a hotplate, which was used for boiling Professor Kelwin's tea—English Breakfast, no sugar, and a squirt of lemon. Professor Kelwin, William Kelwin, was leaning back in his chair eyeing me suspiciously. "And you are?"

"Benjamin, Benjamin Peters. You're my thesis advisor." I jogged his memory. "You've been my advisor for the last year. I'm examining the Christian response to war." Professor Kelwin didn't remember me. He never remembered. He was brilliant, however, in a way that excused his eccentricities. He recalled dead languages, scholars, and theories, but not students. I was fortunate to have him as an advisor. If Professor Kelwin didn't remember me, then I knew that he would, at least, remember my work.

"Ah!" a light flashed in his eyes. "Quite right. Romans 12:14—13:7?"

"Exactly. Do you have any comments on my latest chapter?"

"They were interesting, uh—"

"Benjamin."

"Yes," he nodded. "They were quite interesting, Benjamin. I would caution you against anachronism, however. It's a niggling trouble."

"And where, precisely, did you see anachronism?"

He smiled and absently adjusted his bowtie. "Paul was writing to the communities throughout Rome. He was writing to people living at the heart of the Roman Empire, that is, the *Roman Empire*, not America. Try not to confuse the two."

Blah. It galled me to have my work so succinctly critiqued. "I know, but—" He gazed at me over his glasses. "Okay," I retreated. "The *Roman Empire*. I won't make any unfair comparisons."

"Good," he clapped before handing me a stack of papers. "Here is your chapter. You'll find my notes within."

"What did you make of the section on irony?"

"It's a fringe opinion. I think you're right to mention it, but I wouldn't dwell on it."

"But it makes sense. Paul couldn't openly critique the empire or the emperor; he would've had to code his disagreements somewhat. Irony is the foil to the state's apotheosis. Without it, the section gets stripped of its power. With it, it's a powerful anti-Roman, anti-war passage."

"But neither you nor I can prove that, can we? All we have is two thousand years of tradition."

"Rooted in Augustine's pro-Empire interpretation. An error committed in majority is still an error. Didn't you teach me that?"

"Were we discussing textual criticism or exegesis?"

Does it matter? "Point taken."

Professor Kelwin sipped his tea. "It's better with lemon, you know? Something I picked up in the United Kingdom." He sighed. "Is there anything else that I can help you with?"

"No."

"Well, in that case, why not have your revisions to me by the end of the month? Is that convenient?"

"Yes." I stood.

"Oh, and one thing." I turned. "A few professors and I are interested in exploring the idea of suffering as it relates to war. We've scheduled a brown bag lunch and discussion group in four weeks' time. I would be honored if you would prepare a few remarks. It need neither be profound nor theological, but I imagine, with your experience you would have something to share. Would you be interested?"

I was interested, but intimidated. The minds of seminary professors were foreign objects. The majority of them read monographs in Greek, enjoyed parsing Hebrew, and, I'm sure, ate lunch while conversing in Aramaic. What, if anything, could I say to this group that they hadn't already read, been published on, or translated from the theological German? Before I could change my mind, I blurted: "Yes."

"Splendid."

Professor Kelwin shut the door.

26. Social

THE SKY WAS COLORLESS, burgeoned with snow. At any moment, the clouds would burst. I tightened the scarf around my neck and trudged to the seminary's library. Andrew and Kiera were occupying a corner, whispering. I waved as I passed them and entered our reserved room. I de-winterized and sat. Brian walked in shortly after, as did Karl and Greg, whose beard was weighted down with ice and snow. We talked for a time before starting in earnest.

Andrew and Kiera were expecting. Karl and his wife were contemplating teaching English in China. Brian had recently taken a position at a local church. And Greg was planning on working at an inner-city alternative high school. "I want to mold America's youth," he said, tugging his beard.

My course work would soon be finished with only my thesis to complete. With budding anxiety, I realized I had no plan. I didn't want to work at either a church or a school. I had tossed around the idea of pursuing a PhD, but didn't think I would gain acceptance. And, even if I did, I was stuck in Denver due to my Marine Reserve commitment. No, my only hope was to graduate and propose to Natasha. The rest would fall into place. It was a solid plan.

"Benjamin," Brian said. "You're up. What do you have for us?"

"Alright," I said, pulling papers from my satchel. "Focusing on 13:1–7, I found an interesting piece on Paul and irony. The author posits that Paul wrote to the Romans in some sort of hidden transcript in order to avoid the ire of the empire."

"*The Da Vinci Code*?"

"Did you crack it?" Andrew asked.

"What? No. Paul couldn't critique the empire outright. It would've been the death of him."

"Connect the dots," Karl said.

"How often have you heard a preacher say, 'Submit to the authorities,' without qualification? It's an interpretation that leads to some pretty heinous outcomes. But there was no way Paul could've come out and said: 'the Kingdom of God, not the Empire of Rome, is to be your guiding conscience'—especially during Nero's reign of crazy. So what's he do? He codes his language. It's subtle, but it speaks volumes."

"Caesar is Lord," Kiera said.

"Which meant, ultimately, that all authority lay with Caesar. But listen: 'Let every person be subject to the governing authorities. For, it is not authority if it is not by God, and those that exist have been ordered by God.'"

"Ha!" Greg laughed. "How didn't I notice that before?"

"Easy peasy," I said, stealing Greg's line. "You're only where you are, Caesar, because God chose to order the system in such a way that there is an Emperor, and it just so happens to fall to you—don't screw it up. Not everyone agrees, however."

"If God has ordered the authorities," Andrew started, "then the end of Caesar's power does not lie with him, but with God."

"Even Caesar has to answer to someone," I said. "Which limits Caesar's power. Of course, Paul had to be subtle. 'All authority lies with God, not Caesar,' wouldn't have gone over really well. So the government isn't divine, only divinely intended. So—who knew?—Christians are atheists."

"But," Karl interrupted, "the Greek for 'authorities' could mean either 'angels' or 'powers,' it doesn't necessarily have to read, 'governing authorities.'"

"In context though? I mean, directly after this, Paul dives into the gritty details of taxation in verses 6–7. Do angels care about taxes?"

"This has to be an interpolation," Kiera said. "There's Paul, scratching away on a piece of papyri, when he jumps from virtue ethics to subversive-political discourse. That's strange, right? Do you think he actually wrote this?"

"You're not the only one asking that question."

"I don't think it's a huge stretch to say Paul wrote this," Greg said. "But either way, I'm not sure it matters. Love your enemies and submit to God. No matter the author," he shrugged, "it aligns with Jesus."

"What's the difference," Andrew asked, "between submission to God and blind obedience to the authorities?"

"Um . . . well, Bush asks us to do something contrary to a Christian paradigm, so what do we do? A couple of things. One, peacefully refuse. Two, submit to his right to punish us."

Brian shook his head. "Here it is! We're back to Christians killing themselves. Oh, I know, let's all jump of a cliff. Why? Well, I don't know, Benjamin said to."

"No, we're back to Christians submitting to the authorities' right to execute them. There's a difference. One is suicide, the other follows the example set by Christ."

"No way," Andrew said. "Sounds like a dictatorship."

"What? Look, I understand death. And I understand execution. But that's not the point."

"What is?"

"That this is the norm that Paul was carving out for the new community of Jews and Gentiles united in Christ. Yoder called it, 'Revolutionary Subordination.' I peacefully and nonviolently resist, but then I allow you to punish me. In this way, the systemic injustice of empire is unmasked."

Karl shook his head. "Nope. Don't see it. And I certainly don't think I could live it out."

"In our context, who knows? But in first-century Rome, one couldn't win a war against the empire, but one could unmask its violence."

"That's very Gandhi of you."

"I'm not saying I've embodied this. If I had, then I wouldn't have enlisted in the Marine Corps. But that's what Paul's words mean in our context—refusing to participate in the world's systems of violence."

"But Paul says the authorities bear the sword, right? Of all people, the authorities have the right to wield a big stick."

"But the stick isn't big and it's not really a stick. Karl, you're practically Greek. What does μάχαιραν mean?"

"Uh, it's been awhile. Let me think . . . 'sword,' right? Like a short sword." He held up his hands. "Maybe this long?"

"Not the sword of a Legionnaire. It's more like a dagger than anything else, and most likely a symbol of *judicial* authority. So Paul's not making a statement about the authorities' right to declare war or to execute capital punishment."

"Because the Romans crucified?"

"Exactly. It symbolizes the way a government exercises dominion over its subjects through an appeal to violence. "

"Technologies of power."

"See? Foucault *does* matter," I said. "Anyway, where Paul is flawed is in his assumption that the laws of the state always embody moral principles—not the most historically accurate assumption."

"Just because God orders the powers, doesn't mean rulers always make right decisions."

"Simple," Kiera said.

"But we have examples in our own time, right?"

"Which are?"

"I don't know? Bloody Sunday's one."

"The U2 song?"

"That's different."

"They were beaten and gassed," Kiera said.

"Yeah. But it's an example of living out one's beliefs while simultaneously submitting to the authorities' right to punish."

"That's easy to say, sitting here," Greg said. "But we're white. All of us. At a super white institution."

I nodded. "I don't disagree with you."

"Double negative."

"Funny."

"What do you make of, 'Will bring judgment upon themselves'?" Kiera asked.

I shuffled through my notes. "It's a Semitism meaning, 'to be condemned,' which could mean any number of things: punishment by the state, eternal damnation, or simply living into the consequences of one's actions." I shrugged. "Sometimes all we have are the options."

"Exegesis as *Choose Your Own Adventure*," Greg said.

"I'm looking at it right here," Brian broke in:

For rulers hold no terror for those who do right, but for those who do wrong. Do you want to be free from fear of the one in authority? Then do what is right and you will be commended. For the one in authority is God's servant for your good. But if you do wrong, be afraid, for rulers do not bear the sword for no reason. They are God's servants, agents of wrath to bring punishment on the wrongdoer.

I'm not seeing it, man. I think you're veering into the social gospel, and we've talked about it before. You're missing too much."

"I'm not making this shit up, Brian. Look at the passage you just quoted. What does it say? 'For the one in authority is God's *servant* for your good.' This isn't some spiritual office. The word Paul uses describes menial labor, something all Roman citizens frowned upon, not to mention the emperor. It's coded and hidden language that subverts the emperor's authority. I don't think this passage is straightforward. What's easy about understanding a two-thousand-year old document written in a dead language?"

"Where's mention of the gospel in all that you've said, which, by the way, is the easiest thing in the world to understand?"

I shook my head, stood up, and started pacing. "What's the gospel?"

"The mystery of Christ's death and resurrection," Karl answered. "Which reconciles creation to its creator."

"What about the life of Jesus?"

"Sure," Brian said. "But you can't reduce the mystery of incarnation, death, and resurrection to some sort of social program."

I laughed. "The church is a social program, Brian. Your commitment to a spiritual interpretation of Jesus' life cripples your understanding of Jesus' teachings and death. The atonement, whatever it was, was surely the unmasking of systemic injustice and death. There is nothing else we can verifiably know. Penal substitution, *Christus Victor*, liberation, the embodiment of love—these are metaphors, theories, and readings subject to flaws and changes over time. We can, however, know the historical and social implications of Jesus' death at a given point in time. But that's besides the point, what makes you so uncomfortable is that Paul is taking the teachings of Jesus, coated in dust and blood, and applying them, literally, to the real world."

"Not to belabor the point," Brian said. "But there's more to it than that."

I shook my head. "Maybe I'm wrong and the whole damn thing is about personal salvation. But maybe, just maybe, Jesus' teachings were about whole communities connecting to God while living under the unbearable oppression of empire."

"Then why don't more pastors preach that?"

"Because individualism, as a philosophy, has seeped so deeply into our culture that we're incapable of interpreting our experiences outside of it. We anachronistically, and wrongly, apply twenty-first-century individualism to all of our exegesis. We do it without even knowing it. And, in doing it, we lose the social implications of the New Testament."

"So what does Jesus' death accomplish?" Brian asked.

I poured more coffee before sitting down. "It reveals the fetid reality of systemic injustice and it provides hope for the faceless majority living beneath it."

"What hope?"

"That there's another way to live. The teachings and death of Jesus were always to inform the way we live, not what happens after we die."

"So it's social."

"I have no idea what it is. I'm compiling and reporting data."

"That's it! Don't you see?" Brian asked. "You're spewing facts that sound great, but facts don't change hearts. Jesus wasn't about data, he was about relationship."

"Jesus doesn't care about your heart," I said, frustrated. "He cares about lives both changed and transformed—in community—while embodying the kingdom of God, which means working for and partnering with the oppressed, marginalized, and forgotten. The gospel isn't a twenty-first-century tool for self-actualization."

It was Brian's turn to shake his head. "One, I'm not talking about self-actualization. Two, I don't think you really believe what you're saying." His voice softened. "You're bitter about Iraq."

INTERLUDE

"AND HOW ARE YOU today?" Trent asked.

"I'm well," I said. We were walking along the Highline Canal. Winter had loosened its grip on spring, giving way to summer. The trees around us were in full bloom, overgrowing the path on which we walked. Insects flitted about while birds, overhead, chirped in delight. Trent, who always counseled from the comfort of his office, had suggested, uncharacteristically, that we spend our hour strolling outdoors.

"Summer's here," he said. "You must be prepping for your two weeks with the Marine Corps."

"Yeah."

"Where will you be headed?"

"Korea. The Marine Corps has decided to make my final summer with them memorable. I'll be participating in a two-week war game."

"Game?"

"What would we do if North Korea attacked South Korea? It's a joint game between United States Marines and South Korean Marines."

"How do you feel about that?"

A jogger passed on our left. "I don't have a choice. I could refuse to go and be dishonorably discharged or tossed in the brig. Yes, I disagree with war, but I also know that when I signed up for the Marines, I made a commitment. Seeing my eight years to their end would be a good thing for me."

"It's a matter of staying true to your word, even if your thoughts on the matter have changed."

"Yeah . . . I guess."

"What's most important to you?"

"This is going to sound dumb, but Natasha and I are getting married this summer and—"

"After Korea?"

"Yeah. And somehow being faithful to Natasha is wrapped up in seeing my Marine Corps contract through to its end."

"I see."

"Not exactly logical though."

"Emotions rarely are," Trent said.

"What do you think I should do?"

"I'm not in the business of providing advice."

"I've noticed."

Trent laughed. "Only you can make that decision, Benjamin—conscientious objector or man of your word. Perhaps they're the same thing. Either way, I can't advise you."

"Last summer, at the rifle range in Wyoming, Mexico asked me if I wanted to become an independent contractor with him."

"I remember."

"I'm getting married this summer and I'll finish my course work in the fall. All I'll have left before graduation is my thesis. I have no idea what I'm going to do for work."

"Natasha's a teacher, isn't that correct?"

"Yeah, but I'll need something."

"From what I understand, the role of an independent contractor wouldn't be a great fit."

"No, I don't think it would. But it'd be a lot of money."

"Commitment or belief; values or money—at some point, we all have to make those decisions."

27. Brown Bag

THE ROOM WAS BURSTING. No seat was vacant; people lined the walls. My stomach, for a moment, lurched as I strode to the front table and took my seat with the other panelist.

Professor Kelwin stood and introduced me. He informed the room that I was a Marine who was writing his thesis on just war and pacifism. He introduced the other panelist, Donald, as a Major in the Air Force. "Donald," Professor Kelwin said, "graduated from the Air Force Academy, served overseas, and has now joined us at Denver Seminary so that he might go back into the world as a military chaplain. His rank, if I speak correctly, is that of Major." Donald nodded his head.

An academy graduate and a chaplain—this outta be fun.

"I would like to begin," Professor Kelwin said, "by stating the obvious. This room is filled with learners and, as such, we will respect one another's opinion. We all have different backgrounds and experiences, all of which inform our theology in some way. Be honest, speak plainly, and, above all, be courteous." He was frowning. "I would like to start with the question: what is suffering and how does it impinge or manifest itself in war?" He turned to Donald and nodded. "If you would begin."

Donald cleared his throat and absently adjusted the glass he was clutching. "Suffering can take on many forms: persecution, separation, or the death of a loved one. I deal with it, and have dealt with it, in varying ways. But, in war specifically, I find that suffering makes believers of us all. It's my opinion that a firm reliance on Christ and *his* suffering can help even the weakest bear up under times of crushing weight." Heads around the room bobbed in approval. "War, though evil, is a necessary evil. It upholds justice and the innocent and it both reprimands and judges. Any suffering that arises due to war must be seen from the perspective of a perfect God whose ways are not our ways."

Professor Kelwin leaned forward. "In your estimation, there are times when God uses war to bring about a change in his people?"

"Absolutely. War is never preferable, but, at times, it is necessary."

"And how would you answer, Benjamin?"

I surveyed Donald. He was older than I, balding, and wearing glasses. He was dressed in his uniform, firmly pressed, a deep blue. "I've been to war, and if I've learned anything, then it's this: war is both dehumanizing and arbitrary. In war, there's this profound sense of 'this is not how it's supposed to be.'"

"And by 'it,' you mean?"

"Life . . . human interaction."

"Interesting," Professor Kelwin said. "So God is arbitrary?"

"No. War is arbitrary."

Donald was shaking his head. "God is sovereign and immutable."

Really? "In that case," I said, "I guess we can all leave."

"Before you dismiss us," Donald replied, "let me present just war. I think it'll illuminate this conversation and provide us with the appropriate framework through which to understand suffering in war. You, then, can freely opine. Agreed?"

"Sure."

Professor Kelwin was smiling, titillated.

28. *Just War*

"Let me begin by saying that war is abhorrent. All just war theorists would say as much. The question is not whether war is good or bad or if Christians should take up arms for their nation or cause, but rather, is war avoidable. I would say, 'No, it isn't.' I think war serves a purpose for three reasons: it embodies the love of neighbor; it enacts justice; it is an aegis for the innocent." People throughout the room were either nodding or taking notes.

I started to sweat.

Donald continued: "Just war can be broken into three considerations: *jus ad bellum*, *jus in bello*, and *jus post bellum*—justice before, during, and after war. This might seem like minutia, but these are important distinctions.

"*Jus ad bellum*, or justice before war, is concerned with the justification of resorting to war. People claim that the Iraq war was 'unjust.' The criteria for *jus ad bellum* would prove them wrong. The Iraq war had a just cause, was waged by a legitimate authority, and was fought with the right intention. It was, though not all think so, a last resort. It was proportionate and, of course, we had a reasonable hope of military success. By these standards, the Iraq war was justly commenced.

"*Jus in bello*, or justice in war, examines how nations conduct their war once begun. Don't kill noncombatants, fight proportionately, and honor the legal rights of enemy soldiers and civilians. By these standards, America is conducting its war exceedingly well."

"Yes," Professor Kelwin interrupted. "But we've all seen the images of Abu Ghraib. How is America upholding the legal rights of its prisoners in such an instance?"

Donald nodded. "That was an unfortunate incident, to be sure, but these things happen in all wars. The actions of a few do not represent the whole, nor do they delegitimize the war."

That's putting it mildly.

Professor Kelwin nodded.

"Well, *jus post bellum*, or justice after war, concerns itself with the proper way to end wars and focuses on the re-establishment of both peace and security. Though we haven't reached this stage yet, I'm confident America will do this well.

"Just war theory then, offers guidelines for considering a multi-dimensional war. It's best not to view these guidelines as some sort of public policy checklist, but rather as an embodiment of the Christian life. What's important to understand is that just war is driven neither by hatred nor by a desire for the death and destruction of the enemy, but by the love that desires to bestow the benefits of a just peace upon the enemy."

Yeah, with bombs. "Great summary," I said.

Donald nodded.

"The just war position states that I can kill my enemy as long as he or she is killed in love, correct?"

"In a sense."

"I'm speaking from experience, but one can't pull the trigger in love. Killing the other only happens after a process of dehumanization, which is antithetical to love. The enemy isn't human. The enemy is a beast, less than. Something created by the powers for the solider to prey upon. The soldier, then, trades his or her humanity for the ability to take the life of a human turned enemy turned beast. To pull the trigger, one must hate."

"But God is just," Donald said, shaking his head. "It follows that humans, imitating God, should fight for justice as well. It's a high calling for a soldier, to be sure, but it's a necessary one. God uses force to check evil and bring justice."

"So God has ordained the killing, through his people, of his creation?"

"Well, yes, but that's how God has ordered things . . . society. He has established the socio-political realm in such a way as to appoint the authorities whose job it is to punish evil. You see? The state is a sovereign power, ordained by heaven, which is responsible for the common good, to prevent the worst from happening, so to speak."

"What happens when the state usurps the common good?"

"That's an unfortunate reality, but I believe God then calls an equally powerful state to challenge such despotism. If our neighbor is being slaughtered, we don't just stand by and do nothing. It's the love of neighbor *and* enemy that prompts us to use force in order to stop wrongdoing and to punish wrongdoers. See? War protects the innocent. And a just war limits the violence inherent in war."

"It sounds to me that just war doesn't limit violence, but rather legitimizes it."

"Be that as it may," Donald said, "just war, at least, seeks to bring some good out of the bad. As far as I know, it's the only structured moral context for thinking about war as a practical matter."

"*Some* good? It's the nature of war that third parties die."

"Innocent people, regrettably, are killed in a just war. But—"

"Regrettably?"

"Yes. But the justice of a war is not compromised when the innocent are killed. I can foresee that certain acts of force will kill innocent people without intending those deaths."

"Innocent deaths ought not to be 'regrettable.'"

"Well let's hear your side then."

29. Pacifism

I SHIFTED, LOOKING AROUND the room. Some attendees were visibly angry, some contemplative, and some waiting with pen in hand. I breathed and then started. "War is corrupt. It stands against the revolutionary teachings of Jesus. The Sermon on the Mount isn't practical, but it's essential. Those who minimize or legitimize war and suffering often sideline Jesus' difficult teachings for more politically pragmatic viewpoints."

Donald scoffed.

"Pacifism is often misconstrued as being passive, right?"

"Because it is."

"Well, it's not. Pacifism doesn't mean idling around while political strife rages. It's, rather, the active and often difficult enactment of Jesus' teachings.

"That being said, pacifism, like just war, has a storied past. A pacifist can either be principled or strategic. A principled pacifist is motivated by the belief that violent acts are unacceptable no matter what. A strategic pacifist, however, renounces violence on the basis that the use of violence is illegitimate in some contexts but not others."

"And the implications?" Professor Kelwin asked.

"Well, violence, for a strategic pacifist, is illegitimate because of its likely result rather than because of any absolute prohibition." Donald leaned back and crossed his arms. "Unfortunately, I don't have the time to make all of the necessary distinctions (absolute versus classical; separatist versus politically engaged; or communal versus universal), but, suffice it to say, a middling pacifist would say something like: 'Christians must be pacifist, and the world might become more peaceful through activism in cooperation with other pacifists.' That being said, I think God's original design was peace—"

"On what," Professor Kelwin interrupted, "are you basing that assertion?"

"Well, in the New Testament, both Jesus' and Paul's command to love one's enemies."

"I see."

"Also, the 'gospel,' properly defined, speaks to pacifism."

"How so?"

"The gospel, to me, is the good news of reconciliation, which restores humanity to God, humanity to humanity, and humanity to environment. Essentially, the gospel is the complete cosmic restoration of peace and harmony."

"Even if that's true," Donald said, "governments will still kill their people. So if we are to work towards God's peace—for the least of these—how can one do that without the use of force?"

"I don't know," I acknowledged. "Pacifism's tool for social change is nonviolence."

"Nonviolence?" Donald raised an eyebrow.

"Yeah, nonviolence, which breaks the cycle of violence simply by refusing to respond in kind. Why? Because redemptive violence is a myth."

"All well and good," Donald said. "But that won't protect you when you've a gun to your head or when the terrorists are flying planes into our buildings. War is the continuation of polices by other means. Sometimes, in other words, it's the only practical option that we have. You can wish it away, but that only abdicates your responsibility."

"Wish it away? I don't want to wish it away. There are a lot of terrible realities in the world: hunger, civil war, genocide. Those realities won't magically vanish. But we've been trying to solve those problems through war forever. It's not working. Nonviolence doesn't seek to do away with difficult issues; rather, it reverses the cycle of violence by accepting suffering without retaliation. A way that isn't often used, but when it is, it's successful."

"Give me an example."

"Gandhi, King, Tutu . . . *Lysistrata*. And if these men and women taught us anything, then it's that seeking to achieve peace through nonviolence doesn't happen because people are individually nice; one can't simply pray for change. Nonviolence is, and must be a social, economic, and political arrangement, aggressively and ingeniously forged."

"Are you married?" Donald asked.

"No, engaged. I'm getting married this summer."

"So, after you're married, what would you do if you came home to a man raping your wife?"

Our eyes locked. If the room was silent before, then it was dead now. "I don't know, Donald. I'm no hero. I'm not a savior. What you describe is evil . . . terrible, but I have no way of knowing what I would do if put in that position. What I do know is that we should never glorify killing, especially killing in response to an evil act."

"Okay then," Donald said, "what about Hitler?"

30. Philanthropy

"Why does everyone always ask that?"

"He was wholly evil," Donald said. "A man who could only be stopped through force."

"We all know how Bonhoeffer responded when pushed, but what would've happened in Germany had the church acted like the church? I know, when discussing history, that it's all too easy to generalize a complex situation, but had the church, from the outset, not assimilated its teachings to the National Socialist Party, then would the course of events changed? Who can say?"

"I can," Donald said. "And the answer is, 'No.'"

"Your clarity is comforting."

"Please, if you would, Benjamin, continue," Professor Kelwin said.

"Look, while pacifists are clear in their call for peace and nonviolence, they're also realistic about systemic evils."

"A state, in reality, can neither fund nor support this sort of thing," Donald said. "You can't force people into nonviolence. It's absurd."

"No, but you can reeducate. We currently allow ROTC programs into our high schools. And to teach what? Patriotic violence? We teach our students to do their duty and worship the gods of state. Why not fund programs that teach the way of either nonviolence or restorative justice? What of AmeriCorps, the Peace Corps, or Teach for America? Our defense budget, alone, suggests where our priorities lie. Why not redirect that money into nonviolent education?"

"The state has a responsibility to protect its people and, last I checked, America was the most generous nation in the world."

"We devote a smaller percentage of national income to developmental assistance than nearly any other developed nation. We spend, however, six billion a month on the Iraq War. Why can't we divert some, just some of that money to peacemaking activities? War delivers peace to no one. All we're doing is perpetuating an unsustainable system of violence."

"Well," Donald said. "I don't believe in Christian philanthropy."

"Christian philanthropy," I said. "'Philanthropy?' That's the word you want to use? Not biblical justice?"

"No. The gospel is between an individual and his God; it's neither a social program nor a political system. And biblical justice is an eschatological reality seen in both the future and the present. Christ is coming back; Christ will judge. In the meantime, he's left us to discern who should or shouldn't be judged."

"Who is the 'us?'" I asked. "Are you speaking about Christians or Americans?"

"I am an American and a Christian," Donald said. "I'm well aware what both identities offer."

"Gentlemen," Professor Kelwin interrupted, "I believe we've drifted."

"In the end," I said, "'Christian philanthropy,' reminds us that a nation can't build peace on a foundation of violence and systemic evil. If just war too easily blurs with national interests, then pacifism seeks to correct that trend. To assert a faith that embraces the nonviolence of Jesus is to proclaim oneself an atheist in relation to the preferred gods of nationalism and patriotism."

31. Closing Arguments

"Interesting," Professor Kelwin said. "Do either of you have any closing thoughts?"

"One more thing," I said. "Pacifism claims the appropriate response to war is not an attempt to make war more just, but to abandon war as a method for solving international disputes."

"How on earth would you fight terrorism?" Donald asked. "It has to be combated and just war, at least, provides some sort of moral framework for that."

"I don't disagree with you, Donald, really, I don't. But, I think it is becoming increasingly clear that war is an inappropriate tool to combat terrorism. Eisenhower said: 'Every gun that is made, every warship launched, every rocket fired signifies, in the final sense, a theft from those who hunger and are not fed, those who are cold and are not clothed.'"

"Yes," acknowledged Donald. "What's your point?"

"War doesn't and isn't working. We need another option. Even Colin Powell acknowledged that 'the war against terror is bound up in the war against poverty.' So maybe, if we work towards sustainable development in countries that foster terrorism, we'll see a difference. We don't need war, we need to address the root causes of terrorism: economic and political instability, poverty and hunger, to name a few."

"Well, that sounds like the white man's burden: they're broken, so we'll fix them. There's an obligation to overcome evil, but when you get into economic and political solutions, things get too sticky. I don't know. It just seems that pacifists default on their moral obligation to protect—not fix—the innocent. It might not be the perfect option, but at least just war theorists hear the suffering of the masses and seek to do something about it."

"What's needed is more, not less, political engagement—provided that it's nonpartisan."

"It seems to me that you are abandoning your neighbor to the despot. The church is to serve all and, because Christians believe evil is real, both justice and charity compel us to serve our neighbor and the common good by using force to stop evil."

"The thing is, Donald, I agree with you completely. Where we disagree, however, is the role of violence in serving one's neighbor."

"Well," Professor Kelwin said. "We've moved from suffering to just war to pacifism." He stood up and turned towards the audience. "It's been invigorating."

The audience let out a collective sigh and started murmuring.

I stood and stretched before packing my notes.

Donald stuck out his hand. "It may not mean much to you, but thank you for your service."

"You're welcome," I said, shaking his hand. "I thank you as well."

"Are you still in?"

"Yeah. I have a year left on my contract."

He smiled. "I bet your commanding officers love you."

"It's certainly not the best relationship."

"Well, good luck to you," he said, patting me on the shoulder.

Part Three

1. Korea

"LISTEN UP, MARINES," CAPTAIN said. "After the bus takes you to the museum, a tour guide will meet you. You *will* follow her throughout your tour. Do I make myself clear?"

I had been in Korea for a week, working the night shift for a joint-command annual war game. It was my job to process whatever fake intelligence the computer spewed out and brief the base's Colonel on what movements the North Koreans were making.

I was living in a large tent with forty other Marines. We slept on cots nestled against each other. The tent was constantly dark, because either the day or the night shift was sleeping. We showered in a small water tent and shaved in cold, stale water. The chow tent served MREs. During my shift, I worked next to Mexico, which afforded us the opportunity to discuss our potential futures as contractors in Iraq.

It was muggy and hot. Sweat was trickling down my back. We were headed to Seoul's Korean War Museum. South Koreans, or at least the ones I had interacted with, loved United States Marines. Every time I chatted with one, they told me thank you for defending them in their great war. I would shake their hand and say something pleasant.

"After you tour the museum, you'll be taken to Market Ally," the Captain continued. "You can buy all sorts of shit and souvenirs. There are restaurants and bars. Feel free to eat and drink. But hear me now, Marines: do not get drunk, do not start a fight, and do not spend time with the 'buy-me-drink girls.' Do you understand?"

"Yes, sir," we mumbled.

"You represent the United States. I expect you to act like it." He looked us over before storming off. We boarded the bus. The driver fired up the engine and, with it, his Asian karaoke.

"What the hell is a 'buy-me-drink girl?'"

"Shit, Peters, what do you think it is? It's one of the pleasures of serving in Korea."

"A prostitute?"

"Don't make it sound so dirty."

"What?"

"Look, go into a bar and a girl'll walk up to you. 'Buy me drink,' she'll say. You can buy her a drink or not, it's your choice. But if you do, then maybe you'll get option two."

"Which is?"

"Do I have to spell it?"

"No."

"Hell, Peters, you're getting married this summer, right?"

"Yeah."

"What better way to celebrate?"

"Dude."

"Is your Bible shit getting in the way?"

"'Bible shit?' No. I don't need 'Bible shit' to stop me from paying a woman to have sex, just common decency."

He shrugged. "Well, Peters, for what it's worth, it's not my style either."

"Glad to hear it."

"Hey," Mexico said, "speaking of weird shit, did you read that report last night?"

"Which one?"

"On North Korea's labor camps?"

"Skimmed it. Why?"

"This one guy in the report, Minjun, said he'd served in their military for years. He was some sort of national advisor. Anyway, he claims he retired with honor, but in his retirement started reading and shit. Well, his views change a bit, and he decided North Korea ain't all it's cracked up to be. Kim Jung gets wind of it and ships the poor bastard off to some camp. Thing is, Minjun's like sixty and now breaking rocks every day, eating gruel."

"What happened to him?"

"He escaped through China. Told the whole story to the United Nations. It was their report."

"I can't believe that still happens."

"That's the sort of shit we ought to be going to war for, if you ask me."

The bus stopped. We debarked. Across the street an archery competition was underway. Our tour guide pointed it out before steering us into the museum. She guided us through the Korean War memorabilia. We saw old tanks and uniforms. She discussed the political tensions between North and South Korea, and talked of the Demilitarized Zone. "We are a culture," she said, "that lives in a constant state of war. Because of this, all men must serve in the military."

"For how long?"

"Twenty-one months," she said. Her English was very good.

"What happens if someone refuses?"

"They must go to jail."

Afterwards, we boarded the bus and drove to the tourist strip. We shuffled the streets, constantly ambushed by merchants of various wares. Mexico and I ducked into a small restaurant for reprieve. We waited at the door for a server to seat us. No one came. The Koreans already sitting stared at us. A few minutes passed so we decided to seat ourselves. As soon as we were comfortable, a waitress came over and took our order. She told us that in Korea, the customer must seat him or herself. "Thanks for letting us figure that out," Mexico said. We ate a Korean soup with a side dish of Kimchi. The soup was delicious; the Kimchi wasn't. It tasted like raw sewage.

We finished our meal and met up with a few active-duty Marines from our night shift. They told us of a bar that was nearby and asked us if we wanted to tag along. We said we did and followed through the maze of stalls and merchants. We stopped in front of a dim doorway. Black stairs led down. "Hey," I whispered to Mexico. "Is this one of the places?"

"Come in and look around. If it's weird, we'll leave."

"Alright." We descended.

As soon as we opened the doors, Korean women flowed out and grabbed our arms. They led us inside and sat us at tables throughout the bar. Korean pop music was blasting through the speakers. The woman I was sitting with yelled over the noise: "Buy me drink?" She was beautiful. I looked for Mexico. He was sitting at a table across the bar.

"I'm out, man." I shouted over the music. "We'll see you on the bus."

"Alright. The beer's cheap, so I think I'll stay for a bit."

I climbed back into the fresh light of day and trudged back to the bus. Koreans called out: "Very good price for you!" I waved them off.

Staring out the window—the sights and sounds of Seoul struck me. The sun began to set as the bus slowly filled. The driver started the engine. We waited for stragglers. Mexico boarded and found his seat. The bus pulled away from the curb.

I had one week left in Korea, after which I would have a year left on my contract. Twelve more drill weekends and my commitment to the United States Marine Corps would end. Another bus ride through the dark and winding streets of San Diego had started it all. *You are now property of the United States*

Government. You will not eat, drink, or shit, without the government's approval. That means me, Recruits. I will tell you when and how to breathe. Ambule had been right. I could believe what I wanted, but, in the end, I was a marked man—stamped with an Eagle, Globe, and Anchor. We warred, we killed, and we ruled. I was the system.

A week passed.

I flew home and married my wife.

2. *Street School*

I MARRIED NATASHA AND got a job at the same inner-city high school, the Street School, where Greg taught. He was teaching English and Bible, while I was teaching United States history, world history, and entrepreneurship, subjects that were a mystery to me. But it was a financially hurting school with a high turnover rate, and I needed the money. I planned on juggling my thesis on the weekends. The first semester was painful. Not only were the students difficult, but it was also my first teaching experience. Natasha, who had been teaching for three years, helped me develop my lesson plans and grade papers. We would stay up late, discussing both how to teach and how to relate to my students.

I was underprepared.

"How was your first day?" Natasha asked.

"I have a classroom filled with stereotypes and statistics. I knew it'd be hard, but—"

"What do you mean?"

"Nothing. These kids have nothing. No resources: money, family . . . love. I don't know. And I'm there, to what, save them? So they can climb the ladder of success?"

"No. Teach them."

"Which is so much easier."

‡ ‡ ‡

That first semester, I befriended a student named Miguel. He played the guitar, but struggled with school. One day, he caught me walking to my car after school. He told me his girlfriend was pregnant. "What should I do?"

"What do you want to do?"

"I want to keep it."

"Then do."

"But what about money? Work?"

"You can test out of high school and get your GED if you really need to. You're smart enough for that." He was, though he didn't always apply himself.

"And then what? Work at Autozone for the rest of my life? No way, mister." *Mister* was how my students referred to me. "I'm thinking about the military. You served, right?"

The military? There were a lot of great programs for high school students, but he didn't have the past experience to gain acceptance. One of the services, as long as he had his GED, would take him. *He could use the discipline. But it's the military.* All that he'd heard about the military was that it was a steady job and it would pay for college. What he didn't realize, was the unsaid, that he would be in either Afghanistan or Iraq before the year's end. *Shit, I have to say something.*

I took a deep breath. "It's a steady job and you would be able to provide for your child. That's true."

"But?"

I shook my head. "No 'buts.' Iraq isn't a joke though."

"Shit, mister," he said, smiling. "That ain't nothing compared to what I seen."

I shrugged. "I can connect you with a recruiter."

‡ ‡ ‡

"Who can tell me what Monday is?" It was our first day back after the mid-winter break.

Miguel raised his hand. "Martin Luther King Jr. Day, mister."

"That's right. So today, I was thinking we could read *Letter from a Birmingham Jail.* Cool?"

Silence.

"Okay. Well, that's what we're going to do."

We read:

"You may well ask, 'Why direct action, why sit-ins, marches, and so forth? Isn't negotiation a better path?' You are exactly right in your call for negotiation. Indeed, this is the purpose of direct action. Nonviolent direct action seeks to create such a crisis and establish such creative tension that a community that has consistently refused to negotiate is forced to confront the issue."

"Alright, so what's going on here?"

"King was thrown in jail for protesting whites."

"Okay. So . . . was that good or bad?"

"It's bullshit, mister," Jose, a freshman, said. "You know that. It ain't fair. The white people were treating the black people like dogs or something."

"So what did King do?"

"He, like, used different tactics and stuff."

"Yeah," Miguel said. "He was all nonviolent and shit."

Nice. "Which means?"

Miguel shrugged. "He wasn't into killing."

Jamal, a recent transfer, shifted in his seat and started shaking his head.

"Do you have something to add?"

"No."

"Okay. No pressure. Does anyone else?"

"Actually, mister, I do have something to say."

"Alright, Jamal. The floor's yours."

"That history ain't real, man. There's an alternative to all this shit. King was a dumbass who did nothing but get niggers killed."

"Excuse me?"

"Man, you heard. You want to parade King around once a year and talk about how great whites are, but that's some bullshit. King got us killed. That's all. If I'd lived back then, I'd just start shooting whites, you know?"

I'm loosing control. Should I say something? "Um—"

"There's this video I was watching at home, and it told me all about it, man. You need to expand your understanding, mister. But all that to say, ain't no one gonna get me killed."

I'm an idiot. "Well, Jamal—"

"Whatever, mister."

"Okay. Let's move on."

3. *Goosetown*

We were at the Goosetown, a local pub. Many of us had either graduated or started working. It was late in the day and the atmosphere was dim. Only Andrew and I were still working on our theses. The others still came for enjoyment.

"Do you have an example," Karl asked, "reflecting Paul's pacifistic tendencies?"

I drank from a swarthy pint before answering. "Yeah. Well, yes and no. I'm not actually sure Paul was a pacifist."

The group shook their heads and collectively groaned. "You raised a fricking stink last spring during that brown bag lunch."

"I know. But for precision's sake, I think Paul's teaching more fully embodies a theory called, 'just peacemaking.'"

"Sounds familiar."

"It is," Brian said, "but it's also an unnecessary digression. We're here to discuss your 'first-century test case.'"

"One informs the other," I said. "But it really doesn't matter where we start."

"The test case then," Kiera said.

"Do it."

"Alright, well, you can learn a lot about both violence and religion by comparing different religious groups in similar settings. I'll be looking at how each group chose to disengage from their larger, dominant group. In both cases, the dominant group was Rome. You following?"

They nodded.

"I chose the Christians in Rome around CE 64 and the Zealot movement of Palestine in CE 70."

Greg raised his hand.

"My reasons for doing so will be revealed in time."

He dropped his hand.

"In CE 64 Nero started doing some pretty nasty stuff to the Roman Christians."

"Why?"

"Some sources say that it was because of a great fire that burned a bunch of Roman districts. Nero claimed that it was, you know, the dirty Christians that started it. Most Romans were willing to accept his accusation because the majority despised the Christian community."

"Why?"

"You sound like one of my students." I paused and assumed my best teacherly voice. "Because, Andrew, they were regarded as having usurped the Roman way of life. To the Romans, the Christians were atheists, misfits, and outcasts—the dregs of society. At any rate," I continued normally, "Christianity was certainly no longer under the *religio licita* that it had relished while still considered a Jewish sect."

"And imperial suspicion arose," Kiera said. "They were a mysterious anti-Roman group meeting privately—a secret sect."

"She said 'sects.'"

"Moron," I said, snatching my copy of Tacitus. "Consequently, to get rid of the report—"

"What report?" Brian interrupted.

"A report that claimed Nero started the fire to clear room for his 'Golden House.'"

"*Domus Aurea*," Karl said.

"Can I read now?"

"Continue," Brian beckoned towards me.

I cleared my throat:

Nero fastened the guilt and inflicted the most exquisite tortures on a class hated for their abominations, called Christians by the populace. Accordingly, an arrest was first made of all who pleaded guilty; then, upon their information, an immense multitude was convicted, not so much of the crime of firing the city, as of aversion from human society. Mockery of every sort was added to their deaths. Covered with the skins of beasts, they were torn by dogs and perished, or were nailed to crosses, or were doomed to the flames and burnt, to serve as a nightly illumination, when daylight had expired. Nero offered his gardens for the spectacle . . . even for criminals who deserved extreme and exemplary punishment, there arose a feeling of compassion; for it was not, as it seemed, for the public good, but to glut one man's cruelty, that they were being destroyed.

"This, of course, begs the question: why didn't the Christians of Rome revolt or, at the very least, leave?"

"In the modern sense," Karl asserted.

"Excuse me?"

"You said, 'begs the question.' I was just clarifying that you were using it in the modern sense."

"As opposed to?"

"The Latin: *petitio principia*—'assuming the initial point.'"

"I appreciate your vigilance."

"What was the question?" Greg asked.

"The Christians of Rome," I said, "could've fought back. They could've left. They could've done anything . . . something. But they didn't. Why?"

"Too few?" Andrew posed.

"It's a pointless question. They couldn't have fought back," Greg said. "They would've been massacred."

"Yes . . . and yes," I said, nodding to both Andrew and Greg. "It's also due, partially, to Paul's letter to the Romans."

"You would say that."

"In Rome, there were various house churches meeting. The letter to the Romans circulated amongst these churches. Paul was mainly concerned with solidifying the identity of his base. He wanted both the Jews and Gentiles to unify through their shared interest in Jesus. He also didn't want people either revolting or infighting because of increased taxation and oppression."

"When would you say it was written?"

"Sometime in the late fifties. And if Nero's craziness started in CE 64, then there would have been plenty of time for Paul's teachings to solidify as standard fare. So the Christians were branded as atheists because of their insistence upon monotheism, their regular and secret meetings, and their focus on another king with a soon-to-come kingdom—all of which emperors tend to dislike. So it was cyclical. Because of their beliefs and practices, tension rose between the Christians and the Roman authorities; the more tension that surfaced, the more the Christians disengaged from the larger group."

"Disengagement as survival," Greg said.

"You phrase it so nicely." I raised my glass.

He tipped his pint. "You can quote me."

"So Romans 12:14—13:7 potentially influenced their disengagement tactics, which subsequently influenced their distinct identity, which eventually led to their persecution, and rather than repay evil with evil, they chose to submit to the authorities' right to punish them." I drank heavily from my glass.

The group cheered.

"And the Zealots?" Brian asked.

"Nice transition."

"You're welcome."

"Before you start, let's order another round," Andrew said.

"I concur."

We did. The waitress brought them over, quickly navigating her patrons. The sounds of clinking glasses and humming TVs followed her to our table. Her hair was pinned back with a yellow pencil. She delivered our flowing libations. "Anything else?"

"Nachos," Greg said.

"Nachos," she repeated. "Anything else?"

"Jalapeno Poppers."

"And Jalapeno Poppers. Got it."

While the waitress was gathering our appetizers, we discussed Kiera's growing belly. "When are you due?"

"At the end of the year," she said.

"And how are you both coping?"

"Well," Andrew said. "We're excited."

"Do you know the sex yet?"

"It's a secret," Kiera said. The waitress returned with our food.

Once settled, I continued. "I was always told in church there were four different Jewish groups Jesus had to deal with."

"Yeah."

"Well, that's not exactly accurate. There were the Pharisees, of course, the Sadducees, the Essenes, the followers of the 'Fourth Philosophy,' and the 'Sicarii'—to name a few. But that's not important. Basically, and to grossly simplify, the people in Galilee were both heavily taxed and oppressed by Rome. They had no way to fight back, so they Robin Hooded the Empire."

"Or did Robin Hood Zealot the Prince?" Greg asked.

"Great question. Anyway," I said, "some guys in Galilee left the comforts of society for the crude hills of the countryside and what's called 'social banditry' or 'Robin Hooding.'"

"Robin Hooding?"

"Yeah. When a disenfranchised subgroup disengages from a larger more dominant group and lives out of the law—hence, 'outlaws'—to rob and steal from the rich. There was a group of Galileans who took to social banditry sometime in CE 66. It's important to note, however, that a group typically Robin Hoods for survival, not riches."

"Let's not idealize the Robin Hoods of the world," Brian said. "They're still plundering and killing."

"Just like Rome. Anyway, the social banditry eventually turned into an all-out peasant rebellion. But it was pre-political. They didn't have any larger program in mind; rather, they wanted food and a cheap place to live. The bandits were reacting against the economic, military, and ideological pressures manifested in both increased taxes and occupying forces."

"Sounds like Iraq."

"I don't know anything about Iraqi taxation rates, but the occupying forces certainly sticks. At any rate, the Robin Hoods of Galilee lashed out by organizing into bands that raided and stole to survive."

"From whom?"

"As I understand it, local and imperial elites."

"I'm sure Rome responded well," Greg said.

"In CE 67 they blew the whole thing up. But they didn't leave it there. Once the rebellion in Galilee was quelled, the Romans decided to move south to Jerusalem. On their way down, they burned and raided villages. This all resulted in the original bandits and those running from the encroaching Romans to form up and descend upon Jerusalem."

"So now you have this large group of peasants," Kiera said, "who had been displaced from their homes, filing into Jerusalem."

"Yeah, and it was at this point, around CE 68, that this larger group took to calling themselves the 'Zealots.'"

"And then?"

"And then hell: messianic pretenders and false priests arose, civil war engulfed the region, and Roman sympathizers were assassinated. Jerusalem, with Rome biting at its heels, erupted. Eventually, however, the Jews banded together to fight the Romans. But the Empire proved too much—Titus destroyed Jerusalem."

"So why so much Zealot confusion?" Andrew asked. "It would appear we know a lot of their history."

"There were a couple of post-political groups—groups that did have political agendas—around the time of Jesus that were trying to whip up discontent over Jews assimilating to Roman rule."

"Like?"

"One was called 'The Fourth Philosophy'; the other was called, 'The Sicarii.' The latter of which made their point by assassinating high-ranking Jewish officials, high priests included, who colluded with Rome. They were nasty."

"Sounds like a video game," Greg said.

I laughed. "I think it is."

"So, you have two different socio-religious groups in two similar settings," Kiera said.

"Yep. The Christians in Rome and the Zealots in Palestine. The one is killed in the garden of the emperor and the other is slaughtered by a Roman general soon to be emperor. Both groups were taxed and oppressed."

"Yet they responded differently."

"The Roman Christians chose to disengage from the dominant social power and the civic community in order to solidify their unique identity as a community of Christ followers."

"And the Zealots?"

"The Zealots of Palestine disengaged from both the dominant class and the institutional state, at first, in order to preserve their way of life—pre-political peasant revolt—but later to establish a new socio-political and religious order—the religio-political Zealot party."

"In English?"

"They Robin Hooded with political intent."

"Ah."

"And how does this help your thesis?"

"It's plausible that Paul sought to solidify the Roman Christians' reaction to the possibility of revolution and persecution."'

"That's a lot of 'plausibilities' and 'possibilities.'"

"I know, but it's history. What else is there? At any rate," I continued, "the major difference between the Christians of Rome and the Zealots of Palestine was that the one group, due in part to Paul's previous letter, submitted to God and sacrificed their own lives in order to cement their identity as Christians. The other group, partly due to necessity, partly due to nationalism, and partly due to a heritage of revolt—"

"A heritage?"

"The Maccabees, the 'Fourth Philosophy,' and the 'Sicarii' all provided a history of using violence to counter Rome, which the Zealots assumed, eventually, and enacted against the empire."

"And you think Romans 12:14—13:7, in some way, shaped the Roman Christians' response?"

"Yeah, but while neither characterization holds true throughout history—the Jews have strains of nonviolence while Christians have a history of warring—it does hold true in this particular instance. The one group revolted when faced with opposition; the other didn't. You have to ask yourself: what was the difference?"

"It could've been anything," Brian said.

"Certainly. But it also could've been Paul's letter or, in part, Paul's letter."

"Interesting," Andrew said. "I have to pee."

Part Three

4. *Vanessa*

"THERE'S NO SUCH THING as a free lunch, right? You have to work."

"You really think we can do this?" Miguel asked. "Start a business?"

"It's hard, but it's possible." It was third period, entrepreneurship. My class was working on establishing the student store. They had developed a business plan, bought their inventory, and were now scheduling their daily shifts. There were two a day: one at lunch and one after school.

"I can take Mondays at lunch, because—" Miguel was interrupted by a scream. I ran to the door, locked it, and peered out the window. Vanessa, a seventeen-year-old sophomore was running down the hallway, kicking and screaming. I watched as she tore down bulletin boards, ripped up flyers, and wailed in anguish. She stopped at the door, hair splayed in every direction. Her eyes met mine through the window. She was yelling. "You motherfucking whites. You all don't know me!" I stood back while she continued. "I see you, mister, you white-shit fuck! I'll kill you, I swear to god I'll kill you."

It was about this time the principal, with the police in tow, found Vanessa and escorted her out of the building. I turned back to my classroom, shell-shocked. "What did I do?"

"You gotta ignore Vanessa, man," Miguel said. "She's just trippin. She's got some shit going on at home, you know?"

"Uh . . . no, I do not know."

The following morning in our staff meeting, Mrs. Donna, the principal, told us Vanessa's episode had been prompted by an altercation in her life science class. She had been asked to leave by Mrs. Judy after calling her a bitch. Mrs. Judy was in tears.

"To work here," Mrs. Donna said, "we all have to make sacrifices. Vanessa will back tomorrow."

5. *China*

I WAS ON THE couch, reading, when Natasha walked through the door. "Hey." It was late afternoon. Natasha had started seminary part-time, studying counseling. I was still working on my thesis. We were living in a Denver Seminary apartment. It was spacious and bare, decorated with the few things we collectively owned.

"You're home early," she said. My commute to the Street School each day was an hour and a half.

"It was a crazy day."

"We have dinner with Karl and Mikken in an hour. Tell me about it while we get ready?"

I stood and followed her down the hallway to our room. "The police came to school today and said we needed to evacuate the building."

"What?"

"Yeah. There was going to be a memorial service in the area, but the service was for a gang member who had been killed in a shooting."

"Alright."

"I guess the rival gang threatened to shoot up the memorial service. I don't know. The police talked to the principal. Anyway, they sent us home early. So here I am."

Natasha was shaking her head. "I'm sorry."

"For what?"

"I don't know. It just seems like—"

"As far as I know, they didn't go through with it and everyone's fine." I shrugged. "It was a free day."

"Oh."

Natasha finished readying herself for dinner while I changed shirts. We walked the three flights of stairs to the parking lot and drove to Karl and Mikken's house. Recently graduated, they had decided to move to China.

We sat around a table with lowered lights and open wine bottles. Karl and Mikken were excited. In undergrad, Mikken had studied abroad in Beijing, which is where they would be living and teaching—Beijing Tech.

"But why?" I asked.

Karl and Mikken exchanged glances. "It's something I've always wanted," Mikken said. "Karl loves canoes; I love the East. What can I say?"

"And you?"

Karl held up his hands. "It's a good thing, right? Whether we like it or not; whether we agree with it or not, English is the *lingua franca*. Those who learn it have a higher chance of being successful. I recently read an interesting book on linguistic imperialism. I don't know. It's a strange tension."

"Are you interested in China?" Natasha asked.

"Not really," he said. "It's just that I have an innate skill that can help people rise out of poverty. What are a few years of my life when compared with that?"

I nodded.

Karl smiled. "You should join us."

I looked at Natasha. We both shook our heads. "No."

"Sounds miserable."

"Well, if you're interested," Mikken said, "There's an informal presentation next week. You should attend. If for no other reason, then you can get all the information you'll need to send us packages."

"Okay."

6. *Miguel*

"MIGUEL, YOU'RE LATE. LIKE, really late."

"Oh, hey man, look, it wasn't my fault."

Miguel had strolled into class forty-five minutes late. First period—world history—was almost over. "Just sit down. Wait. Come here." His eyes were on fire. "You need to go Mrs. Donna's office, Miguel."

His shoulders slumped. "Oh, hey man, that's not necessary. I'm cool. I promise."

I shook my head. "Sorry, but you have to go." He turned and walked out as I resumed my lesson.

Ten minutes later, Mrs. Donna came and found me. "Can you join me in my office?"

"Sure."

In her office, I found Miguel steaming. He was pacing back and forth, screaming obscenities. "Fuck you, bitch. You can't suspend me."

"Miguel," Mrs. Donna started, "I already have. If you don't calm down, then I'll have to call the police." She turned to me. "Can you calm him down?"

"Miguel—"

"And fuck you, too," he said, shoving his nose in my face. "This your fault. So what if I came to school high. You didn't have go and tell nobody."

"Miguel, those are the rules. You know better."

"Oh, I know better, do I? What? So I'm stupid?"

"That's not what I'm saying, Miguel. Just calm down and we'll figure this out. Deal with it like a man." It was the wrong thing to say.

"Deal with it like a man?" he screamed. "Fuck you, Marine motherfucker. I'll kill the fuck out of you!"

I took a deep breath, realizing I had made a mistake. "Miguel—" but before I could finish my statement, he pushed me.

"You ain't nothing, Mister!"

I steadied myself and looked at Mrs. Donna. "We're done. Call the police." I turned and went back to class.

INTERLUDE

"SHE TOLD ME THAT both her grandfather and her uncle abused her—sexually. I sat there. I had no idea what to say. How do you respond to that?"

"That's why you took the position, right?" Trent probed.

"How's that?"

"You told me you either have to embody your beliefs or be left empty."

"Well, yeah, that's why I said 'no' to Mexico. After Korea, I couldn't—not in good conscience—accept a position as a contractor. I want to do something in the world. Maybe it's naïve or hopeful, but I feel like I have something to offer. That, and . . . you know . . . I want to make reparations."

"Reparations?"

"Yeah, for Iraq. We did something bad there. We carved out space for evil in the world. I want to try making peace."

"What does that look like?"

"I don't know. We all have different contexts and experiences," I said, while shifting in my seat. "For me it means accomplishing what we sought to accomplish in Iraq without the bullets."

"What did you set out to accomplish in Iraq?"

"To protect the innocent, right? Or so we were told. We were to protect the innocent from the mighty hand of Saddam."

"So you took the alternative school position to protect the innocent?"

"It's all bound together for me. If the war on terrorism, foundationally, is a war on poverty, then why can't I participate in the war on terror in a different capacity?"

"As a peace fighter?"

"Don't make it sound so stupid," I said smiling.

"It's not and, believe me, I understand."

"But then I hit a wall."

"How so?"

"Well, like I said, this girl in class shares she'd been sexually abused by both her grandfather and her uncle. Her mother had died and her father was in jail. So there she is, fifteen, growing up in America, but with a total lack of resources, a total lack of support. The school I work at is a Christian school. But what am I supposed to say? 'Put your faith in Jesus and it'll all go away? You'll be healed?' That's bullshit. You and I both know that's not true."

I took a breath.

"And then I asked myself: what the hell are we actually offering, as Christians? Where's the holistic peace and rest that's shoveled down our throats every Sunday? And how's that shit supposed to be the answer to a girl, weeping, in my classroom?"

"Maybe it's not an answer."

I bit my cheek. "I don't think it is, not anymore. There has to be something else."

"Like what?"

"I don't know. But we live in a system in which a girl is placed, by the state, with her grandfather who then abuses her. No one checks?

"And her grandfather," Trent offered, "we live in a world in which a grandfather can freely rape his granddaughter."

"Jesus," I shook my head, "that's not acceptable. And what does Western, evangelical Christianity have to say? 'Believe in Jesus. Be freed from your sin.' It's no wonder wars rage on."

"You're blaming the wars of the world on evangelical Christianity?"

I thought for a moment. "I'm blaming a population of ignorant and uncritical thinkers on evangelical Christianity."

"You don't find that to be a bit harsh?"

"Generalizations typically are."

Trent scribbled in his notebook.

"What are you writing?" I asked.

"Wouldn't you like to know?" He smiled.

"Yes, yes, I would."

There was silence as Trent sat down his pen. "In the Talmud," he started, "it says: 'and whoever saves a life, it is considered as if he saved an entire world.'"

"Meaning?"

"Each human can be seen as the population of the world; that, in each of us, there is something of the larger and the greater. If you can make a difference in one life, then it's as if you made a difference throughout the world."

"Is the inverse true?"

"In school, I read a case study about a girl, no more than six, who was adopted. She had been abused her whole life. One night at dinner she heard an ice cream truck blaring its song throughout her neighborhood. She asked her new parents if she could run outside and buy some ice cream. Her parents said 'no,' but that—maybe—after she ate her dinner she might be able to have a treat. The girl threw a fit, stood up on her chair, and lifted her sundress over her head. She wasn't wearing any underwear. She asked, 'can I go now?' What do you think her adopted parents did?"

"I don't know."

"They took her back to the adoption agency, because, as they claimed, she was irreparably broken."

I shook my head. "What the hell am I supposed to do with that, Trent?"

"A world in a life," he said absently. "Each time I tell that—" he cleared his throat. "Let's shift gears . . . how's marriage?"

I waited a moment before answering. Wind lapped against the window, jarring leaves from their summertime strongholds. "It's strange. My parents are divorced. I don't remember them being married. The first night in our new apartment," I started laughing, "Natasha asked me to hang up these curtain rods. I'm no handyman, but I tried. The next thing I know I'm flinging screwdrivers across the house and bashing pillows into the wall, which was pockmarked with drill holes. The curtain rod was hanging crookedly. Natasha must have contemplated annulment."

"Why were you so angry?" asked Trent, leaning forward.

"I don't know," I said. "It was my first house project as a new husband. I'm supposed to be some masculine guy, right? A Marine, which people never seem to forget: 'Come on, Benjamin, aren't you supposed to be a Marine?' they'll ask. 'It's not cold. It's only seventeen degrees.' Dumb shit like that. Anyway, it was my first house project. I wanted to do it well."

"That's all?"

"No."

"I can't stand things that aren't perfect."

"What do you mean?"

"There's symmetry in perfection, wholeness. I desired a wall with no holes and a curtain rod that was perfectly level. Instead, I got me—chinked and crooked."

"That's life."

"Is it?"

Trent shrugged. "What would you tell the young woman in your class?"

"What would you tell the adopted girl?"

Trent was quiet.

I crossed my legs while scanning the books on the shelf behind Trent. "How do you comfort without minimizing suffering?"

"You listen," he said.

"How do you change suffering?"

Trent didn't answer.

7. Conversation

ANDREW AND I WERE at Stella's on Pearl. We had decided to grab an early morning coffee to discuss our progress. It was a cold, spring morning. We had lost track of the germane, however. "He was a living breathing man," said Andrew. "He ate, he drank, he shat—dusty and dirty. We too often forget that side of Jesus. He was a great man."

"And divine?"

"Does it matter?"

"What do you mean?"

"Even you say Jesus' life and teachings are the important things—that which carries weight. His death was important for, as you've said, unmasking the powers of corruption and oppression that afflict us all. But the rest? The deification? How do we know it isn't some first-century way of saying: 'Take notice—this man was a Rabbi worth following.' It's not that strange, is it? The emperor himself was deified. And Jesus' coming kingdom was always held up as a counter weight to the empire. Couldn't it be then, that what was true for one was true for the other? Caesar is Lord; Caesar is deified. Jesus is Lord; Jesus is deified. Caesar's empire reigns on earth and is characterized by violence as a way to peace. Jesus' empire is found amongst you, linked in solidarity, and is characterized by love as a way to peace. Is that so strange?"

"No, I guess not." I paused. "What about other religions: Islam, Buddhism . . . whatever?"

"What about them? They do what they do and Christianity does what it does."

"I'm not sure I follow."

"History, tradition, liturgy—these are good for the soul of the community. They make us whole. They allow for participation in the lives of others, which is essential for life. If a religion can do this—create space for mutual and holistic engagement in the lives of others—then who cares where it came from?"

"I'm not saying I disagree with you, but surely justification has to be the same for everyone?"

"Why? Why can't justification be different?"

"I don't know."

"Why are you a Christian?"

"Uh . . . well, I didn't become a Christian until after I turned eighteen. Christianity, prior to my life in the Marine Corps, was an emotional response to a perceived solution to brokenness."

"Come on," Andrew said, "that's a book answer. Be truthful: why are you a Christian?" He sipped his café au lait.

I laughed. "It's funny, you know? I ask myself that all of the time. I once had an experience, which I would say was God, that . . . moved me. I don't know how to describe it. But I feel like I was made aware of a new reality. How can I go back on that? Though war, death, or violence."

"That's better, Benjamin. You can't go back, you're stuck. That's why you're striving to bring both your experience and your theology in line with your Christian paradigm. You're seeking to reduce the dissonance."

"What dissonance?"

"Between being a killer and a Christian."

"I'm not sure the reality of being a Christian has fully sunk in yet."

"So you write this thesis on war and you wonder about things like justification."

"Yeah."

"Complex shit."

I nodded. "Oh, hey. How's the baby, little Ollia? You digging fatherhood?"

"Did you know my father died when I was sixteen?"

"No."

"Well, he did. It was hard growing up, figuring a lot of stuff out on my own. So with Ollia, I didn't know what to expect. There were a lot of emotions. What is parenthood? How does one be a father? But . . . "

"What?"

"I had this realization I don't want Ollia to be happy. I want her to be good."

"What do you mean?"

"I look around and all I see are people trying to be happy. Trying to feel good. But are we? I don't know. We're, most of us, depressed and sad and overweight. Most likely because we don't drink enough vodka." He smiled. "But also because we're constantly in search of happiness, of something else. We're discontents. I don't want that for Ollia. Part of me doesn't care if she's happy at all. But I do care if she's good. A person who knows how to make moral choices."

"Isn't that what we all want?"

8. Cambodia

"Do you want to go?"

"I think so," I said.

"I'm not going to do this if you 'think so.' I need you to know."

New flowers were breaking through the stale, winter ground. Natasha and I had attended the Asian Language Teaching forum. We had heard all about Karl and Mikken's coming trip to China. ALT, as it turned out, placed teachers both in China and throughout Southeast Asia. We had listened to the presentation on Cambodia with interest. It was a country reeling from genocide, years of civil war, and systemic poverty. Natasha, an English teacher by trade, was intrigued by the idea of teaching English at a foreign university. For me, I was interested in reparations. Cambodia was war torn. And I was a warfighter who wanted to help. We were excited, hopeful, and naïve. Natasha would have to quit her job, however, and place seminary on hold. I would have to pause my thesis.

"Okay. I know. I want to go."

"Like that, we're going to uproot and move halfway around the world?"

I nodded. "Yeah, why not?"

"Because it's crazy."

"True."

"And because I like my job."

"Sure you do. I . . . kind of like mine." She laughed. "But this is a once in a lifetime chance. We don't have kids. We don't have a mortgage. We haven't been at our jobs for very long. I mean, when else are we going to get a chance to just go?"

Natasha was silent, staring out the window. "I thought my life would be different."

"What?"

"I thought I would marry a normal guy. Instead I got some twisted up veteran who wants to save the world. How did that happen?"

I laughed. "This is going to sound stupid, but I feel like I'm missing something—that there's a prewar Benjamin and a postwar Benjamin. I don't know how to explain it, but I want the other one back. Maybe this'll help. Maybe I'll find myself in Cambodia."

"We're the same wherever we go. Geography has nothing to do with it."

"Still. I want to go."

9. *Finished*

I DROVE TO BASE and dressed in my Marine Corps utilities with a lighthearted eagerness. What I had started eight years ago was coming to a final and irrevocable end. I was tired of the Marine Corps being a part of my identity. I had stuffed my seabag full of old Marine Corps gear. I would be handing it back to my supply officer today. The rest, that which they wouldn't take or didn't need, I was planning on burning in a trash can behind my apartment complex. It would be a form of a celebration, a passing—a death. I entered Buckley Air Force Base that Saturday morning as a Marine. I would leave a civilian.

I parked my car and stood in formation. We marched around the base and yelled off our roll call. I was a sergeant and a squad leader. I was in charge of squad three. Mexico was in charge of squad two. We had grown. After roll call, we filed inside and sat behind our workstations. To keep us sharp on our drill weekends, we often drafted false imagery targets. We were waiting for our targets to be assigned.

"What's next?" I asked Mexico.

"I took that job in California, Peters. I leave next week. I'm officially a contractor."

"No shit? You're a mercenary."

"A contractor, Peters. A contractor who makes sixty thousand for only working six months out of the year—sixty un-taxable dollars."

"Congratulations."

"And you?"

"Natasha and I are moving to Cambodia to teach English."

"What?"

"Yeah, the opportunity presented itself. I feel good about it."

"Is this more of your Bible shit?"

"Yeah, maybe. We'll be helping people."

"So will I."

"Sort of."

"Oh, I will."

"Maybe not."

"Peters, Mexico," a voice yelled through the door. "Report to the major's office."

"Here it is," I said. "You ready?"

"Born."

We marched to Bravo Company's Office and stood at attention. "At ease," our major barked. In real life he was a civilian pilot for American Airlines. "I hear you two are leaving us today. Is that right?"

"Yes, sir."

He nodded while shuffling through papers on his desk. "You're two of my leaders. You're sure you want to do this?"

"Yes, sir."

He looked us each in the eyes. "It's a terrible economy out there, gentleman. The Marine Corps Reserves is a steady paycheck. You willing to give that up?"

"Yes, sir."

He shook his head. "If you ever want to come back, then we'll be here for you." He signed our discharge papers and handed them back to us. "Good luck."

We walked back to our work stations and said goodbye to the other Marines. Some of them were happy to see us leave, because it meant two lucky corporals would be promoted to sergeant. We shook their hands and walked outside.

"You remember when they forgot to call us?"

"How could *I* forget?"

"I thought . . . " Mexico shook his head. "I don't know what I thought, Peters. I was scared . . . I think."

"That was a long time ago. I think I'll grow my hair out."

"Shitbird."

I shook Mexico's hand. "Stay in touch."

"I will, Peters . . . I mean, Benjamin. It's not me you have to worry about. You never return a phone call."

I laughed. It was true. "Fair enough. Take care, Luis. Be safe."

We went our separate ways.

I started my car and drove home. Natasha was out for the day. I took off my uniform and placed it on my bed. It was all I had left. I had said I would be happy to watch it burn. Instead, I packed it into a few grocery bags and drove to a nearby Goodwill. I left it with an attendant. My Marine Corps uniform, forged in sweat and blood, was nothing more than an anonymous Halloween costume.

I drove home in silence.

Finished.

Part Three

10. Abandoned

I HAD TO TELL Mrs. Donna that I wouldn't be returning. Natasha and I had made our decision. *What are my students going to say?* Charis, who at the beginning of the year had shared with me about her grandfather, was doing well. She would graduate the following year, a year early. She was planning on attending Denver Community College before transferring to Metro State University. Her dream was to graduate college with a nursing degree. She wanted to help people.

The door to the principal's office swung inward.

"Benjamin," Mrs. Donna said. "What are you doing here? Don't you have class?"

"I do. In a minute. I wanted to talk to you quickly, if I could." She beckoned me in.

"What can I help you with?"

I launched into my speech. "My wife, Natasha, and I have decided to teach English in Cambodia next year. I won't be coming back to the alternative school. I'm sorry. It's not you or the students, it's just that—"

"Benjamin," she interrupted. "I don't need your excuses. It's alright. This job isn't for everyone, and it's certainly not a long-term career."

Relief. "Well, okay then."

"Would you like to tell the students or should I?"

"I guess I should, right?"

"It's typically better that way. They'll be hurt, at first. But that's to be expected." I turned towards the door. "Benjamin," she stopped me. "Good luck."

"Thanks."

‡ ‡ ‡

"So that's it, huh?"

"I'm sorry, Miguel. But, yes."

He nodded. "You teachers always be leaving, mister."

Miguel had found me in the parking lot after I announced to the students that I wouldn't be returning. I was standing next to my car. "I thought it might be different this time."

"I'm sorry."

"It's cool, mister."

"Hey, any word from the Army?"

"Nah. I popped the test, mister. I ain't going anywhere."

11. *Initiative*

"Benjamin," Professor Kelwin said, smiling. We had grown friendly with one another since after the brownbag lunch. He had become an academic mentor and confidant. "Come in, come in," he was saying as he cleared away his tea dishes and placed them in their rightful location on his windowsill. "What brings you here?"

I sat down, folded hands in lap. Sun was streaming through the window. "My wife and I have decided to move to English." The words tumbled out of my mouth.

"Move to English?" He raised an eyebrow.

I collected myself. "My wife and I have decided to move to Cambodia to teach English."

"Ah," he absently adjusted his bowtie.

"It's just that—"

He cut me off. "It's just that you want to see if your thesis is accurate—a case study of your own life. Would that be correct?"

"Yes." I shifted. "That would be correct."

"So you'll be pausing your thesis?"

"Yes."

"How far along are you?"

"I'm done. I only have my conclusion to finish. I thought it might be best if I left it until after Cambodia."

"How long will you be staying?"

"Two years."

He breathed deeply. "In some ways, I envy you. It's been a long time since I've embarked on an adventure."

"It's less about adventure and more about the common good."

"Benjamin," he smiled. "I wish you luck."

"Thank you."

"Now, if all you've left is your conclusion, then you must have finished your section on just peacemaking."

"I did."

"Let's discuss it." His eyes sparkled with excitement.

"Okay. Let me think . . . well, there are a lot of theories about war and not war: pacifism, just war, nonresistance, preemptive war—"

"Yes," he interrupted. "And just peacemaking . . . tell me something I don't know."

"Well, the goal is to achieve a just peace between two nations, which happens through the use of nonviolence."

He stood and began brewing water for tea.

"At its core," I continued, "is a distinction between 'transformative initiatives' and 'the culture of violence.'"

"Explain." His back was to me.

"In a culture of violence a group dominates others by force, which can be responded to a number of ways: violence, accommodation, to name a few, but also transforming initiatives."

He squirted lemon into his tea. "Interesting." I had the distinct feeling that he had heard this before.

"In a context of violence," I said, excitement welling, "the oppressive power holds the initiative, and others simply choose how best to respond. Jesus, however, calls the oppressed to seize the initiative. If you follow the teachings of Jesus, then you are to *act*, therefore initiating a new set of events to which the dominant must respond."

"Like the act of killing?"

"No."

"Why not?"

"In the Sermon on the Mount, Jesus does this thing where he states a traditionally held piety before unmasking it as a mechanism of bondage."

"Mechanism of bondage?"

"Yeah, like when Matthew writes: 'You have heard that the ancients were told that everyone who is angry with his brother shall be guilty before the court and whoever shall say, *You fool*, shall be guilty enough to go into the fiery hell.'"

"And the gears of bondage grind."

"But in this section, as in most, Jesus takes the mechanism of bondage and turns it on its head—a transforming initiative. 'Leave your offering before the altar and be reconciled to your brother.' Jesus is laying the groundwork for just peacemaking. He's telling us that what's really important is the difficult work of peacemaking and reconciliation. Actually, I think you could even make the case that both peacemaking and reconciliation, worked out in community, are acts of worship."

"Worked out in community?"

"You can't just throw money at a problem. On some level, you have to identify with those you're working for. Identity. Solidarity. Only happen in community."

"The wealthy move; their wealth redistributed."

"What we call redistribution Jesus would have called 'prophetic justice.'"

"Which I call anachronistic."

"I know. It's the essence of the thing though. The rightness of it."

"The rightness of it," Professor Kelwin said. "Hmm." He sipped his tea. "What else comprises just peacemaking?"

"I'll guess you'll have to read my thesis."

He raised an eyebrow. "Well done, Benjamin. You're coming along quite nicely."

"Well, not everyone agrees with me."

"No?"

"But Jesus himself launched a . . . why do I feel like you already know this?"

He shrugged. "I haven't the foggiest."

"Jesus knew what it meant to live under the reign of an occupying force. And, like so many freedom fighters, he sought for a better tomorrow."

"And this applies to war?"

"Yeah. It teaches us to do something. I could wallow in anger and self-pity, I could put false hope in Jesus and his followers, or I could do something."

"Peace is a much deeper reality than violence," Professor Kelwin mused before leaning forward in an uncharacteristic display of clarity. "But what are we to do?"

"But if your enemy is hungry, feed him. If he is thirsty, give him a drink . . . overcome evil with good."

"You ask much."

"So did Paul."

"How romantic."

"It is, kind of."

The sun set, casting its crimson hues across the mountain sky. Our conversation dwindled. Professor Kelwin shook my hand and wished me luck. I thanked him and told him I looked forward to working with him after I returned from Cambodia. He chuckled and, for my sake, said he hoped it was true. "All too often," he said, "students leave without finishing. It's rare that one comes back."

"I will. I promise."

He adjusted his bowtie. "We shall see."

12. Unexpected

Natasha and I were greeted at the airport by the ALT liaison. We were in California with what few possessions we could bring—our lives crammed into two large suitcases. We had said our goodbyes in Colorado by hosting a bon voyage party. The Tinklings had attended, as well as Natasha's family. It was an evening filled with hopeful lament. We were both excited about the future's untapped potential and saddened at leaving behind such great friends.

In Pasadena, we were shoved into a van with two other ALT teachers. One was a twenty-eight-year-old man with a shaved head. He was from Alabama. His name was Ethan. The other was a twenty-six-year-old woman with blonde hair and blue eyes. She was short. Her name was Lauren.

"Hey," Ethan said with a thick southern drawl. "I'll tell you what, I'm excited 'bout this little trip here. From what I understand the four of us'll be teaching in Phnom Penh together." The van rocked back and forth as it wove its way through LA's rush hour.

"Really?" said Lauren. "That's great. Have any of you been to Cambodia before."

Natasha and I shook our heads.

"I have," said Ethan. "A few times. I also grew up next to a Khmer population in Mobile."

"Can you speak Khmer?"

"A little." We found out later he was both fluent and modest.

"Well," started Lauren, "I've never been to Cambodia, but I did live in China for a while, right out of college."

"Where did you go to school?"

"A small liberal arts school in West Virginia. You wouldn't have heard of it. You?"

"Colorado State University," Natasha said. "Benjamin graduated from a small school in Kansas called Bethany."

Lauren nodded as the van came to a stop. Our liaison slid the side door open. "Grab your bags and check in at the front desk. Your orientation starts in an hour. Rest up."

Inside the hotel, Natasha unpacked her suitcase. "You going to unpack yours?"

"What's the point? We're leaving in a few days for Hanoi." She shook her head.

"Ethan and Lauren seemed nice."

"Yeah. It'll be nice having them in Cambodia." I flopped on the bed and absently flicked on the television. We didn't have cable at home, so it was a luxury surfing through the endless channels.

Natasha was in the bathroom.

I stopped floating through the cable-verse and rested on ESPN and a European soccer match. I didn't know anything about the sport, but, as an America traveling abroad, I thought I should learn. The play resembled a jumbled food court.

Ten minutes passed.

I stood, walked over to the bathroom door, and knocked. "Everything okay?" I was greeted with silence. I jiggled the handle. It was locked. "Hey!"

"I'm here," she called through the door. "I'm fine."

"Well, open up." She was pale and holding something, an unfamiliar thermometer. "What's going on?"

"I'm pregnant."

INTERLUDE

"CONGRATULATIONS," TRENT SAID. "HAVE you told your parents?"

"That's the thing," I said. "They don't think we should go. But what can we do? We've quit our jobs, sold our cars."

"You're stuck, huh?" He was distracted, driving. I had called him to tell him the news, but also to work through all of my unexpected emotions.

"Yeah, I guess." The phone crackled. "Can you hear me? Are you there?"

"I'm here," Trent said. "I'm driving, though, and I don't normally conduct sessions over the phone."

I sat down on my hotel bed. The reality of leaving America, for the third time, and becoming a father was sinking in. *Am I ready for this?* What kind of world was I bringing my child into? I had fought, I had killed, and now I was trying to make reparations for those transgressions. *Where does a child fit?* My father had once told me that everyone was a revolutionary until the day they became parents. "I'm sorry," I said. "I know you're busy. I'll let you go."

"You'll be fine, Benjamin."

"Okay."

"Any idea when you'll be back in the states?"

"We'll be in Cambodia for two years, at least."

"Do you have any way that we can stay in touch? A blog or something?"

"Yeah. I'll send you the link."

"Anything else?"

"No."

"Take care." He hung up the phone.

13. Doorknob

I HEARD THE DISTANT and muffled ringing and roused from sleep. "Hello." The voice on the other end was hysterical. I heard clanging and shuffling in the background. "Who is this?" There was silence. And then a voice erupted.

"It's me, Lauren," her voice was shrill and wracked with sobs. "He's here."

I sat up. It was two in the morning and my mind was slowly firing. "Who?" I muttered.

"I don't know," she said, before launching into a tale too quickly for me to understand.

"Slow down, Lauren," I said. My wife opened her eyes and rested on her elbow, awakened by the commotion.

"Who is it?"

"Lauren," I whispered out of the side of my mouth.

We had been in country for four months. We were residing in a three-story house in the city's center, near Cambodia's Independence Monument—a granite reminder championing Cambodia's independence from the French. Though we were living in the city, our school, and eventual home, was tucked into the Cambodian countryside forty-five minutes outside of Phnom Penh. We had not begun teaching, however. The university in which we were to teach had told us: "We commence the academic year upon students arriving." We asked when that would be, but received only a smile and a nod.

While we waited for our classes to begin, we toured the city and read books on parenting. We had also taught a two-week English course at a university in Cambodia's coastal Kampot region. It had been a good experience, but hadn't lasted. At the end of our course, our students, if nothing else, were well versed in the art of the definite article. The university in Kampot had been run by South Koreans and, as such, I was also able to overcome my fear of Kimchi—radish, not cabbage.

While we waited for our permanent classes at the National Polytechnic Institute of Cambodia to begin, we also visited Angkor Wat—a sprawling twelfth-century temple built by King Suryavarman II. My wife, burgeoning with three months of life, trekked the ruins with intensity, thinking it would be her last adventure without children.

As expatriates in the doldrums of life abroad, we played the tourists. We tried new foods, shopped at the market, and rode in Cambodia's Tuk-Tuks—a kind of motorbike horse-and-carriage taxi. We entered into community with Phnom Penh's Episcopal church and spent long afternoons drinking at the Cambodian coffeehouse, Java. Boasting a vine-encrusted balcony, Java overlooked Cambodia's main thoroughfare, which was alive with motorbikes weaving in-and-out of traffic, seeking gravity in larger trucks that bent traffic to their will. For an American, Cambodia's traffic was overwhelming. Once settled in country, we had purchased a used Jeep Cherokee. It took me some time, however, to adjust to driving with no traffic laws. Hurtling down the road, I was the bigger car that motorbikes sought out, like chum to whales they would follow in my wake.

"Benjamin," Lauren screamed. "You have to come—now."

"What?" I shot a glance at my wife. "It's two in the morning. Slow down and tell me what happened."

Lauren breathed. "I was watching a movie in my living room; I feel asleep. When I woke a few minutes ago, there was a man staring at me through the window. He threw a beam of light in my face with his flashlight and started to shimmy open my window. I ran out, shut and locked the door to my living room, and called you."

"Where are you now?"

"In my room. But I'm afraid he might break in. You have to come now. You have to do something."

I looked at Natasha who had overheard the conversation. "What am I supposed to do?"

"Go over there," Natasha said. "Wake Ethan and take him with you. He speaks Khmer. Maybe he can figure out what's happening."

Ethan roomed with us. He lived on the third floor. I slipped on my shoes and trudged up the steps with Lauren on hold. I shook Ethan awake. He startled. I explained the situation and told him to dress. We met up on the first floor and mounted Ethan's motorbike. I straddled him as he zipped out and into the empty streets.

Phnom Penh was dark and bare. Humidity, even at two in the morning, weighed us down. Piles of garbage lined the streets, which were lit by the few working streetlamps of Phnom Penh. When we had landed in the capital I had been told Westerners should stay indoors after sunset. Yet, here I was speeding through town in the middle of the night. I thought about the Dragon Boys, a motorbike gang of rabid teens who ravaged the empty streets of Phnom Penh by night. At least, that's what I had been told. "Are we safe out here?" I yelled in Ethan's ear. The throttle was pinned.

"Sure," he said in his thick drawl. "Besides, if we get mugged and die, we get mugged and die. Ain't nothing we can do about it."

I nodded to his sage advice.

As familiar fruit stands whizzed by, I knew we were close to Lauren's home. We turned left at a large pile of chicken dung and stopped in front of her house. I hopped off and knocked on the door. She opened it, tears streaming down her face. "He's locked in the living room. I can hear him banging around. I've never been burgled." Her normally well-groomed hair was hysterical.

"What should we do?" I turned to Ethan. "Call the police?"

He laughed. "They wouldn't come. And if they did, they wouldn't be here 'til sun-up."

"You know Khmer best," I pointed out. "You want to try talking to him?"

"No way, you're the Marine. You outta just charge in there and demand answers."

"What?" I asked, shocked.

"It's true," Lauren said. "You have military training."

"You're both kidding, right?"

They shook their heads. I shrugged. "Alright, give me your flashlight." I reached for Ethan's Maglite.

"What are you going to do with that? Whack him?"

"If I have to . . . shit, I don't know. Just give it to me." I was flustered. He handed me the light. It was heavy in my hand. I sighed and crept to the locked door. "I don't hear anything."

"He's in there. I know it," Lauren said.

I rested my ear on the door and listened. Nothing.

Bang!

Something slammed into the door. "What the hell," I jumped back. Both Lauren and Ethan were standing feet away, behind a couch. "This is ridiculous," I said. "We have to call somebody."

"Who?" Lauren asked.

"Say something in Khmer, Ethan."

He shouted in Khmer.

"What did you say?"

"I said: 'Who goes there?'"

"Really?"

"Yeah, what else was I gonna say?"

We waited for an answer.

Nothing.

"You're up, Marine."

I had been trained to kill, true, but that was behind me.

"Dude," said Ethan. "You gotta go."

I shuffled to the door. My hands were wet against the cold flashlight, which I was brandishing before me. *This is insane.* Creeping closer to the door, I willed my situation to evaporate with the dawn. *Regan.* That was the name Natasha and I had decided upon. It meant "strong one." It was from Shakespeare's *King Lear*. Regan was Lear's horrid daughter who had sought to kill her father and wrest control of his kingdom. I loved both the name and it's meaning—not its legacy. I had decided to write a story reclaiming the name. It was eponymously titled and featured my daughter as the heroine. *Will she ever read it?*

I closed my eyes, but opened my lungs for a deep and steadying breath.

I reached for the doorknob.

Flinging the door open, I made a last-second decision. I charged in, screaming at the top of my lungs. Three steps into the room, I stopped. It was empty. I looked up and out the window. Crouched down and peering through the now-broken screen was a Cambodian teenager. "Come here," I said. He shook his head. Ethan, Lauren, get in here."

"Is it safe?"

"All clear."

Ethan walked in first with Lauren trailing behind. I pointed to the window. Ethan spoke in Khmer. After a few minutes of discussion, the young Cambodian man climbed back in through the window. "What's going on?"

"He's the security guard of this complex," Ethan said. "He's never seen a white person before. He said he recently came to Phnom Penh from his village—his uncle helped him find work." The Cambodian security guard interrupted and rattled off something in Khmer. "He said he was confused by Lauren's white skin and blonde hair. He wanted a closer look, that's all."

"That's all? He scared the shit out of me. I want him fired."

"You can't fire him," Ethan said. "He didn't know any better."

Lauren turned to me. "What do you think?"

I had no idea. There were cultural differences at play, differences in which I had no experience. What was appropriate in Cambodia—knocking on someone's window at three in the morning—wasn't, clearly, appropriate in the United States. I couldn't think of an answer to Lauren's question. *I'm tired.* What would I have done if the intruder had been hostile? Would I have swung the Maglite? Would I have injured him? At what point does one risk his or her safety in pursuit of an ideal? "Let him go, Lauren. If Ethan said he didn't know any better, then he didn't know any better."

"So that's it? He gets away?"

I dropped my shoulders. "I guess."

Lauren was frustrated. "Well, I can't stay here. Can I sleep on your couch tonight?"

"Sure," Ethan said.

We asked the night guard to leave before securing Lauren's house and piling on Ethan's motorbike. We drove home on the darkened and bare Norodom Boulevard.

"Well?" asked Natasha as I slid back into bed, "what happened?" I explained the situation. She laughed at my unease. "I'm sure you acted with the utmost bravery."

"It's not funny." I was still shaken up. "What if he would've had a gun? What then? What if a knife?"

"You worry too much."

"I'm not sure I could've used violence."

Natasha rolled beneath the sheets and pillows and closed her eyes. "What about Hitler?"

"Very funny."

14. NPIC

THE SUN POURED ITS beating rays on top of us. It was a muffled submersion, like being clothed in a swimming pool. "It's hot."

"Damn right," Ethan said. "Reminds me of Mobile."

We were in the back of a Tuk-Tuk—Natasha, Ethan, and I. Summoned to our official posting at NPIC, we were preparing to meet the South Korean president of our university. NPIC had a Khmer president as well, but as it was both funded and run by South Koreans, the South Korean president, President Kim, was the one we had to deal with on a regular basis.

We had been traveling for two hours when we arrived, sticky with dust and sweat. The South Korean president greeted us with his wife and staff. "Hello." He bowed. "We have very good news for you. The students arrive now, so school starts in three days." It was mid-November. We had been in Cambodia since August. We were both relieved to finally start our classes and frustrated that we were only receiving a three-day's notice. We had prepared our lessons, but, within the next three days, we'd have to move from the city to the countryside.

"Wonderful news," I said.

"Yes, yes. Very good for you. We now show you dormitory." Kim and his wife, who was short with graying hair, led us to student housing. We paused at the stairwell where we found a small four-year old boy, naked.

"Who's this?" Natasha asked.

"He live here," Seung, the president's wife, said.

"In the dormitory?"

"No," Kim said. "In stairwell."

"No," said Ethan.

Kim looked confused. "This true. He live underneath stairwell with mother. She clean dormitory."

"His mom's the janitor," I said. "And they live underneath the stairs?"

Kim and Seung nodded while the boy hopped into the grass and relived himself. Done, he strolled back to the stairwell and crawled inside his hammock. He was darkly skinned and disheveled.

"Does he have a name?" Ethan asked.

"Good question," Kim said.

We left the boy to his mid-morning nap and climbed the three stories to our dorm room. Kim and Seung had readied three rooms for us. Natasha and I would live in one, Ethan in one, and the third would function as our common space. We unlocked the doors to find bare rooms filled with nothing but gecko shit. "You will move in tomorrow," Seung said. "You make look very nice." Kim and Seung left us to explore after telling us a student would be hauling up beds and portable closets later that day.

"Well, this sucks," Ethan said.

Natasha started crying. She was four-and-a-half months pregnant. "I don't know if I can live like this."

I shook my head. We hadn't expected this. We assumed, at first, that we would be living and teaching at the city university where Lauren was teaching. Weeks into our stay, however, our organization revealed that we would be teaching in the countryside with Ethan at NPIC. I didn't know how to respond, so I grabbed my wife and held her close. *How American are we?* I felt guilty for expecting more, for wanting more, when three stories below there was a child with nothing but a hammock and a broom.

We finished exploring the dormitory and found Kim and Seung, along with their South Korean staff, and drove to a nearby golf course for lunch. Kim ordered for the table. The waiter brought soup with a squid-like creature floating towards the top. The president pointed to the soup. "Very good for you."

"I'm sure."

His wife reached under the table and pulled out a Tupperware dish of Kimchi.

"They do not know the pleasures of Kimchi in Cambodia," she said. "You like?"

I nodded and turned to Kim. "Mister President, do you know what classes each of us will be teaching?"

He smiled. "When all of students arrive, we sort out details."

"I thought you said they were here," Ethan said.

"Ah, yes, but not all."

I looked at Natasha who was growing increasingly anxious. "Isn't there a schedule? An academic calendar?"

"You discuss with Mister Cho, yes?" The president acknowledged our colleague across the table. It was a subtle dismissal—now was not the time to discuss business.

‡ ‡ ‡

"Good 'ole, Kim," Ethan said. "Man, that was weird." We were on our way back to Phnom Penh.

"Why would they bring us all the way out here and then tell us they aren't ready?"

"Who knows?" We had a long ride back; Ethan changed the subject. "What did you think of that kid?"

"Unbelievable," Natasha said. "I can't believe he lives like that."

"I can't believe he pooped in front us."

"Seriously, Benjamin?" Natasha said. "Do you think there is anything we can do for him?"

"Like what?" Bear asked.

"I don't know," she said. "It just seems . . . it seems strange to not do anything."

"Have you been to Toul Slang yet?" Bear asked.

"No. It's on our list though."

"Pol Pot," Bear said, "was a bastard. He killed millions of people. You should definitely see it. A kid living in a stairwell is a tragedy, for sure, but Toul Slang will make you weep. Place is imbued with helplessness. What would you've done about Pol Pot, you know, with your leanings and all?"

"I don't know," I said. This was a conversation to which Bear and I often returned. He was a conservative, Southern Republican with a penchant for social justice. He wanted to work a good in the world, but not at the expense of his understanding of the gospel. And as he often said: "Sometimes you just gotta use force against force." I looked out of the Tuk-Tuk. We were still in the countryside. The rice fields stretched out before us, temples, dotting the landscape, broke the horizon. "I'm tired of violence, that's all. Mass killing is wrong and so is a child growing up in abject poverty. I think the two are connected and that if you can right the system—"

"But you can't, Benjamin," Natasha said. "No one can. If you want to change the system, then you have to do what is in front of you. The kid is in front of us, not Pol Pot."

"I don't know 'bout all that," Bear said. "But if I'd had the chance, then I'd have killed Pol Pot. Shot his damn eyes out—thank you very much."

"A wrong is a wrong, no matter the reasoning," I said. "Would killing Pol Pot make you a hero? Or only someone who had killed? People might call you a hero, but I can guarantee that when you closed your eyes at night, you would be haunted by the images of an eyeless Pol Pot. Humans weren't created to kill."

"Yeah, yeah" said Bear. "I've heard it before. You're a one hit wonder."

We were in the city now and Ethan had to raise his voice to be heard. Cars and motorbikes sped around us as we dashed in-and-out of traffic. We acknowledged our driver's skill at the next intersection that forced us to a stop.

"Ethan," Natasha said. "Can you ask our driver his name?"

"He says it's Surin," Ethan said. "You know? Like, 'Sir-in.'"

"Hello, Surin," Natasha said in her best Khmer. Surin smiled and waved to us by placing his palms together and slightly bowing. His clothes, long pants with a long shirt, matched his hair—black. The heat only affected foreigners.

We arrived at our house and paid Surin. "I heard about this restaurant called, 'Gasolina,'" Ethan said, "It's some kind of French-fusion joint. Good food, apparently, and internet. You want to meet up for dinner?"

"We have a doctor's appointment," Natasha said, "but after?"

"It's a plan."

15. Blood

"NAME?" THE NURSE ASKED, handing us a sticky note. "Age?"

Natasha grabbed the notepad and wrote down her information, before taking a seat next to me in the waiting area. "Is that," Natasha elbowed me, "blood?"

The clinic's walls were lined with red smudges.

"Um . . . maybe?"

Both the waiting room and the halls of the clinic were deserted.

Finally, after what felt like an hour, a small Cambodian man greeted us and beckoned us to follow him. "You Americans?"

"Yes."

He nodded and clicked his tongue. The room was bare except for three chairs and an ultrasound machine. "What bring you?"

"I'm having strange pains," Natasha said.

He clicked his tongue. "Pull shirt," he illustrated what he meant. Natasha lifted her shirt above her belly. The doctor placed his hands on Natasha's stomach. He pressed; Natasha winced. He looked at me, clicking his tongue, and started the ultrasound machine. "This your baby," he said, pointing to the screen. "Maybe everything not okay."

"What do you mean?"

The doctor stood and left the room. We sat in silence for a moment before he returned with a tome. "Medical book," he said. "English. You read." He pointed to a paragraph with the heading: Preeclampsia. We read. Preeclampsia, as it turned out, is a form of gestational hypertension that is associated with significant amounts of protein in the urine.

"You need call American doctor."

"Okay," we said, and left.

"What the hell is preeclampsia?"

"You read it," Natasha said.

"Yeah, but I have no idea what it meant."

"I don't know," she said. "I'll call our pediatrician in the States."

"I'm sure it's nothing."

"You're probably right," she said. "But the isolation is making everything worse."

"Isolation?"

"We have no family here, Benjamin. We're alone in this."

I was defensive. "This was a joint decision."

"Don't be that way."

"What way?"

"You know exactly what way. I'm just scared. If something happened—"

I cut her off. "Children are born in Cambodia every day, Natasha."

"So I can't be scared?"

"That's not what I'm saying."

She turned on me. "What are you saying?"

I was frustrated. It was difficult enough to navigate one's first pregnancy, but to do it overseas in a developing country was madness. "We're here to make sacrifices. People live and die in Cambodia. If we can't move past this, then how are we going—"

"This isn't about affecting change, Benjamin. This isn't about your thesis. You have a wife and child. That has to sink in. Peacemaking isn't everything."

"Isn't it?"

"No."

"It is," I said. "What else is there?"

"Family, friends, work . . . love—life."

"None of which matters if you're part of an oppressive system. We have a life in America because these people," I was shouting and flailing my arms, "make it—our clothes, our cars, our oil. And what do we give back? Bullets and movies. We have all the power and wield it for *our* gain. We're selfish, fat, and lazy people. And when we try to do something good, you want to run at the first sign of trouble. We have a responsibility not only to embody that which we believe, but also to repay the affluence into which we were born."

"Give it up, Benjamin. You're not Paul. I need to know that you're with me."

I drooped. "I don't know what to say."

"Then don't say anything." Natasha marched off.

At the front desk, we asked the receptionist how much our visit would cost. "Three hundred and fifty Riel."

"That's cheaper than coffee at Java," Natasha said.

The nurse shrugged. "You pay now."

I paid.

16. Class

"MISTER." I LOOKED UP to a staring classroom. It was the first day of class. I was in a long, narrow room. The windows were wet with humidity; the walls were bare; the floor was cement. I stood behind a wooden desk while forty eager students waited.

"Mister?"

Beelzebub, McDougal, Mexico—faces flashed in my mind. Beelzebub's angry glare, McDougal's red hair and freckled cheeks, and Mexico dressed in his Marine alphas, escorting me to my room in San Angelo. The setting Iraqi sun, Grace's warm smile, and Swift's lifeless body. I could never escape. Shaped and formed, I was because of the Marine Corps.

Can I?

A hushed murmur filled the room.

I closed my eyes and breathed deeply.

I was unsure of my ability—to teach, to lead, to make peace. I had wrestled with the realities of violence, death, and killing: poverty, hate, and anger. I wanted desperately to do good, to be good. *Could I be?* I had killed; I had participated in killing; I was the perfected system of violence.

I am not a natural killer. I'm a trained killer. And yet, what was I but the sum of my experiences?

Swift. A dusty street, garbage floating in the wind, dogs prowling the sidewalk. Blood seeping out, pooling.

I opened my eyes. It was a moment of nothingness, a moment bursting with possibility.

I had a present. I would set right.

It seemed small, teaching as vengeance—teaching as my answer to a bullet in Fallujah.

17. Damson

"Mister Benjamin," Damson, a student, said after class. "I am very happy to be studying with you."

"Thank you."

"To study with native English speaker has always been dream."

"Really?" I sat my bag down.

"Yes. You see, when Pol Pot came, my family all killed."

"Your whole family?"

"Yes," he said. "Grandfather, grandmother, mother, and father. I have no one left."

"Do you have any siblings?" He tilted his head in confusion, so I clarified, "Uh . . . brothers and sisters?"

"Ah. Yes. One sister. We go to refugee camp in Thailand. We stay for many years. We come back, go to college. We very fortunate."

"And what are you studying at NPIC?"

"I study information technology. I graduate; get job. But having English skills, especially having studied with native, will help me secure better position."

"I see. Well, I'm glad to be here." I grabbed my bag.

"Mister," Damson said, "why you come Cambodia?"

"I'll tell you what, Damson. Why don't you walk with me to my dorm room? I'm hungry for lunch. You can stay and eat with us, if you'd like. I'll answer all of your questions."

"Really?"

"Yeah."

He beamed. "This means much."

We left the classroom and strolled across the small campus. At our door, I paused and looked out over the rice patties. It was harvest and the rice farmers were busy. A woman was crouched—one hand behind her back—slowly filling an oxcart. *Tedious.*

I opened the door and introduced Damson to Natasha who had held her first session that morning as well. While I was teaching the information technology students, Natasha was teaching English to the hospitality and recreation students. "How was class?"

"Great," she said. "When I walked into the classroom, my students stood to greet me."

"That would never happen in the States."

"No. They were strangely formal. It was nice."

"Damson," I shifted the conversation, "have you ever eaten a tortilla?" We had recently discovered both the secret of homemade tortillas and a local market that sold canned refried beans. In our excitement, we were devouring bean burritos like Cambodians rice. We made our own tortillas by mixing flour, water, and salt and rolling the dough flat with empty wine bottles. It was a comfort to eat something familiar. Damson had never seen a tortilla.

"No rice?"

"I need a break from rice," I said. He was confused. "How many times a day do you eat rice?"

"Everyday. Every meal. It what we eat. You same?"

"No," I laughed. Back home I eat rice *maybe* three or four times a year." He was scandalized, but watched as we rolled and fried our tortillas. Stuffed with beans and cheese, he took a bite and set it down.

"Thank you, but maybe I wait for rice. You like Michael Jackson?"

"I take it you do?"

"Yes. Michael Jackson is Cambodian hero. Wonderful music. *Billy Jean*. *Thriller*. *Car Wash*. Very good for you."

"I listen to Michael," Natasha said.

"Can I ask," Damson began, "why you in Cambodia?"

"To teach English," Natasha said.

"And have baby?"

"That was more of an accident."

"When your baby born, I ask for blessing."

"Blessing?"

"Yes," he said. "Babies very lucky."

"Oh. Sure."

"What America like?"

"It's very big," Natasha said. "There are a lot of people and a lot of big cities."

"Like Phnom Penh?"

"Like Phnom Penh."

"Someday," he said. "Maybe I go America."

"You want to go to America?"

"Yes. I want to attend university in America. After, I come back to Cambodia and make better place."

"Do you know where?"

"I have uncle in California. He left when Pol Pot came. He cleans things."

"He's a janitor?"

Damson nodded. "What favorite football team?"

"Football?" I asked.

"Hmm, how you say . . . soccer?"

"Oh. Football, maybe, isn't so popular in the United States."

He tilted his head. "You watch Manchester United, yes?"

"No."

"So you watch the Barcelona?"

Natasha laughed. "Who do you think we should watch?"

"Easy," he said. "You watch the Arsenal. Best team."

"Okay," I said. "We'll watch Arsenal."

He nodded. "Very good for you."

Natasha and I finished eating and cleared our dishes. Damson remained sitting. "Do you think that maybe I come once a week and you teach me English better?"

"You want me to tutor you?"

"Yes," he nodded. "You tutor me."

"I'll tell you what. I'll tutor you, if you teach me about football. Deal?"

"Deal," he said. "We will also listen to Michael Jackson."

18. Abroad

I SLAMMED THE DOOR on our Jeep Cherokee. Natasha was in the passenger seat. We were headed into Phnom Penh to buy groceries.

I turned the key.

Nothing.

The car had been roasting in the sun all day and I started to sweat.

I turned the key again.

Nothing. "Great."

"Give it a minute," Natasha said. We rolled down the windows and waited as our clothes slowly soaked through with perspiration. "Try it now."

I turned the key.

It started.

I backed out of our parking spot at the end of campus, shifted into drive, and drove by the cafeteria on our way to the front gate. Students were queued waiting for their daily rice. Our Jeep stalled and jerked to a stop. The students waiting in line moved towards us.

I turned the key.

Nothing.

Blood rose to my face; frustration pulsed through my veins.

We waited. The students were pointing.

I turned the key.

The car started, drove six feet, and died. Laughter wafted into our windows.

I was wet with sweat. Natasha, seven months pregnant, was sitting next to me in misery. The Jeep we had bought was clearly broken, but, not being a mechanic, I didn't know how to fix it. In America, we would have called a tow truck and paid for any necessary fixes. In Cambodia, I didn't know what the hell to do. *Does Cambodia even have towing companies?* Even if they did, how long would it be before they arrived? More than anything, I was baffled at how such a small problem, in a foreign culture, became a large problem.

I turned the ignition to the same result.

We were halfway to the front gate. At this point, I could exit the car and push it back to its parking space or I could continue on and see how far we might make it. I chose to continue.

Turning the key, the Jeep started.

"We're good now. I can feel it."

I bit my cheek and eased the car forward. We passed both the milling students waiting in line and the administrative building as we drew near the gate. When we were fifteen feet away, the Jeep stalled.

I lost control.

I slammed the steering wheel.

I raged.

I said bad things.

After calming, I saw that the middle console was broken and Natasha was in tears.

"I'm sorry."

"What's wrong with you?"

"I don't know."

I turned the ignition.

The car started. The air conditioner blasted cool air.

I took a deep breath as clouds broiled overhead, opened up, and poured. Rain came down as Natasha and I drove into Phnom Penh. The road was slick with mud and grease. The ditches overflowed.

It was a long, slow drive.

Halfway to Lucky Mart, Natasha asked: "Is it war stuff?"

"No. It's not that. I just . . . I hate not being in control."

"Culture shock?"

"That's too easy."

"Oh."

"Sometime I feel ashamed. That's all."

"Ashamed?"

"Yeah. We're supposed to have it together, right?"

"Because we're Americans?"

"Maybe. At least foreigners. But look at us. We're poor English teachers in a developing country with a baby on the way."

"We'll be fine."

"I don't even know how to fix a car. And everyone was staring."

"You sound like a six-year-old."

"Maybe I am," I said. "What are we doing here?"

"What do you mean? Teaching."

"Yeah, but we're barely doing that. I feel like this whole damn thing was a swing-and-a-miss."

"I wouldn't say that," Natasha said. "We've changed. We met Damson. NPIC has native English teachers. It's not a loss."

"In the States people our age are buying houses and progressing in their careers. I don't know. I thought . . . I'm the same here as I was in the States. Shouldn't I be better?"

"Better?"

"When I was in Iraq I always thought if I were on a peacekeeping mission and not a war mission, I would feel noble. You know? Brave and useful. Then I wrote my thesis . . . I wanted to atone. But this can't be what it feels like."

"What?"

"Atonement."

"How does it feel?"

"Helpless."

The rain stopped as quickly as it had started. Within moments, it was a hot and humid outside. We pulled into Lucky Mart's parking garage and sat for a moment. "I don't feel like shopping."

"We haven't toured Toul Slang yet. The groceries can wait."

Natasha handed me her phone. I called Surin. "Ja," he answered.

"Surin," I said. "This Benjamin. At grocery. You come?"

"Ja." He hung up the phone.

Ten minutes later, Surin rounded the corner in his Tuk-Tuk. We boarded and asked him to take us to Toul Slang. "Okay. I know."

At the entrance of the museum sat a man with no arms or legs. Around his neck hung a sign that read: *land mine victim*. Natasha placed twenty dollars worth of Riel into his bucket as we shuffled into the school's courtyard. It was empty except for a few tourists, thick and muggy. There was no tour guide.

We spent the next two hours exploring the rooms and courtyards of Pol Pot's security prison. It was here that 17,000 Cambodians were imprisoned and tortured for the purpose of providing the names of friends and family members whom were anti-Khmer Rouge. From here, the prisoners were hauled to The Killing Fields, shot, and thrown into mass graves.

The complex consisted of five buildings shaped into a horseshoe. Many of the rooms remained as they did during S-21's active days. Spring beds without mattresses filled the rooms, as did chains and wrist cuffs. Dried blood stained both the floors and walls. In one room, we found hundreds of pictures of victims—Cambodians whose only crime was to be Cambodian. Near the photographs of prisoners, hung a list of S-21's rules and regulations:

1. You must answer accordingly to my question. Don't turn them away.
2. Don't try to hide the facts by making pretexts this and that, you are strictly prohibited to contest me.
3. Don't be a fool for you are a chap who dare to thwart the revolution.
4. You must immediately answer my questions without wasting time to reflect.
5. Don't tell me either about your immoralities or the essence of the revolution.
6. While getting lashes or electrification you must not cry at all.
7. Do nothing, sit still and wait for my orders. If there is no order, keep quiet. When I ask you to do something, you must do it right away without protesting.
8. Don't make pretext about Kampuchea Krom in order to hide your secret or traitor.
9. If you don't follow all the above rules, you shall get many lashes of electric wire.
10. If you disobey any point of my regulations you shall get either ten lashes or five shocks of electric discharge.

"How could this happen?" Natasha asked.

"I don't know."

We were in Surin's Tuk-Tuk driving to our favorite restaurant—Gasolina. We had decided that we would eat and then return to Lucky Market for groceries.

As we ordered our food, a woman at an adjacent table overheard us speaking English and asked if she might join us. We obliged. The expatriate community was a small and accommodating one. We introduced ourselves. Her name was Patty.

"What are you doing in Cambodia?" I asked.

"I'm on business. I work here."

"Oh, where are you from?"

"England, if you couldn't tell from my accent."

"I didn't want to assume," Natasha said.

"An unassuming American. That's rare."

"There are a few."

"And what do you both do for work?"

"Teachers," I said. "At the National Polytechnic Institute of Cambodia. You?"

"Lawyer."

"Really? Business lawyer?"

"No. Defense attorney." Both Natasha and I responded with quizzical looks. "I'm in the employ of Mr. Kang Kek Iew."

"Who?"

"Comrade Duch, the one-time officer in charge of S-21."

"Wait . . . you're defending Duch?"

"He's a right to a fair trial, doesn't he? I knew things were changing in America, but I didn't realize they were changing that deeply."

"No," Natasha said. "It's just that . . . he deserves to be imprisoned. Doesn't he?"

"Half of the world's political leaders deserve prison, but they've still a right to a fair trial. Besides, it pays well."

I withheld judgment. "Has the trial started?"

"In a few weeks. Actually, it's near NPIC. The United Nations and the Government of Cambodia are selling tickets. I can retain a pair of tickets for you, if you'd like?"

"I'd like that very much," I said. "But we'll be leaving for Thailand soon." I pointed to Natasha's growing belly.

"Congratulations."

"How long will you be in Cambodia?" Natasha asked.

"The trial should take a year or so and then I'm off to The Hague."

"For what?"

Patty looked up from her spaghetti carbonara. "Another trial, I assume."

"So you just . . . travel the world defending war criminals?"

"Yes." There was no emotion in Patty's answer.

"Fascinating."

We finished our meal and thanked Patty for the conversation. Surin, who had been waiting, drove us back to Lucky Market. We shopped and then made the long journey back to NPIC.

It was dark when we turned onto the ill-paved road that would lead us to the front gate. We were five minutes away from NPIC. As we started to accelerate, a rock crashed into our windshield. Natasha screamed. *Is this an ambush?*

"Drive," Natasha said.

I mashed the pedal. The Jeep's tires flung dirt and mud as we hurled into the night. I drove recklessly, searching the horizon for the welcoming lights of NPIC.

Our hearts pounding; we pulled into safety.

The following morning we recounted our adventure to President Kim. He smiled. "Maybe countryside not so safe for Americans. We buy AK?"

"Excuse me?"

"AK," he said. "AK-47—pop, pop, pop."

"Uh . . . no thanks," I said. "I only wanted you to know that it happened."

He shrugged and went back to work.

19. Regan

We traveled to Thailand for Regan's delivery, because both necessity and insurance demanded it. Natasha flew a month early while I finished the Khmer semester. Once in Thailand, we stayed in Chiang Mai. At five in the morning Natasha's water broke. We rushed down the stairs and into the first Tuk-Tuk we could find. Thirty-four hours later, at the Chiang Mai RAM Hospital, Regan Elise Peters was born. She was alien and blue—something Natasha and I had made, but wholly other. I was filled with both joy and doubt.

The day we were to discharge, however, the doctors told us Regan was sick.

Doctor Pia wasn't sure what it was, but he knew Regan needed a lumbar puncture followed by a ten-day antibiotic cycle. We were new parents in a foreign country, scared and out of our depth. My thesis turned adventure had mutated into a dirty, ugly thing. The consequence of which could be both terrible and lasting.

Natasha was weeping outside of the operating room when Doctor Pia told me to hold Regan down. He was preparing to puncture her lumbar.

"What you do in Phnom Penh?" Doctor Pia asked.

"Teach English."

"Hmph. Why Cambodia? Why you not come Thailand and teach?"

Thailand and Cambodia had a difficult and complex history. "Well," with my hand on Regan's neck, I tried to balance the conversation. "It's where I was placed by my organization."

"Hmph. Why you come Thailand deliver baby?"

Flattery. "I heard the Chiang Mai RAM was the best hospital in Southeast Asia."

"Really?"

"That's what I heard."

"Excellent," Pia said, before clapping his hands. "Let's begin."

It was terrible, worse than water boarding. While I held Regan down, Doctor Pia rooted four-long needles into Regan's back, draining her spinal juice into a small vial. My daughter, my perfect and beautiful daughter, shrieked—her face purple, her screams haunting.

This is my fault. I'm the one who convinced Natasha to live in Southeast Asia. If I had only . . . this never should've happened.

Doctor Pia finished the procedure and began Regan's intravenous drip, which was to continue two hours a day, twelve hours apart, for seven days. After which, he said, "Maybe we see."

Natasha and I left the nursery to find our room and rest. "We can't stay."

"In Thailand?"

"No. Cambodia."

I stopped and turned towards her. "Not now, Natasha. This could've happened anywhere."

"But it wasn't anywhere. It was Cambodia . . . it was Thailand. In the States they test for Group B Strep. They don't here. Our doctors would've caught it. Now our daughter might have meningitis." She opened the door to our hospital room. "We can't stay here."

Regan was born February 1st. We were home by July.

20. Culture

THE FAN OVERHEAD, WHIRLING on its axis, created a haven of respite from the stifling heat and suffocating humidity. Geckos scurried along the walls as Natasha and I lounged on Java's balcony, waiting for our Cambodian hamburgers. Regan, ten-weeks-old, was resting in her car seat. The sounds of Norodom Boulevard drifted over the balcony's edge—motorbikes, SUVs, and Tuk-Tuks seeking out their Friday night haunts. Natasha and I were taking a break from the countryside for the weekend and staying at a hotel with both consistently running water and air-conditioning.

Our meal came as an American woman walked out onto the balcony with a Cambodian child and flopped onto the couch opposite us. Her eyes were rimmed red. She ordered a coffee, but, before it came, fell asleep with her child resting in her arms. It wasn't until later, after the woman woke and offered a spoon to her child, that Natasha struck a conversation. "Not to presume, but we have a lot of toys if your child would like to play with one."

"Yes," she said, breathing with relief. "I'd appreciate that."

Natasha handed her one of Regan's toys and asked the woman her name.

"Juliet," she said. "I'm from Tennessee. Where are y'all from?"

"Denver," Natasha said. "What brings you to Cambodia?"

"I run a community center in a small village north of Phnom Penh."

"Are you adopting?" I asked, gesturing to the Cambodian baby, which she was now cradling.

"No. This," she looked down at the child, "just sort of happened."

"Happened?"

"I met with the grandparents of a student in my program. They had this baby, Lutroo. They couldn't care for her, and I couldn't help myself. I said I'd adopt her, but the process is excruciating."

"How long have you been in Cambodia?"

"I've been here a year," she started to cry. "Now the government is telling me that it might be another two years. I'm not allowed to leave with her. My parents—her grandparents—want to meet Lutroo so badly." Natasha placed an arm around Juliet, who had tears streaking down her face.

We were both new parents, struggling to sleep each night. I couldn't imagine meeting the demands of a newborn alone.

Throughout the rest of our meal, we discussed parenting, Cambodia, and living abroad. Juliet, not expecting to acquire a child in Cambodia, was short on resources. We offered her what we could—a Baby Bjorn, pacifiers, and a few blankets. Grateful, she asked if we would be interested in touring her school and community center. We said we would and made plans for visiting the following morning.

‡ ‡ ‡

We drank jasmine tea in the courtyard of our hotel, the Frangipani, as the sun rose over Phnom Penh. Surin and his Tuk-Tuk arrived. "Can you take us here," Ethan, who had joined us, asked in Khmer while pointing at a map of the surrounding area.

"Yeah, I know," he said, which was a common Surin-ism. He fired up his motorbike and waded into Phnom Penh's sea of traffic.

At a stoplight halfway to our destination, a beggar stumbled over to our Tuk-Tuk. He asked for money and we obliged with a few hundred Riel—the equivalent of three or four U.S. dollars. As I handed him the money, he noticed my arm hair. He caught my hand and tugged on it. When I didn't wince, he met my eyes and pulled my hair as hard as he could. I let out a cry and jerked my hand back. Surin rounded on the beggar and hit him on the head. My eyes were wide with shock as Surin sped away.

"What was that?" Natasha asked.

I blinked and rubbed my arm.

"That's some weird bull," said Ethan.

We left the city behind and followed a small river alongside a dirt road for what seemed like hours. Natasha struggled to both keep her breasts hidden from Ethan and feed Regan as the Tuk-Tuk bounced our daughter up and down. She had just closed her eyes and greedily drifted to sleep when Juliet's compound came into site. Surin pulled through the gate and lurched to a stop. The community center was comprised of three buildings: one for teaching, one for recreation, and one for eating. Juliet greeted us with Lutroo resting on her hip. We followed Juliet as she led us on a tour of her program. At lunch, we stopped in the kitchen and ate a simple meal of rice and chicken.

"Why this village?" Natasha asked. I was holding Regan while Natasha finished her lunch.

"The organization I'm with, Promise International, chose this village because of its unique situation."

"What's that?" Ethan asked.

"We work with children aged four to twelve. The parents of our children are trapped in a cycle of poverty, so, often, they sell their children."

"What do you mean 'sell'?"

"Uh—" Juliet hesitated, "into sexual encounters."

"They sell their own children?"

"What the fuck?" Ethan asked.

"I'm not being clear," Juliet said. "It's not a permanent arrangement. Each night, many of our children will be prostituted. After their encounter, they will return to their home. We see them the following day."

"Wait," I said. "So these kids are being sold into sex each night and then showing up here in the morning?"

"Yes," Juliet said.

Ethan shook his head. "I don't understand."

"I don't either."

"Who buys them?" Natasha asked.

"Cambodian men, mostly."

Hearing little voices, we moved outside to find Juliet's students had arrived. Her yard was filled with beautiful and healthy Cambodian boys and girls—dark haired and skinned. They were smiling and laughing, kicking around a soccer ball. One of Juliet's colleagues was among them, playing goalie. I looked down at my own daughter. She was small with clear eyes and black, fuzzy hair. Regan's harsh entry into the world had passed. She was healthy. But holding her fragile body in my arms, I couldn't imagine another man—in four years' time—ravaging her. Anger welled up within me as I watched Cambodian children enjoying an impromptu soccer match. They were happy, living in the moment, as if their night horrors were a thing of dreams. I was dismayed by their strength, dumbfounded by their resilience. *Unbelievable.*

We watched the students in silence until Ethan ran out and onto the makeshift pitch. "It ain't 'bama," he shouted. "But I'm gonna learn me some football."

I turned to Juliet. "How do you do it?"

"What?"

"Live with it."

"I'm not trying to."

"You're a—" I started to say, but was drowned out by the roar of students scoring on Ethan.

Part Three

21. Angkor

I HAD BEEN ALONE in Cambodia for two months. After Regan's hospital scare, Natasha and I had decided to move back to the United States. We were cutting our journey a year short. *Was it worth it?* Change takes time, relationship . . . expertise. *But living overseas?* Is the truth of a thing changed because one can't measure up to it?

Before Natasha boarded at the Phnom Penh airport, we shared a scoop of ice cream and discussed our return. She would finish her master's degree; I would stay home with Regan. I would transition from killer to educator to stay-at-home dad—a strange path with an unknown end. I kissed Regan on the forehead and waved goodbye to Natasha before driving back to NPIC and spending a lonely two months filled with teaching and reading.

It was my last session with Damson. "Next year, you come back?" He asked.

"My daughter—" I stopped. "I don't think I'll be back next year, Damson. I'm sorry."

"You no come back?"

"No."

"Maybe I come America."

"If you visit America, call me."

He scrunched his forehead. "Why you no like Cambodia?"

"No, Damson, I like Cambodia very much, it's that . . . I have a family." I stopped. Why had we come here? To make a difference. Had we? To Damson maybe. *To change a life is to change a world.* It was arrogant to assume Cambodia needed us. It didn't. If we had affected any great change in the world, then it was surely in ourselves more than our students. Was that enough? Would that end war? I shook my head. "I'm sorry, Damson. I wish I could stay."

"In Cambodia we say, 'Drop by drop fills the bamboo.'"

"Thanks?"

"I know why you come. You come see big change. But maybe you don't." Damson shrugged. "Maybe you see tomorrow, yes?"

"Yes."

"I think Michael Jackson proud."

"Thanks, Damson."

Later that night Ethan and I found our way to a Cambodian tavern. We drank Angkor beer and discussed our year at NPIC. He wouldn't be returning either. He was planning on attending nursing school in Alabama.

We held up our beers. "Well, we tried."

"That we did."

"Are we assholes?" I asked.

"Why?"

"We think we have something to offer the world; we think we can change the world. Does that come from being Christians or Americans?"

"It aligns with the teachings of Jesus—we do good; serve the poor."

"To serve, yes, but to see a difference? That we aren't promised."

"Well," Ethan said, "maybe you're an asshole."

"Why nursing?"

"I don't know. It's like the Good Samaritan—serve people while they're down."

"Why does it always come back to that?"

"It's a powerful story—"

"Yeah, yeah, yeah," I said.

"It's both simple and incomprehensible," Ethan said. "Things should be right, but they aren't."

"But what's 'right'?"

"I wonder if the Samaritan ever felt that way."

"Or Jesus?"

"Him, too."

The next morning Ethan, Lauren, and I drove to the airport. We would be on the same flight out of Phnom Penh, but would diverge at the Bangkok airport. Students from both Phnom Penh's Royal University—where Lauren had taught—and NPIC came to say goodbye. We hugged our students, some of who cried. Damson made two western gestures—he shook my hand and looked me in the eyes. I told him I'd miss him and I was happy we'd met. He thanked me and said goodbye.

I passed through security and boarded the plane.

22. Write

"Okay," I said, "have a good day."

I watched Natasha shut the door on our Subaru. We were home and living in the basement of my in-laws. I was a stay-at-home dad. Natasha was finishing her master's degree in counseling at Denver Seminary. She started the car and drove off through the falling snow. I turned, scooped up my crawling daughter, and descended into the basement. It was naptime, which meant I had an hour-and-a-half to work on the conclusion to my thesis. I popped Regan's pacifier in her mouth and laid her down. She cooed while I sat down at our desk and powered up the computer. Her cooing turned to gentle cries as I opened up a blank Word document. I had spent the last week reading over the finished chapters of my thesis, reacquainting myself with it. *I can do this*. I looked at the stacks of books lying around me and waited. Regan's crying died off. She was asleep. I wrote.

‡ ‡ ‡

"How much were you able to do today?" Natasha asked. We were eating dinner. Regan was flinging her mashed peas across the table.

"I finished my summary. Tomorrow I'll start writing the section on contemporary applications. And then I'll be done."

"That's exciting."

"It's weird. In some ways, it feels like the end."

"I, for one, will be glad it's over."

Weeep, Regan screeched. A pea landed in my eye. I wiped it off. "Yeah, I know."

Three weeks passed before I found the time to write. *Beelzebub. Swift. Major Donald. Damson.* I had come a long way—read a lot and written much. But the problem with biblical studies is found in the complexity of applying ancient texts, filtered through personal experience, two-thousand years after they were written. What did Paul have to say, today, on matters of social issues and foreign policy? What were the implications of loving or not loving my neighbor in an age of nuclear weapons, terrorism, and robot monkeys?

And so I went back, back to the beginning, the reason for my research. There was a question, all those years ago: was I justified in what I did? I excessively mulled over this question. I reflected on justifications, reasons, and implications. It kept me up at night. I wanted clarifications, a streamlined response. I wrestled with words.

And then, I stopped.

The answers would come or they wouldn't. I would find a way forward, or I wouldn't. Either way, with a small and simple word—a first hesitant step forward—I would create something difficult and complex, poignant and beautiful. I would craft my response to war. I had earned that, if nothing else.

‡ ‡ ‡

I leaned back and watched as Natasha read my conclusion. It didn't take long.

"You were certainly clear," she said. "What do you think Professor Kelwin will say?"

"I have no idea. It's due in a week."

"What's left?"

"I have to write one more section: *The Way Ahead*."

"Which is?" Natasha asked.

"I guess you'll have to wait and see."

Regan stirred. We were sitting on a blue couch in the basement of my in-law's house. It was cold and snowing outside.

"Let's bundle her up and make some snow angels," Natasha said, her eyes glittering.

We changed into winter clothes before squeezing Regan into a polar bear bunting. Her round, pink face was peaking out, unaware.

INTERLUDE

"YOU'RE DONE?"

"Yeah. I finally finished."

"How does it feel?" Trent asked. We were sitting at Stella's on Pearl Street, drinking coffee. He wanted to hear about Cambodia and agreed to break the rules of counseling. We were in public and he wasn't charging me. *It's almost like we're friends.*

"Great, actually. It's nice to be done."

"So what's next?"

"Oh, I don't know." I sipped my coffee. "I've been asked to teach a small, four-week course at my church on war and peacemaking. So I'll do that. It'll give me something to do while I'm at home with Regan."

"How much longer does Natasha have?"

"She'll graduate in the spring. And then we'll have to decide about work and parenting. But, for now, we're just enjoying being home."

He smiled. "Do you remember when you fist came to see me?"

"Yeah. Why?"

"You told me you sought wholeness."

I chuckled. "Perhaps I was being overly dramatic."

"It's a common enough desire. Most of us feel it at one point or another."

"Maybe."

"So?"

"You want to know if you were successful, right? If I'm healed?"

He looked down at his mug. "No, not that. I'm only curious."

"When Natasha's at work and it's just me and Regan at home. I sit her in her bouncy and read *Paradise Lost* to her."

"I bet she enjoys that."

"We both do." I sipped my coffee. "Anyway, there's this scene, near the end, when the archangel takes Adam atop this mountain so they can both look out, east of Eden."

He nodded.

"Michael reveals the course of human history in light of the apple. And what does Adam see? Violence through all the plain, 'and refuge none was found.' I don't know," I said. "Maybe there's no such thing as wholeness."

"Ah," Trent smiled. "But the purpose of that section, if I recall, is the eschatological triumph of Christ. There's hope, in the end."

I laughed. "But in the here and now? No. We're all death's ministers. Eschatology's nothing but a theological loop-de-loo. Even if you believe, it's meaningless."

"Why's that?"

"'Already here, but not yet.' Bah! Last I checked the 'already here' was a war in a desert and the raping of kids."

"You need to read *Paradise Regained*."

"No. I need *you* to tell me to read *Paradise Regained*."

"So you didn't find it?"

I sipped. "I found great subtlety. Complexities. But no certainties."

"Does wholeness require certainty?"

23. Teach

Driving through the snow-encrusted streets of Denver, wisps of white powder blew across my windshield while Natasha and I navigated the mountainous storm. Regan was sleeping at her grandparents. It was the last session in my four-week seminar on the issues of peace, justice, and war as they related to the Christian faith.

There had been a nominal turn out. There were four others, besides me and Natasha: Cole and Christie, a married couple resembling two thinly framed pixies, Ethan, who was visiting from Mobile, and the former Tinkling, Greg. We followed, through assigned readings, the outline of my thesis. This week, we were tackling the conclusion.

We were huddled around a modern table dominated by a long window. The lights outside were bright, casting the flitting snow into an ethereal nether.

Everyone was present except for Greg, who was committed to driving a Camaro throughout Denver's winter. "Did everyone finish their readings?"

"Yeah," Cole said. "But I was hoping for a little more clarity." He was leaning forward, elbows on the table.

"Meaning?"

"How do you take ideas and concepts generated in the first century, slap a little theoretical paint on them, and apply them in our time? Too much is lost in translation."

"Hold on," Ethan said. "The Bible's always applicable."

"How? That's my question. Is it abstract? Is it practical?'

Snow stormed into the room as the door swung open. "Sorry," Greg said. "I had trouble with my car."

"Surprise," Natasha said.

"Yeah, yeah," he said. "What did I miss?"

"We were questioning the legitimacy of biblical application to our modern context."

"*You* were," Ethan said.

"Southerner." I clapped my hands in excitement. "Alright, let's recap. First, Christians should repay evil with good."

"Which ain't some sort of bullshit hippie policy," Ethan said. "It very well might be troops on the ground."

"We differed on that point."

"That's what *you* said."

"Paul's peacemaking ethic—"

"Look," Ethan said, slapping his hand on the table. "You said that even if our enemies are seeking to harm us, we should just lie down. That's stupid. I don't think God wants innocent people to die. Someone has to stand up for justice."

"Vengeance is mine," Greg said.

"Blah, blah, blah. I've heard it before. But I'm putting my money on the church. You know why? Because it's God's tool for reaping vengeance."

"That's absurd," Christie said. "Watch *The Godfather*. Violence only creates more violence."

"I see Ethan's point," Cole said. "What you say sounds great. Of course I don't want to create more violence in the world, but how does one, in actuality, accomplish that . . . reducing violence while creating peace?"

"I'm for real solutions," Natasha said. "Pragmatics. Our longing for vengeance is really a longing for justice. The question, for me, is can perfect justice be attained?"

"Eschatologically?"

"I don't know. I would prefer the here and now."

Cole nodded.

"Real solutions are nice," Greg said, "but complex."

"In Cambodia," Natasha started, "we met this Floridian whose life revolved around working with kids living in Phnom Penh's dump. He'd develop a relationship with a kid, drum up some aid for him or her, only to watch as the child contracted, every time, some rare, infectious disease and died. I'd call that complex."

"Or when I taught at the Street School," I said. "Every day my students greeted me: 'Morning, dumbfuck.' It was really encouraging. But part of saying 'no' to violence, is saying 'yes' to death."

"Which makes a whole lot of sense," Christie offered.

"Point," Greg said.

"The thing about peacemaking, though, is that it's infinitely creative—"

"Continually seeking," Natasha broke in, "new ways to overcome evil."

"Systemic evil." I clarified.

"Both individual and systemic," she smiled.

"Both *personal* and systemic."

"A lover's quarrel?"

I nodded. "Either way."

Natasha patted my cheek.

I shrugged her off. "If I may." I picked up my now completed thesis and read: "This study has endeavored to prove the thesis that Romans 12:14—13:7 is an appeal to reconciliation, active peacemaking, and political critique not a proof text for governmental theology." I sat it down. "There's only one question left."

24. Representations

I STOOD AND WROTE the question on the whiteboard opposite the window. "This world is filled with an enormous amount of violence, hate, and war. Does anything we've discussed, does anything I've written, make a difference—in the real world?" I sat. Outside, the ethereal snow continued to congregate at the corners of the window. Our view was shrinking with each passing moment.

"I think it *can* make a difference," Christie said.

"It's gray," Cole said. "I'm not sure how clearly we can, you know, see . . . through a glass, darkly. It's like Plato. All we experience are the shadows of the real objects that, even if upgraded to high def, only *represent* the thing."

"We have to try though," Greg said.

"What are we talking 'bout?" Ethan asked.

"Three things," I said. "First, Christians do not fight in wars." I smote the table in a rousing display of confidence.

"Reality says different," Ethan said. "Christians have and do fight in wars. I don't agree with you."

"That's just stupid, Ethan. Of course Christians have fought in wars. That doesn't make it prescriptive. We can own up to the past and not repeat it."

"Repeat yourself."

I moved on. "So, one, Christians shouldn't kill people. Two, the church should partner with the government and local authorities on peacemaking initiatives."

"Yeah, I still don't agree with you."

"I'm shocked."

"What would that look like?" Cole asked.

"For me," Greg said, "it's rethinking our response to events like September 11th. We were attacked. It was horrific. A lot of innocent people died. Paul writes, however, to 'bless the persecutor.' In light of the Twin Towers, those are difficult and complex words. Were we to seek vengeance, start a war, or send in elite troops to assassinate Bin Laden? I think the corporate message should've been one of forgiveness and reconciliation, focused, in part, on the redemption of the instigators."

"I don't think you should belittle anyone's suffering," Ethan said. "It's kind of offensive."

"I'm not. I'm just answering a question."

"Well that's batshit crazy," Ethan said.

"Is it?" I stepped in. "Is it crazy to mourn something, to be greatly offended by something, but also to admit one's role in it, no matter how complicit?"

"Yeah!" Ethan stood and began strolling around the table.

"Wait," Cole said. "Are you talking about redeeming Osama?"

"No. Not redeeming," Greg said. "He's got his own damn religion. I'm talking about reaching out in reconciliation, not violence. The logical conclusion to be drawn from Paul is that we're to live at peace, to be makers of peace, no matter what. In fact, that's supposed to be the church's role within society. It's to serve as a reminder that violence doesn't always have to be the answer."

"Yeah that's batshit," Cole said.

"It sounds better in the abstract."

25. Knowing

"The poor," Christie said. "If what you're saying is accurate, caring for the poor is synonymous with Paul's peacemaking initiatives."

"It might sounds harsh," I said. "But no matter how frequently they practice their religious rituals, those who neglect the poor and oppressed are not God's people."

"Home of the generous and openhanded."

"The church isn't America; America isn't Christian."

"Oh, but we want to believe," Greg said.

"Like so many other cultures."

Ethan circled around the table and stood next to his chair. "The Constitution is rooted in Christian principals."

"That's not a fun argument," I said. "Actions prove values. I'm interested in understanding how—today, right now—we conduct ourselves in the global arena."

"You make it sound like we're bad."

"Bad?" I leaned back and gazed out the window. The snow was pelting the glass in hushed thumps. "It's not about bad or good."

"What're we talking 'bout then?" Ethan sat.

"In a world where 1.2 billion people live off a dollar or less a day while another 1.6 billion are very poor, living on two dollars or less a day; where thirty thousand children die every day of hunger and preventable diseases; where thirteen million people die every year from infectious—"

Greg interrupted with a laugh, reciting: "I don't know half of you half as well as I should like, and I like less than half of you half as well as you deserve."

"Exactly," I smiled. "Stats are stats. But if they reveal anything, then they reveal we're rich; we've the means to rectify systemic injustice; and yet we don't. That's not to say we don't put forth effort—we do. But I believe the way in which we spend is a reflection of our collective values. Our defensive budget would suggest something other than biblical values guiding our decisions."

"Like what?"

"Our own interests—material, political, ideological. We've insulated ourselves to a degree that most of us are divorced from the realities of the world. Jesus moved among the poorest of the poor. He was a poor man who taught that when we act on behalf of the poor we are actually acting both for him and with him. The world is filled with impoverished people being strangled by the wealthy. And in case you missed it or I'm not being clear—that's us . . . that's me. We're part of a system that perpetuates the suffering of the poor."

"So," Ethan said. "We earned it."

"But at whose expense?" Christie asked.

"I'll bore you with facts and figures," I said. They groaned. "Don't blame me, blame the bald one." I pointed at Ethan. "In 2001 the Program on International Policy Attitudes at the University of Maryland—"

"The who?"

"PIPA . . . they're a thing," I said. "Anyway, they reported that Americans, on average, believed that foreign aid accounts for 20 percent of the federal budget, roughly twenty-four times the actual figure."

"Which is?"

"Much smaller. In fact, when one adds churches and other faith-based organizations it's still only .18 percent of GNP. In contrast, our defense budget is—."

"That's a lot of acronyms," Natasha interrupted.

"Can't help it—military. What's important is that our .18 percent lands us at the bottom of the list for first-world countries. Again, and this is really important, I'm not saying redistribution of wealth will result in the eradication of evil—that's absurd. We must, however, acknowledge our misconceptions and short fallings so we can begin a dialogue on how to move forward. After all, if we're supposed to love our neighbor, then I would say we're doing a terrible job of it."

"Neighbor?'" Ethan asked. "Isn't our neighbor, literally, our neighbor? Should Nigeria be our concern?"

"We live in a global age," Christie said. "Flip on your computer, television, or radio. As long as you're made aware of the suffering of others, you're accountable."

"So the governing principle when considering the definition of one's neighbor is awareness?"

"Sure," she said.

"War doesn't solve economic despair, social injustice, or political oppression and," I said, "our military doesn't equal our security. Loving my neighbor, strategically, has to mean more than violently protecting him or her."

"We all believe, abstractly, in human rights," Greg said. "But they're not necessarily universal. Even human rights charters are written from positions of power."

"But what's the alternative? Terrorist hotbeds are unstable societies beset by poverty, unemployment, rapid population growth . . . hunger."

"Nothing can solve that stuff," Ethan said. "Not war, not social justice, not anything."

"But the four hundred and fifty billion dollars the U.S. spends on our military won't buy us peace. So what should we do? If we can agree war is a problem and that poverty is a key issue in cultivating war, what should we do? Maintain the status quo?"

"You can't make people change," Ethan said. "And, besides, who the hell knows where that money goes?"

"Seriously though, what's the alternative?"

"I don't know." He shrugged.

26. Streaming War

"Are we allowed to say 'third-world'?" Natasha asked. "Is that offensive?"

"Yes," Greg said. "It is."

"I'm sure it is. But with affluence comes responsibility, right? If the statistics do anything, then they surely point to our own misconceptions."

"You bemoan Western affluence," Ethan said, "but apparently want every other nations to have it. So which is it?"

"In a world where children grow up beneath a stairwell in Cambodia, affluence and its partner, opportunity, have to come with some kind of responsibility."

"Why?" he asked. "Why can't we let people solve their own problems? And you didn't answer my question."

"We can," I said. "And there's a lot of interesting work being done with sustainable development. But the teachings I believe in say the poor are my concern. There's no escape clause. So regardless of what development might look like, as a Christian, I do have to care and I do, in some way, have to make myself available."

"Well, the teachings I ascribe to are about salvation, not philanthropy or sustainable development."

"Which is where evangelicalism led you astray, Ethan. It sold you a false gospel."

"You can't say that."

"Just did."

"You're a shitty teacher."

"Maybe. But when a society is economically dominant, it's easy to assume that such dominance reflects a deeper superiority—whether religious, racial, genetic, cultural, institutional . . . whatever. We've succumbed to a complacency in which belief trumps body. And we love to justify our ignorance by defaulting to false views of prophecy and health and wealth gospels."

"That's harsh."

"But necessary."

"I don't know," Cole said. "We struck out to do good."

"Its after prom," I said. "And the church is humping the state. What's that? Whoops. They gone and made a baby—Western evangelicalism."

"That's ridiculous," Natasha said.

"Is it?" Greg asked.

"I remember watching as we invaded Iraq in college," Cole said. "I never thought in our age . . . war was supposed to be something our grandfathers lived through, not us. I wasn't prepared for that . . . and I didn't even fight. It was like reality television. I don't know . . . how should we have responded?"

"America repays evil with precision-guided bombs," I said. "In contrast, Christians repay evil with good. The two are diametrically opposed."

"'Good' is vague," Ethan said. "And we've talked about this. That could mean anything."

I shrugged. "It serves as a reminder that religion isn't meant to be a self-help, self-serving entity, but rather a community committed to the community."

27. Empire Wins

"I'm waiting for something other than theory," Christie said.

"We've all done the readings," I said. "What do you think?"

"If we're going to say war is always bad and Christianity should always be opposed to it, then to me the next logical question is: how should the church interact with the world?"

"Well—"

"Let me answer."

"Alright."

"The church has to remain independent. It can't promote any *one* party, for when it does, it forfeits its right to critique."

"Anyone else?"

"We have to start calling war what it is," Greg said. "Evil. And we can't keep siding with the empire or else we just create an us-versus-them mentality that, at its core, breeds violence."

"Hold it," Ethan said. "Aren't you forgetting the men and women who died so you could hold your precious ideals?"

"I don't think so."

"My experience shouldn't trump your opinion, Ethan," I interrupted. "But it can serve as a reminder. A reminder that violence won't leave you the way you encountered it. PTSD implies that both violence and war aren't healthy pursuits. After all, we don't often pursue corrective counseling for the good, fulfilling things in our lives. If PTSD is the symptom, then war is the disease. Is that really an unpatriotic message? An un-Christian message? People who kill by profession are jacked up. And yet we glorify it. We glorify it in both our schools and pulpits, which is a nasty rhetoric that compromises the nature of Christianity. Rectification can only begin when we start calling war what it is—sin, depravity, humanity run amok."

"But what's the alternative? War happens."

"A friend of mine, we enlisted together, came home from Iraq . . . different. I'm not saying I had it easy, but this guy, McDougal, he was jacked. He couldn't sleep, be with his wife, work. You name it. When the Fourth of July rolled around, he thought every firework was a fucking insurgent hunting him down. He needed help."

"And your point?"

"My point is that war and violence fundamentally change a person, and not for the better. It's okay . . . it *should* be okay to say that out loud."

"If not war, then what?"

"All people," Natasha said, "should have access to the resources necessary to earn a decent living and be dignified members of their community."

"And that would stop war?"

"Wouldn't it?" The snow had built up around the window. The street was barely visible. What I could see was clean and pure. It lay perfectly unaware of its surroundings. "All I'm saying is there's a better way than violence, and the church, as its founder proposed, should look to promoting that better way."

"Or what?" Cole asked.

"The empire wins," Greg responded.

I snorted. "For seventeen-hundred years we've been trying to answer this question." I paused. "Maybe the empire always wins."

"You haven't seen Star Wars."

Our hour was up. We packed our bags. No one spoke as we filed out of the conference room.

Do words have the power to affect change?

I shook my head. I was at the end of a long journey, a journey that had started nine years previously on a dark night in San Diego. That night had culminated in the question: was I justified in what I did?

We opened the door to a silent blizzard raging quietly.

Epilogue

FRAMED IN THE OUTLINE of a large oaken door was Luis. We hadn't seen each other since our final day in the Marine Corps. He was smiling, holding a bottle of fifteen-year Dalwhinnie. "What's up, Devil?"

I hadn't been called that in years. I smiled and escorted Luis into my in-law's kitchen. We pulled cast iron stools from underneath the kitchen's island and sat. He poured the highland scotch, neat. Our glasses clinked. We drank. "It's been a long time," I said.

"So it has."

"Who are you working for these days?"

"Logistical Aeronautics," he replied. "You?"

"My daughter." I paused. "What are you doing for LA?"

"You know me, Peters, I'm holding down the insurgency in Afghanistan."

I lifted my glass off the granite countertop and swirled it. "How many times have you been over now?"

"Besides the Marine Corps, six. All told, eight."

"Why do you keep doing it?"

"It's my job, Peters. Not to sound cliché, but it's what I do."

"You in danger?"

"As much as anyone, I guess." He sighed and looked around. "Nice house."

"It is. We live in the basement."

"Well, look at us," he said. "We've come a long way." Mischief filled his eyes. "You remember that old gunnery sergeant in San Angelo?"

I nodded.

"Good God, I thought his eyes were gonna shoot out of his damn sockets when he inspected our room after you won Marine of the Quarter. It was filthy."

"Yeah," I laughed. "But it was definitely your filth. I was an innocent bystander."

"Didn't matter." Luis was laughing, too. "You outranked me and you'd just come from the Marine of the Quarter banquet. It was your job to keep me in line."

"Didn't gunny bring that captain with him? To show off?"

"That's right! I'd forgotten that. Shit, Peters, those were good times."

I sipped. "You ever talk to anyone from the reserve unit?"

"Oh, a few people. Most of them are boots. The real Devils got out when they could. This new breed . . . well, they've not seen Iraq."

"And those who have?"

"Well, there are various levels of civilian competence. Some are fine, working and functioning. But there are others, you know, who can't even walk outside without seeing an insurgent."

"Who?"

"Corporal Quixote, for one. He locks himself into his closet and drinks until he passes out." Luis shrugged. "Can't handle it, I guess."

"And you?"

"I'm like anyone else, Peters. I get by." Luis shifted in his seat. "So what's next for you?"

"Oh, I don't know. I'm researching PhD programs—"

"You finished your master's?"

"Yeah," I said.

"And?"

"And what?"

"Is war good or bad, Peters?"

"Eight times? You tell me."

"If America's waging it, then it's good." He winked. "Seriously, a little of both . . . I guess."

"We've experienced the bad," I said. "But how is it good?"

Luis leaned forward. "Look, here's the thing, and you know this. I don't care about insurgents or their damn countries; I do care about Marines on the ground. At LA, I get to protect them. And when I do, I feel like it's a good thing."

"And the money?"

"Well, that's a perk," Luis said, leaning back.

"You really think it's okay for people like you and me to go overseas and make large sums of money without government oversight."

"*Shoulds* and *oughts* is your realm, Peters, not mine."

"So if a contractor kills civilians, then who pays the cost?"

"The contractor, I guess. The company. I don't know."

"Well, to answer your question," I said. "War is bad."

"I figured. I don't disagree, but I don't agree either."

As I filled both glasses, Luis changed the subject. "How was Cambodia?"

"It was a learning experience," I said. "My wife and I came away changed; Cambodia stayed the same."

"You had high hopes?"

"Too high, maybe. I don't know . . . a bomb destroys in the blink of an eye; rebuilding takes a lifetime."

"So you failed?"

"No. While our presence made a difference to a few, it definitely transformed us. It was peacemaking as redemption."

"For you."

"For me . . . maybe for others."

"That's dismal," Luis said. "I mean, if you were in charge—you had the president's ear—what would you say? How would you end Iraq? How would you have avoided it?"

"But I tell you: love your enemies."

"Funny."

"I'm no foreign policy expert and I certainly won't pretend that I understand the complexities of the presidency, but in the end, peace will always trump violence."

"Two roads diverged," Luis recited.

"Peace or violence?"

"You're a strange one, Peters."

I sat my glass down with a resonant *clunk*. "Well, there you go. You traveled your road, and I mine."

"But where do we go from here?"